# TOWARD OTHER WORLDS

## Borgo Press Books by MICHAEL R. COLLINGS

# TOWARD OTHER WORLDS

## PERSPECTIVES ON JOHN MILTON, C. S. LEWIS, STEPHEN KING, ORSON SCOTT CARD, AND OTHERS

by

### Michael R. Collings

Emeritus Professor of English
Seaver College
Pepperdine University

### THE BORGO PRESS

*An Imprint of Wildside Press LLC*

MMX

FIRST EDITION

# CONTENTS

# ACKNOWLEDGMENTS

Many thanks to the following for initially providing a forum for presenting or publishing the essays, subsequent permission to reprint, and/or other assistance in completing *Toward Other Worlds*:

Dave Hinchberger, publisher of Overlook Connection Press;
*Deep Thoughts* and "Life, the Universe, and Everything": The Marion K. "Doc" Smith Symposium on Science Fiction and Fantasy;
EnderCon, 2002;
George Beahm, ed., *Demon-Driven: Stephen King and the Art of Writing*, *Phantasmagoria*, and *The Stephen King Story: A Literary Profile*;
*MythLore* and the Mythopoeic Society;
*Star\*Line* and the Science Fiction Poetry Association;
Stephen Spignesi, ed., *The Shape Under the Sheet: The Complete Stephen King Encyclopedia*;
*Sunstone: Mormon Experience, Scholarship, Issues & Art* and the Sunstone Symposium;
*The Lamp-Post* and the Southern California C. S. Lewis Society;
*The Leading Edge: Magazine of Science Fiction and Fantasy*;
World Horror Convention, 2008.

# INTRODUCTION

This collection emerged naturally from the directions I have taken as scholar, critic, educator, and writer over the past thirty years. While not resolving into a strictly chronological sequence, the essays nonetheless retain an overall sense of chronology; by and large, the earlier essays appear first, the later ones toward the end of the book. And, while there is not a strict division according to subject, the essays in general follow the development of my interest in the fantastic—in science fiction, myth and fantasy, and horror.

The first essays introduce two broad areas of special interest: horror and poetry. While I have written a fair amount on non-horror-related works and authors, the bulk of my work over the past twenty years has been devoted to authors such as Stephen King, Peter Straub, Dean R. Koontz, Clive Barker, and Robert McCammon. Their dark imaginations have exerted a powerful attraction on my own, both in the area of critical/scholarly inquiry and in creative writing. Probably more than half of my published books, chapters, articles, and reviews deal with these writers, with their themes, landscapes, characters, and social commentary. And certainly more than half of my creative writing—two of my three novels, all of my short stories, the preponderance of my poetry—are drawn from the same sense of darkness. It is entirely fitting, then, that the first essay in this collection, "The Persistence of Darkness," directs the readers' attention to the long tradition of horror in English literature, from the earliest times to the present. As the Author Guest of Honor Address at the World Horror Convention in 2008, it speaks to my largest audience, providing a kind of capstone to my interests, activities, and directions over the preceding decades.

The next essays seem to shift ground entirely. "Quantum Memories: Notes Toward an Anti-Definition of Science Fiction Poetry," suggests something quite different. Its title seems distanced, objective, clinical, yet its subject matter is the most personal, subjective, and emotional of the genres I enjoy writing—poetry. And specifically science fiction poetry, that strange amalgam of subjects, styles, voices, and themes that in some important ways speaks more directly of and to the final decades of the twentieth-century than much of its mainstream poetry. It is the world of science, of knowledge, of technology both theoretical and applied, and of the infinite possibilities that world offers. And it is simultaneously dark, potentially as dark and as horrific as any Gothic tale. In preparing a collection of my poems of science fiction, myth and fantasy, and horror, *In the Void*, I was aware of the applicability of the title to nearly every poem. In each, there was almost invariably a touch of darkness, of dread, of fear, of death—of the void that surrounds us in the larger universe. So in spite of the seeming disparity between prose horror and science fiction poetry, the two frequently overlap in my imagination...and in my writing.

Given that, it might seem unusual, then, to find two subsequent essays on a non-horror, non-science-fiction, non-fantasy writer, the seventeenth-century genius, John Milton. But he is in fact a logical place for me to begin discussions of specific authors and their works. In addition to my love affair with the epic (which resulted in my own 6,500 line Renaissance-style religious epic), Milton actually provided the initial point for my earliest explorations of science fiction and fantasy. During my graduate studies, one of my courses—a directed reading course superintended by one of the world's leading Miltonists and an unusually broad-minded academic for the early 1970s, John M. Steadman—developed into an attempt to track the fortunes of literary epic following the publication of *Paradise Lost* in 1667. Over the next two centuries, poetic epic virtually disappeared in English, but many of its purposes and much of its spark appeared to me at least to suddenly resurge in the form, not of traditional prose fiction as exemplified by the novel, but of prose *fantastic* fiction—an umbrella term which includes fantasy, science fiction, and horror. The emerging genres allowed for the scope, sweep and power of epic; they encouraged heroes who fought, not for personal glory alone, but to save a nation, a planet, a galaxy...and occasionally a universe. They invited clear-cut divisions between heroes and villains, between warring nations and, again occasionally, warring gods. The result was, for me, a clear path from Milton's climactic achievement to the finest works of J. R. R. Tolkien, Frank Herbert, Piers Anthony, Stephen King, Dean R. Koontz, Robert McCammon, and Orson Scott Card—to drop but a few of the dozens of possible names.

From Milton, it seemed inevitable that my attention should move to one of his finest twentieth-century apologists, C. S. Lewis. His *Preface to Paradise Lost* staggered my imagination long before I read any of his fiction, even though now I treasure the fiction above all else. He knew Milton works, understood Milton's purposes, could reveal Milton's secrets in ways few other critics could…and he chose to write mythic, fantastic, and science-fictional novels. What could I do but study them? When the opportunity came to edit *The Lamp-Post of the Southern California C. S. Lewis Society*, it was something I could not resist. From that experience came the next sequence of essays in this book: studies of Lewis's techniques, themes, and literary choices.

Shortly after my tenure as editor of *The Lamp-Post*, I was asked by the publisher of my monographs on Brian W. Aldiss and Piers Anthony to write a series of short studies of Stephen King, and subsequently stepped effortlessly into my next consuming interest. King represented an apparently radical departure from my work on Lewis; but in fact, the connections between them were, for me at least, compelling and strong. Both were master craftsmen, honing their skill over decades of preliminary work. Both were men of enormous imagination. Both worked within visions that encompassed immensities, linking story after story. Both were writers of intensely moral fictions that, despite their surface differences, demonstrated their concern for human society and community. In many ways, they *did* differ, not the least being King's clear-cut preference for darkness, for horror, occasionally for "the gross out." But the more I worked with his stories, the more convinced I became that he, perhaps more than any other single writer, was speaking to, for, and in behalf of late twentieth-century America, with all of its strengths and failings. His horrors became as much metaphors as attempts at shocking or terrifying. His monsters at times seemed even less potent than the monsters each of us must face daily: war; disease, especially for King, cancer; loss of community; loss of authority in the family; failing educational systems; and many more. In the end, I've written more on King than on any of the other writers that have drawn my interest.

In addition to being an academic, I have a strong religious background. My predilection for Lewis's stories probably gained much of its dynamism by that fact. Similarly, my own sense of morality and spirituality drew me with equal power to King's epic struggles between the Dark Man and the Light—the latter his term for what I read as approaching an apprehension of God. It wasn't surprising, then, when I discovered in the early 1980s that one of the writers I had recently read and figuratively devoured equally dealt with similar concerns. In some way, he was the most diverse of the three authors. He wrote fantasy, but fantasy with a hard edge; he wrote science fiction, but science fiction with an overtone of darkness; he occasionally wrote horror, but imaginative, purposeful, ultimately and paradoxically redemptive horror. And he was a co-religionist.

Thus Orson Scott Card's stories became the object of my shared attention, divided between his works and King's. But Card had one distinct advantage over King. I had met King briefly at a conference and had corresponded with him freely for several years while working on the Starmont studies. He was open, gracious, friendly, helpful—everything I could have wished for. But Card...I actually knew. We initially met at a BYU conference (the source of a number of papers in this collection) and formed a strong friendship. We talked about literature, about religion, about art, about life. And out of our conversations came insights that enabled me to approach his stories from perhaps a slightly different angle than other critics. The result of that friendship was *In the Image of God: Theme, Character, and Landscape in the Fiction of Orson Scott Card,* and later, *Storyteller: The Official Orson Scott Bibliography and Guide.* Along the way, his stories led me to exciting and unexpected conclusions about science fiction, fantasy, and horror—many of which are incorporated into the next major set of essays here.

There are, of course, many other great writers of science fiction, fantasy, and horror...more than I could possibly read in a dozen lifetimes. Many of them I *have* read; some of them have become subjects of chapters, essays, notes, and reviews published elsewhere. Many of them I return to and re-read as often as I do Lewis, King, and Card. Some will appear sprinkled through the texts before you, as evidence, as exemplars, as sources, as inspirations. A few are even represented by essays devoted to their works along.

As eclectic as this collection of essays may seem, it is in fact reasonably unified. *Toward Other Worlds* progresses through a series of imaginations, a series of stories, striving to drawn from them a sense of the human and the infinite that each writer seems to have wished to convey.

Most of the essays appear essentially as they were originally presented or published, with minor editing or revising for style and clarity; a few are published here for the first time. In a very real sense, they represent three decades of engagement with science fiction, fantasy, and horror, and conclusions reached over the course of those years.

—Michael R. Collings
Meridian, ID, December 2009

# THE PERSISTENCE OF DARKNESS

[This essay was presented as the Academic Guest of Honor Address at the World Horror Convention, Salt Lake City UT, March 26-30, 2008. Portions were earlier presented during the Arts Festival, Seaver College, Pepperdine University, on November 19, 1991, as part of the opening celebration for the Cultural Arts Festival. A much shorter version appeared as the introduction to George Beahm's biography of Stephen King: "Introduction: The Persistence of Darkness—Shadows Behind the Life Behind the Story" in *The Stephen King Story: A Literary Profile* (Kansas City: Andrews & McMeel, 1991), 1-6.]

Several years ago, the Humanities Division at my university sponsored an Arts Festival to commemorate the opening of the new Cultural Arts Center. Colleagues from the division—English, History, and Philosophy departments—were to present papers relating to their current research.

I was a bit taken aback when my division chair asked me to present one. He knew that my research centered primarily on horror—and on Stephen King in particular; and I knew that many in the division looked upon my activities as an aberration of an unsettled mind. One colleague, for example, noticed a King novel among the books one of his advisees was holding during a meeting in his office. He took the opportunity to explain to the poor benighted child that such books were not appropriate on a college campus and certainly not welcome in his office. The student—to my enormous gratification—calmly explained that the text was required reading for one of his classes (mine, to be precise) and that even if it weren't, he would be reading it anyway.

Another colleague, whose attitudes toward any sub-literary forms, including science fiction, fantasy, and horror, were less than enthusiastic, took great pains to explain to the rank, tenure, and promotion committee the extent to which she felt I was wasting my time and the university's money in such trivial pursuits. She even objected to the fact that my early Starmont House King studies were printed in courier font—obviously the work of amateurs among the great unwashed. She made her point. Over my thirty years at the university, her attitude and similar attitudes among others cost me several promotions.

Given his constant support for my work, however, I shouldn't have been surprised when the division chair extended the invitation, but I was. And a bit trepidatious, since I knew that the audience would include not only fellow professors but faculty from across the University; administrators, including most probably the president himself; wealthy potential contributors from nearby Malibu; and members of the board of regents...not a few of whom easily fit the category of conservative little old "blue-haired" ladies.

After some soul-searching, I decided, "Well, what have I got to lose?"

So I opened my presentation with the simple statement: "William Shakespeare was the Stephen King of his day."

I swear you could hear neck-bones snap as heads jerked up. I tried not to look at those colleagues from the English program whom I knew had no senses of humor; but I did notice a mischievous twinkle in the division chair's eye.

I recall that experience because it has influenced my approach to most of my work since. I continued to write about Stephen King...and Orson Scott Card, Dean Koontz, Robert McCammon, Piers Anthony, Brian Aldiss, and pretty much anyone else who caught my interest. My subsequent division chairs, all three of them, continued steadfastly to support the directions of my research. And those persistent colleagues continued to try to block any promotions or advancement ... rather successfully, I'm afraid, and that in face of the fact that I had pretty much out-published the entire division combined. And the conclusions expressed in that presentation about the role and nature of horror continued to color everything I taught and wrote, whether it related directly to science fiction, fantasy and horror, or to Edmund Spenser, John Milton, and the Renaissance epic.

For that reason, I would like to recall, restate, and expand upon a couple of those points today. And, as then, instead of trying to be theoretically cutting-edge or to 'deconstruct' the genre until it becomes clear that I really hate horror but figure I can get publication credits by writing about it, I would like to make some suggestions about the continuity of horror—both the monsters and the motifs— in literary history.

But first, a plot synopsis:

*A handful of people have gathered in a building in the center of a small, isolated community. Inside, they have found safety...or at least the illusion of safety. Outside, there is only darkness, and fear, and death. Daylight is dying. With the night will come the monster. The people huddle close for warmth, for comfort. They know that by the time the sun dawns again, some, or most—or all—of them may be dead.*

Is this an outline of a Horror novel? Koontz's *Strangers*, perhaps, or *Phantoms*? Or better yet, King's early novella, *The Mist*? Those would be good guesses. They seem logical. To a degree even probable.

But this summary doesn't actually speak to any of these. The story I had in mind was written a few years before King assumed the mantle, willingly or not, of "King of Horror," or before King, Koontz, McCammon, or the others began writing...or, for that matter, were even born. This story goes back somewhere between 1,200 and 1,400 years.

I'm speaking of *Beowulf*, the earliest and greatest of the surviving Germanic epics that helped to form our literary heritage. It is the exciting story (as long as you can read it in a good translation) of a small group of people forced to confront terror and horror. The building is the golden mead-hall, Heorot (upon which J. R. R. Tolkien modeled Edoras in *The Lord of the Rings*). The cluster of people are the warriors—the *comitatus*—of the Germanic king Hrothgar. And the monster is Grendel. The monster has visited the great mead hall before, at night, and each time he has left a trail of blood and death. The poem survives in a single manuscript from the 10th century, preserved, probably not because it was obviously a masterpiece of early English writing, but because it was about a monster. Hastily written, it was bound with four other texts, including stories of adventures, wonders...and monsters.

It is intriguing and instructive, I think to notice how closely *Beowulf* and, say, *The Mist*, represent departures from a similar narrative point. Both focus on small groups, the core of a culture that defines characters dually as individuals and as parts of their community. Both groups are isolated by the physical darkness of the landscape and the internal darkness of their fears. Individuals in both must work together for communal strength, protection, and survival—but their gathering does not work. In spite of everything, they must emerge and confront head-on the monsters...the darkness, and the fear, and the specter of death.

There are differences, of course. In *Beowulf,* we quickly learn that the poet has found a hero, a single warrior with the courage and prowess to combat monsters. Grendel has devoured thirty of King Hrothgar's retainers:

> Straightway he seized a sleeping warrior
> for the first, and tore him fiercely asunder,
> the bone-frame bit, drank blood in streams,
> swallowed him piecemeal: swiftly thus
> the lifeless corse was clear devoured,
> even feet and hands.... (XI)

The hero Beowulf, symmetrically enough, is endowed with the strength of thirty men. In the fury of single combat with Grendel, he rips the monster's arm from its body and nails the bloody trophy to the wall above the mead-hall door:

> For him [Grendel] the keen-souled kinsman of Hygelac
> held in hand; hateful alive
> was each to other. The outlaw dire
> took mortal hurt; a mighty wound
> showed on his shoulder, and sinews cracked,
> and the bone-frame burst. To Beowulf now
> the glory was given, and Grendel thence
> death-sick his den in the dark moor sought .... (xii)

In *The Mist,* events do not proceed quite as smoothly. There is no single hero, no outlander suddenly arrived to kill the beast and rescue the community. In a technologically oriented world such as ours, individual heroism is generally not encouraged; nor does King insult his reader's intelligence by importing one—not even from the distant, almost mythic shores of Geatland (Sweden). There are individual battles fought against the monsters that inhabit the mist, to be sure, but King's vision allows no simple ending. His characters are stripped of everything until all that remains is the courage of a few to face the darkness directly and to attempt to discover the extent of the mist...and the monsters.

And then the next wave of monsters strikes, in *Beowulf* as well as in *The Mist.* Even Beowulf, the impervious hero, ultimately suffers defeat in battle with the Firedrake. All that he has accomplished—the deaths of Grendel and Grendel's dam; the consolidation of his kingdom; his fifty years of faultless rule, summarized in a single phrase, "he was a good king"—all is called into doubt as his body burns and the forces of darkness gather once again. In *The Mist*, the time frame has been condensed from fifty years to hours and days but the effect is the same. Humanity may raise buildings, construct moral and civil codes, and create a veneer of civility, but in the face of the darkness most of that counts for little. The implications of such stories, ancient and contemporary, are consistent with a pervasive theme in Western literature, captured by both the *Beowulf*-poet and modern Horror writers: 'Here there be monsters,' here in the darkness of the human soul, and here in the darkness of the worlds we imagine.

Nor did this concern with explicit horror die out with the passing of the culture that generated the *Beowulf*-poet. Throughout the middle ages, writers—and by implication—audiences appreciated the creation and re-creation of horror. One enormously popular form, the "metrical tragedy," incorporated tales of the "fall of great men" in rhymed verse that reveled not only in horrific details but in a particularly graphic—and thus, presumably, more spiritually elevating—death. According to one scholar, such tales did not simply conclude with a death scene but expanded far beyond to a "general loosening of the forces of death, a repercussive slaughter led up to by earlier bloodshed." One author felt impelled to describe the ghost of Pompey, face disfigured by smoke and seawater, while

> a huge slaughter was accepted casually by Chaucer's Monk as the natural end of the tragedy of Samson.... This had to be so because tragedy was meant to illustrate the essential horror of life and the reasons for a Contempt of the World morality. In its essential aspects medieval tragedy was...a Dance of Death. (Baker, *Induction*, p. 172)

Beyond the more-than-coincidental fact that King borrowed a variation on the phrase for his own quasi-scholarly history of horror as genre, *Danse Macabre*, is the more salient fact that in many ways our world is also concerned with bringing some kind of moral value out of an increasing sense of the "essential horror of life." A society struggling under the weight of such disparate collective burdens as nuclear weaponry (with their threat of devastation even when used for peaceful means), disease, the implicit horrors of technology and its wildfire proliferation, and the constant threat of terrorism, might also search for illustrations of the idea—held in common with the *Beowulf*-poet—that after the short and bitter struggle comes a welcome death.

But enough of the middle ages.

Let's try another story.

*Plot Summary:*

*A frightened man confronts a midnight apparition, a specter that by all logic cannot exist, but does. He speaks to it, he demands that it speak to him, and it reveals tales of darkness and fear and death. It grants him visions of murder, blood, revenge, and—again—death.*

Does this describe King's *The Dark Half?* Or a segment of *It?* Koontz's *Phantoms?* McCammon's *Stinger?* Perhaps. Certainly the synopsis could apply equally to a number of contemporary horror novels. But again, none of those was the story I had in mind. Instead, I was thinking of *Hamlet.* There, three times in the course of what is now almost universally hailed as the greatest tragedy in English literature (some would broaden that to include Western literature), we find...a ghost. A specter. A haunted shade whispering of murders past and murders yet to come.

By all accounts, the audiences of Shakespeare's day loved the play. They flocked to the Globe Theater to watch it, standing for the full four hours of its performance (unlike modern audiences, they were not subjected to editors and rewriters who know more about dramaturgy than the Bard himself). They might have stood in the rain to see it. They might have paid the equivalent of a week's wages for the privilege.

Why? Did they come to watch a performance of the greatest play by the greatest English playwright?

Hardly.

F. E. Halliday begins his *Shakespeare and His Critics* by noting that at the time of Shakespeare's death, there were no popular newspapers to herald the tragic tidings from shore to shore; and even if there had been, "it is more than probable that the death in the provinces of a retired actor and writer of plays which could scarcely be considered as serious literature would have passed unnoticed" (1). In fact, until the middle of the eighteenth century—a century and a half after Shakespeare's death—there was remarkably little evidence of the "bardolotry" that has since colored our assessments of his works.

No, the Elizabethan playgoers went to see a *drama*, and not coincidentally to see blood, and fear, and death...and a ghost. Samuel

Johnson, writing over a century after Shakespeare's death about another of Shakespeare's initial theatrical successes, *Titus Andronicus,* urged that the play not be considered part of the Master's canon: "The barbarity of the spectacles, and the general massacre, which are here exhibited, can scarcely be conceived tolerable to any audience; yet we are told by [Ben] Jonson, that they were not only borne, but praised. That Shakespeare wrote any part...I see no reason for believing" (Halliday 142). In spite of now being frequently excoriated as among Shakespeare's worst plays, to the point that many critics struggle to demonstrate that Shakespeare only contributed part—or perhaps none—of the lines, *Titus Andronicus* was unusually and undeniably popular in its time. G. B. Harrison notes in his edition of the plays that it remained in the stage repertory for two full decades after it first appeared. Based on tales preserved for over a thousand years in classical myth and specifically in Seneca's Latin revenge tragedies (one of the more popular genres of the Elizabethan period), the story was sensational and horrific even for the Elizabethans, full of graphic representations of blood and death. Many of the more objectionable episodes were eliminated in variants written by Shakespeare's contemporaries, but, again in Professor Harrison's words, "Shakespeare spared his audience nothing."

Shakespeare's audience—not being 'modern playgoers' and lacking the foreknowledge that they were in the presence of a work by one of the premier dramatists of Western culture—found nothing absurd in the presentation of horrors. Alexander Legatt summarizes the blood-soaked episodes that—not coincidentally—find close parallels in King's *The Stand* (1990 edition), with its extended passages of bloodletting in the face of global plague: Titus's initial, ritual sacrifice of a gothic prince to "appease the ghosts of his sons"; his daughter's rape and mutilation in retribution; Titus's euthanasic killing of his daughter; the trapping of his sons in a "detested, dark, blood-drinking pit" with the body of a murdered noble; the deaths of his sons; his manipulation into chopping off his own hand—and his revenge on Tamora, Queen of the Goths, for these atrocities. He kills Tamora's sons and serves them up to her baked in a pie (28-29). For Shakespeare's audience, the highlight of the play must have been the on-stage removal of Titus Andronicus' hand, after which the character puns on multiple meanings of 'giving one's hand' as a symbol of loyalty. One of my undergraduate Shakespeare professors, in fact, lectured at length on that scene, noting that the actor portraying Titus Andronicus would often wear a bladder of pig's blood beneath his arm and, at the climactic moment, spray blood onto the footlings surrounding the stage.

Many critics today argue that the play fails miserably although, in a society in which horror is an increasingly popular genre, the play is also increasingly accepted as having been written by Shakespeare. Harrison writes, for example,

> Few critics can seriously defend *Titus Andronicus*; but its failure is not solely due to a revolting and fantastic story. Modern playgoers may regard rape, mutilation, and severed heads and hands as unsuitable for stage presentation; yet there are scenes quite as painful in plays which are among the very greatest—the blinding of Gloucester in *Lear* for instance, or the conclusion of Sophocles' *Oedipus the King;* these are horrible but still justifiable in their contexts. The horrors in *Titus Andronicus* are too much; if ever presented on a modern stage they would move the audience not to shudders but to guffaws. (296)

For us, perhaps. But Shakespeare's audiences apparently loved it.

Nor did his audience's responses differ substantively from the assessments of most of Shakespeare's contemporaries. Following Shakespeare's death, two acting companions of his, John Heminges and Henry Condell, put together a volume of his plays. The act of collecting plays was itself an anomaly during the period, since plays were considered ephemeral, certainly not 'literary' in the sense that poetry might be. As was the custom, they invited commendatory verses, of which only *one*—Ben Jonson's—suggested the status Shakespeare today enjoys:

> Triumph, my Britain, thou hast one to show
> > To whom all scenes of Europe homage owe.
> He was not of an age, but for all time. (Donaldson 454)

Marchette Chute's biography of Jonson (itself aimed at a popular rather than a scholarly audience) notes in passing that

> This judgment of Jonson's is the only contemporary piece of writing on Shakespeare that assigns him the position he now holds. Several other playwrights—Drayton, Beaumont, Heywood and Webster—wrote favorably of Shakespeare and his work,

but there was usually a touch of patronage in their remarks and never any indication that here was a giant who towered over them all. In general Shakespeare's contemporaries did not take him seriously as an artist or give him the praise that is now considered his due. (275)

In fact, Chute argues, Heminges and Condell were taking a calculated risk by publishing Shakespeare's works at all; he was not "one of the writers whom it was correct to admire and whom every gentleman of the period was expected to know" (271). In other words, Shakespeare had spent his career writing, not for scholars and critics, but for his *audience*; he was a "common playhouse poet" writing sensational, unrealistic, often horrific, commercially successful but artistically flawed works, and would thus have been considered to some extent "academically incorrect":

> …the plays of Shakespeare stood for everything that Jonson disapproved of in the theatre and everything he had fought against in his long career as a playwright….in general [Shakespeare] had produced an untidy, sprawling body of work that a true classicist could only regard with something approaching despair. (273)

Jonson's remarks—coming as they did from a Royal pensioner (the equivalent of Poet Laureate) and the generally acknowledged arbiter of English poetic taste—clearly indicate that during his own lifetime, Shakespeare's reputation paralleled that of writers like King, Koontz, McCammon, and others: immensely popular with the masses but largely ignored or slighted by the critics and scholars. And there are good reasons for this. Jonson's avowed aim was to reform the English stage by restoring the virtues, values, and structures of classical drama; Shakespeare ignored such things entirely, concentrating instead on plays that elicited his desired responses from his audience. In Jonson's words (related by William Drummond of Hawthorndon, a Scots poet Jonson visited in 1619, three years after Shakespeare's death), "Shakespeare wanted art" (Donaldson 596). Whether by dramatizing ghostly visitations that lead to revenge and bloody death, or more directly by the on-stage removal of body parts, Shakespeare shows himself acquainted with the age-old techniques of fear, terror, and horror—including what

King has described in his own works as the "gross out."

Now, let's examine yet a third story:

*Plot Summary:*

*For a paltry price, a mysterious stranger offers the things dearest to a man's heart. The man accepts. For a while—a short while—he enjoys the pleasure his desire brings...but then the reckoning falls due, and he discovers that the thing he desired will ultimately cost him something even more precious: his soul.*

Again, the summary strikes a familiar tone, suggests King's *Needful Things*, for example, in which a mysterious stranger sets up shop in the small town of Castle Rock, where a steady stream of customers enter and leave one by one, each with a small parcel clutched under a protective arm, each with an oddly trance-like expression. As the narrative progresses, Mr. Gaunt, the proprietor of Needful Things, extracts from all of his customers fulfillment of the bargains struck. leading to an intensifying spiral of violence, viciousness, mayhem, and murder. At the end, the town itself explodes in a metaphorical eruption of the private emotions its inhabitants have been tempted to release. More than a little reminiscent of Mark Twain's "The Man Who Corrupted Hadleyburg," *Needful Things* becomes a powerful statements of horror's persistent analysis of the forces of light and dark as evil struggles to possess human souls.

Yet—perhaps no surprise at this point—King's *Needful Things* was not the title I had in mind when I wrote the plot summary.

Instead, I was considering another Elizabethan drama, nearly contemporaneous with Shakespeare's *Titus Andronicus*, and written by the leading pre-Shakespearean dramatist: Christopher Marlowe's *Dr. Faustus.*

To return for a moment to Shakespeare and Renaissance revenge tragedy, King's *Needful Things* develops a close parallel. Each character is entrapped by the seduction he or she defines—Gaunt does little except provide them with an external, physical device by which they can explore and develop their own internal weaknesses, corruption, guilt, and obsessions. This pairing of action and morality echoes a similar pairing—coupled with frequent and violent death—that extends throughout the revenge play tradition:

In *Antonio's Revenge* [the revenge killings] are lurid and sensational, but purposeful in that the victim is punished for good reason. In *Titus Andronicus*, where Tamora is made to eat her sons, in *Hamlet*, where Claudius is killed with his own poison, and in *The Revenger's Tragedy*, where the Duke is made to kiss the poisoned lips of the woman he lusted after and killed, the manner of the killing is morally logical. Aesthetic design and nemesis come together. Even in the crazy last scene of *Women Beware Women* the individual deaths, using tricks like poisoned love-darts and showers of gold, are significant judgments on the victims. (Legatt, 162)

This sense of judgment recurs throughout horror as genre. Human societies become corrupt, greedy, unfeeling, willing to pollute, destroy—and they are visited by appropriate monsters. On one of the narrowest levels, we see this in any number of horror novels and films when young people—too young to understand and consciously accept adult responsibility for their actions—engage in illicit sex ... and die horribly as a result, often during the act itself. A general social consensus (admittedly one more honored in the breach than in the keeping) has been ignored; justice is served...immediately.

Like *Faustus,* horror literature frequently anatomizes greed, avarice, vanity, lust for power, repaying a heedless humanity in a coin of our own choosing. McCammon's *Swan Song* makes this sense concrete as character after character emerges from a mask-like growth that has covered their faces, only to discover that they have altered physically. What they are truly like *inside* has become their *external* identity...and monsters are born.

Like *Faustus,* horror literature focuses on central fears of the society it anatomizes. *Faustus'* audience was concerned with matters of heaven and hell. Catholicism. Patriotism. Witchcraft. Damnation. And they took such concerns quite seriously.

In a rabid attack on the theater published in 1633, *Histriomastix,* William Prynne recounted a performance of *Dr. Faustus* at an inn-yard theater, referring to "the visible apparition of the Devill on the Stage at the Belsavage Play-house in Queene Elizabeths dayes (to the great amazement both of the Actors and Spectators) whiles they were there prophanely playing the history of Faustus" (Tucker Brooke, 45). Not only did the onlookers think they saw an extra devil capering on the stage but they also fled the inn-yard *en masse* and refused to re-enter it for a year and a day.

We see different concerns confronting our society: the breakdown of home and family; the break down of educational institutions (King for one has always portrayed schools as places more dedicated to destruction than elevation); lack of ethics in politics, in government, in authorities; lack of central spiritual guidelines and a concomitant quest for spiritual truth—again, King provides a superb example of the latter in *Desperation*.

Marlowe's England—Shakespeare's England, the *Beowulf*-poet's Britain—were cultures experiencing turmoil similar to ours. They too experienced physical and spiritual threats, internal and external. They too confronted a future in which traditional standards and beliefs would be increasingly questioned, if not destroyed. They too stood on the threshold of a world in which everything they accepted would be challenged, in which their very conceptions of the universe itself would undergo radical alterations.

And they, like us, found a means of symbolizing, confronting, and adapting to that world: the images, emotions, and vicarious purgation of literary fear, terror, and horror.

# QUANTUM MEMORIES:

## NOTES TOWARD AN ANTI-DEFINITION OF SCIENCE FICTION POETRY

[The original version of this essay was published as: "New Words for New Worlds: Notes Toward an Anti-Definition of Science Fiction Poetry," *New York Review of Science Fiction,* No. 17 (January 1990). A revised version, "Quantum Memories: Notes Toward an Anti-Definition of Science Fiction Poetry," was presented to the Brigham Young University Symposium on Science Fiction and Fantasy, Life, the Universe, and Everything VIII, Provo UT, February 9, 1990; and subsequently appeared in *The Leading Edge: Magazine of Science Fiction and Fantasy* No. 24 (September 1991). The revised essay is reprinted here.]

\* \* \* \* \* \* \*

When the wordmonger came
and spread his wares beneath
our alien shade
we wandered one by one
toward his ship
to touch our tongues
on new, exotic shapes.
We fondled and we fell in love,
we started back in shock,
we grew and changed.

And when he packed and left,
spinning out to planets
far from ours,
we shared our purchases,
cultivated them, watched them grow.
And after many days
the newness atrophied.
The words no longer touched

as much,
as deeply...
But we were different
and we knew it would happen once again
when the wordmonger returned.[*]

Recently, Andrew Joron and M. J. Engh have published lengthy articles centering on the question of definitions: what is Science Fiction poetry? Their responses to that fundamental issue vary widely, as do the kinds of evidence each adduced to support specific points of view. Interwoven throughout both articles were elements of cultural, economic, political, and literary history; references to contemporary "establishment" poetics; and considerations of the role and value of rhyme and meter in contemporary poetry in general as well as in SF poetry in particular.

While I found much to agree with in both—and much to disagree with—it seems that the central issue in the debate has perhaps been distorted.

In spite of my professional title (Professor of English), in spite of the fact that much of my own publishing is critical and theoretical, in spite of the fact that I am to some degree part of the "academic establishment" referred to by both Joron and Engh—in spite of all, I really have little interest in *defining* what Science Fiction poetry *ought* to be. I am far more interested in exploring what those poets who refer to themselves as "Science Fiction poets" actually *do*.

Prescriptive definitions present a fair degree of difficulty, for the simple fact that most attempts at defining—particularly in literary areas—consist primarily in determining what *does not* fit a specific preconceived definition. Katherine Hume demonstrates this tendency admirably in her study of the fantastic, noting that each of the definitions she incorporates in her opening chapter attempts to limit the number of texts that could actually be categorized as "fantastic." Certainly the more rigid paradigms radically limit possibilities; Tzvetan Todorov's, for example, would admit only a handful of texts as fantastic throughout, with the majority fitting somewhere on an extra-fantastic continuum, depending upon whether the final resolution establishes the text as Uncanny or Marvelous. Significantly, he rejects out of hand even the possibility of a fantastic po-

---

[*] "When the Wordmonger Came" originally appeared in *The Leading Edge* (Fall 1987), 17.

etry:

> We see now why the poetic reading constitutes a danger for the fantastic. If as we read a text we reject all representation, considering each sentence as a pure semantic combination, the fantastic *could not appear*: for the fantastic requires, it will be recalled, a reaction to events as they occur in the world evoked. For this reason, the fantastic can subsist only within fiction; poetry cannot be fantastic (though there may be anthologies of "fantastic poetry"). In short, the fantastic implies fiction. (60)

By virtue of the fact that we automatically read poetry figuratively, Todorov argues, it is impossible to embed within a poem the structural guideposts that define fantasy.

Similarly, a prescriptive definition of SF poetry such as Joron's inadvertently acts to limit what is possible within the genre (or subgenre, depending on how one looks at it). By the strictest interpretation of Joron's stridently modernist definition, all rhyming, metrical, or narrative poetry simply could *not* be SF poetry—and, to his credit, Joron meticulously adheres to these proscriptions in his own writing, demonstrating at least the viability of one form of SF poetry.

But such a radical limitation is not, I think, what he had in mind when he discussed the role of rhyme and meter in SF poetry; nor was Engh's intention to limit in other ways what might be possible. Still, the fact remains that the simple *act* of attempting to determine a comprehensive, definitive paradigm for SF poetry in a real sense militates against the *fact* of SF poetry.

More useful, because more practical, are less didactic, less programmatic approaches that focus on characteristics rather than prescriptions (or proscriptions). Suzette Haden Elgin—poet, novelist, and founder of the Science Fiction Poetry Association—simply and ambiguously defines SF poetry as having "a narrative component and a science component" (Green x); Scott E. Green notes wryly that

> Elgin's law...has become a widely used but by no means universally accepted definition for science fiction poetry. It is also an ongoing source of argument among poets as to its accuracy (116)

Green's own pragmatic attempt at defining SF poetry entails categorizing existing poems, based on their responses to specific criteria:

> 1. The *science fiction narrative poem* is any poem that tells a story, frequently using the conventions associated with science fiction literature, such as time travel, planetary exploration, and human/alien communications.
> 2. *Poems of science* are poems that speak about scientific phenomena, the lives of scientists and the relationships of science and society. These poems frequently find markets outside of genre publications, especially in Britain.
> 3. *Poems of commentary* are poems that critique or comment upon themes in science fiction literature and film rather than narrating a story.
> 4. *Speculative poems* relate themes associated with science fiction such as time travel and interstellar exploration but use language and structure associated with mainstream poetry. They are often written by mainstream poets and appear in mainstream publications. Their primary concern is the human condition, not adherence to traditional science fiction plots. Certain fantasy and horror poems also fall under this definition. (Green, xi)

"Notwithstanding," Green concludes, granting his categories a necessary element of fluidity, "a poem may embrace one or more of the above definitions."

Generally, when a literary movement can be clearly (and rigidly) categorized, codified, and canonized; when its chief characteristics and proponents can be neatly established; when its impact on the surrounding culture and society can be assessed and verified with any degree of accuracy—in a word, when it can be *defined* in any limiting or academically abstracted sense, that movement is dead. For example, the English Literary Epic appeared in multiple manifestations over many centuries, each writer moving the form slightly off center (or better yet, by establishing new norms, moving the *center* itself), each emphasizing a particular structure or theme or subject or approach. Only with the appearance of Milton's *Paradise Lost*, however, was it possible to *define* comprehensively what the English Literary Epic was—what it attempted, how it functioned, how it was structured, and how it fit within the cultural context that developed it. But *Paradise Lost* was also the *last* successful English Literary Epic.

Certainly long narrative poems on lesser biblical or historical subjects, couched in imitative and excessive Miltonic blank verse, most often written in twelve books, continued to appear throughout the eighteenth and nineteenth centuries (and a few well into the twentieth).[*] While poets on the order of Pope, Byron, Wordsworth, Tennyson, and Browning understood the vital epic impulse that survived beneath the rigidity of form, and willingly modified that form to meet the requirements of their genius (often overtly parodying the excesses of traditional literary epic), lesser poets fell into the trap of assuming that imitating formal requirements equated with producing effective poetry. Literary fossils such as Timothy Dwight's *America; or, A Poem on the Settlement of the British Colonies* (1780) and Joel Barlowe's ambitious but numbingly conventional *Columbiad* (1807) attempted to recreate the majesty of Miltonic epic by adhering to a rigid formulation of rules. As a consequence, they are static, virtually unreadable artifacts; they are social, historical, or cultural reconstructions of a lithified literary form, complete with catalogues of dead devices and appropriate Latinate diction. But in an age when the epic impulse had transferred itself from narrative poetry to the novel (and ultimately, as I have argued elsewhere, to the Science Fiction novel), those poems remained little more than novelties, footnotes to a literary form. Interesting to look at. Unusual. Sometimes even intriguing.

But they ceased to make any difference to the culture. They were dead.

(Parenthetically, much the same thing happened to the epic in the other cultural contexts as well; in Greek, the *Iliad* and the *Odyssey* were not only the greatest but the first—they simultaneously established and completed the epic impulse. In Anglo-Saxon alliterative poetry, *Beowulf* occupies an analogous position as earliest, greatest, and last epic statement.)

Joron defines science fiction poetry by stating that it is a "modernist form of poetry, a kind of writing that experiments with the very substance of language itself—its sound and syntax." To specify that SF poetry is a subset of "modernist" poetry implies that it conforms to specific, demonstrable paradigms; the inescapable sugges-

---

[*] Including, not coincidentally, my own, *The Nephiad* (Borgo/Wildside Press, 2010).

tion is that poems relying on *non*-modernist paradigms (for example, the traditional devices of rhyme and meter) cannot—or at least *should* not—be classified as SF poetry. By the critical act of establishing such rigid boundaries, Joron encapsulates SF poetry. Yet what Engh notes about the evolution of modernist poetry itself is also true: The very forms that were explorative and extrapolative and iconoclastic a generation ago are now considered *de rigueur*. The radicals have become the establishment. And if SF poetry can be simply incorporated under a general rubric as a "modernist form of poetry," it may have already lost much of its viability as an extrapolative or speculative form.

A corollary to this bit of literary investigation is that I do not *wish* to see SF poetry defined. I do not *wish* to be able to look at the form or content of a poem and say, with the confidence of a distanced, unchanged scholar making academic pronouncements over a dead artifact, that *this is a Science Fiction poem.*

Instead, I am far more interested in seeing how different minds respond to the needs of a new world. Because that is what Science Fiction is, and by extension I think that is what Science Fiction poetry must be (and here, of course, I contradict my own thesis by offering *my* notes toward a definition of the form).

It has been argued that Science Fiction is not the same as Science Fiction poetry. Some have in fact gone so far as to suggest that the extrapolative, narrative impulse underlying Science Fiction is almost automatically inimical to poetry. Yet if we are going to use the term, it would seem that we must accept the full implications of that term.

Science Fiction poetry is poetry that at some level engages science fiction.

Granting for the moment the obvious tautology, I would argue that there is in fact some merit in examining the terminology, not in terms of what SF poetry *must be,* but rather in terms of what it has generated in different writers.

First, *science.* This may be the easiest of the three terms to accommodate. SF poetry is a poetry of today; it reflects our obsession with technological developments, but more importantly, it reflects our awareness of an increasing dependence on them. In some senses, we already live in a science-fictional world. If a particular extrapolative element has not yet appeared, wait a few moments and it will. The impact of technology is so far-reaching, so profound, that one might argue with some justification that there is perhaps no such thing as 'science fiction' itself—that the literary form we have traditionally identified by the label has expanded to become *the* literary form for the last quarter of this century (one of my colleagues at Pepperdine, Dr. Michelle Langford, has in fact articulated this position). The cross-generic writings that touch upon science fiction from multiple directions are legion: mainstream fiction, westerns, fantasy and horror, romance—again and again, we find subtle elements of extrapolation that suggest the importance of the future, of technological change. Many such touches are almost subliminal; others are increasingly overt, as when essentially mainstream writers such as Doris Lessing, or horror writers such as Stephen King and Robert McCammon, or cross-genre writers such as Dean R. Koontz incorporate clear technological extrapolation into their novels.

To expand the *science* part of 'Science Fiction' this widely suggests that Science Fiction poetry need not necessarily be limited as to subject or theme. The scientific element may be overt and pronounced; just as easily, it could be subtle and assumed, part of the necessary background of the poem without which the work could not exist. But somewhere, no matter how layered, the poem must confront perhaps the central issue of human life in our generation: assessing the technology that continuously shapes and reshapes our world.

If that were all the SF poets needed to be concerned with, of course, it should be sufficient to speak not of SF poetry but simply of "Science Poetry." Robert Frazier, himself an important SF poet, has in fact used the term—in such a way, however, as to suggest that there are essential differences between the two forms.

And I think that there are, because—as Elgin's Law implies— we *do* refer specifically to "Science *Fiction* poetry."

It would be a mistake to concentrate too narrowly on the "fiction" portion of the phrase, of course. Joron is correct when he writes that "many SF readers have a prejudice against any kind of writing that doesn't tell a story, including most of modern poetry." He notes also that fan poetry tends to be bad, not because it is poorly imagined or handled but because (among other things), it simply recycles "all the standard SF storylines and situations." I would not argue that SF poetry is as responsible for telling stories as SF prose.

But I would argue that the kernel of fiction must be present— that a narrative must exist within or through the poem. The SF poem need not *tell* a story; many of Joron's best works do not. But it can itself *be* a story—a fictive re-creation of a world that does not exist but might, or a world that should exist but doesn't, or a world that must not exist but possibly (even probably) will. Throughout, whether communicated through symbol and image, or through more traditional narrative forms, SF poetry *does* tell story—what Orson Scott Card defines simply as a series of causally related events.

And that emphasis on story—which requires teller and listener, creator and auditor—is crucial. My private objection to much modernist poetry is precisely that which Joron sees as a strength. It does *not* communicate story. Poetry needn't be overtly narrative, of course, but when poetry becomes so private and involuted and self-referentially symbolic that its audience is incapable of understanding what the poet is saying, how can the poet justifiably condemn that audience for not listening? When the poet tramples on traditional forms, condemns and contemns centuries-old devices for creating emotion and image, then how can the poet complain that no one listens any more? I recently had a student in my creative writing classes who was frustrated by responses to his poetry. He is unarguably a brilliant poet, capable of striking imagery and powerful emotions—but his works were so internalized that even though the brilliance was obvious, the meanings of the poems were not. When only one person can even hope to apprehend the poem, poetry ceases to be a communal act and thereby distorts its primary purpose.

I would argue, then, that Science Fiction poetry should not be defined in terms of adherence to or deviation from literary forms. Such forms are virtually timeless. Even relative latecomers, such as syllabic meter and end-stop rhyme, extend back nearly a thousand years. To employ *any* of the established forms is not necessarily reactionary; it is rather to make full use of the arsenal that is the birthright of any poet. Frequently, a SF poem may look simultaneously in two directions, as I attempted in one of my most successful pieces, "The Last Pastoral." The poem—nominated for the Rhysling and recommended for the Nebula (in the short-fiction category) several years ago—consciously juxtaposed the static, formalistic rhythms and rhyme of Renaissance pastoral love poetry against a futuristic, extrapolative setting; one of the unspoken points of the poem *was* the contradiction between the two, the inability of the past to answer all of the questions the future might pose. Without a deliberate concentration on rhyme and meter—at the same time attempting to fragment and disintegrate that absolute pattern as completely yet as subtly as possible—the poem could not have come to life. As Scott E. Green has noted about this work and others, the language and structures have "an archaic flavor that clashes with futuristic themes. The result is that the reader is made aware that the future is not some distinct entity that is independent of the past and present. Future, past, and present are all of the same cloth" (104).

It is also the poet's right, of course, to deny those historical precedents. SF poetry may indeed focus on stylistic exploration—as long as the poets are aware that even that iconoclasm has itself become a variety of historical precedent. Much good SF poetry is written in free verse; much good SF poetry explores possibilities of typographical arrangement and white space. But those elements by themselves do not establish the pieces as "Science Fiction poetry." Rather, they simply represent specific stylistic and formalistic (or anti-formalistic) choices individual poets have made.

Reading through *Star\*Line*; the Rhysling Anthologies; anthologies as disparate as Frazier's *Burning With a Vision,* Steve Rasnic Tem's *Umbral Anthology,* and Lee Ballentine's *Poly*; and the collected and individual works of Bruce Boston, Andrew Joron, Robert Frazier, W. Gregory Stewart, Jonathan vos Post, Tom Digby, and others, what I find is not a similarity of form or approach but rather a similarity in direction and complexity of responses by individual minds to technological world-view. Individual poems may incorporate new, widely varying patterns—Joron's superlatively created verbal surrealism, or Susan Palwick's Rhysling-winning narrative approach, or Robert Frazier's historical and personal poems that assume rather than assert science, technology, and extrapolation.

On certain obvious levels, the poets that make up the growing SF-poetry community will diverge in their allegiance to or rejection of specific approaches and forms; on more subtle, deeper levels, they do in fact adhere in their concerns for forging a poetry that communicates the needs of the age. Not every SF poet will be concerned with whether or not it is technically possible to write an SF haiku (as was debated hotly in *Star\*Line* some years ago). Not every poet will wish to explore the poetic potentials in the often unpronounceable polysyllabic, inherently non-metrical, non-imagistic, often stultifyingly jargonistic technical vocabulary that clutters our non-literary communications. Not every poet will be interested in poetically structured stories of space flight and ray guns.

But all of those possibilities—and an infinity of others—by right belong to the poets speaking to the contemporary audience about a contemporary world that is itself expanding almost beyond comprehension. The final criterion for assessing SF poetry should not be merely the *kind* of form chosen to express a science-fictional idea, but rather the facility with which the poet controls, develops, and deepens whatever form the poem requires. Traditional narratives, couched in meter and rhyme, may in fact become innovative, forward-looking, exciting; modernistic imagistic fragmentation can become as trite and stereotypic as any other literary device. The difference should, and must, lie within the poet.

# WRITING THE
# FANTASTIC AND RELIGION:

## SOME RUMINATIONS ON THE ROLES OF POETRY

[This essay was presented to the Brigham Young University Symposium on Science Fiction and Fantasy: "Life, the Universe, and Everything, XIV," Provo UT, February 2, 1996; and subsequently published in *Deep Thoughts: Proceedings of Life, the Universe, and Everything, XIV, January 31-February 3, 1996*, edited by Marny K. Parkin and Steve Setzer (Provo UT: LTU&E, 1998): 25-41.]

I am here in a kind of dual role—as a poet of Science Fiction, Fantasy, and Horror, and as a life-long member of the Church of Jesus Christ of Latter-day Saints. As a member, I can recall moments of intense pleasure when something I have written has—if only for myself—illuminated an important point of belief; a number of my earliest exercise poems were unabashed verse paraphrases of scriptures. I can recall the pleasure, only marginally less intense, of seeing or hearing something of mine performed before a congregation that seemed to take from the piece precisely what I had hoped. I can also, however, recall moments tinged with something akin to vicarious horror—certainly astonishment, puzzlement, more than a little curiosity—when a member of my ward has discovered that I read Stephen King, Dean R. Koontz, Robert McCammon, and others of that ilk.

Or worse, that I write *about* Stephen King.

Or beyond worst, that I *write* things like Stephen King's.

I suppose that my first moment of enlightenment occurred back while I was in graduate school, attending the Institute of Religion at my university. Up until that time, most of what I wrote was innocuously mainstream, with a bit of dabbling in marginal SF, or the occasional mythic fantasy. Certainly nothing approaching horror. Nor had I yet formally been introduced to Stephen King's novels; that would have to wait for another few years.

I had, however, become enamored with Milton's *Paradise*

*Lost*—actually, I had loved the poem for years and had only recently been given the opportunity to study it closely under an internationally known scholar. As I worked through scholarship and criticism devoted to the nature of the epic, it seemed to me that the most logical way to understand what Milton intended in the poem was to write something like it.

So, being rather naive at the time, I did.

The consequence, finished about eighteen months later, was a twelve-book, 6,000-line poem on Nephi and the brass plates of Laban, complete with all of the epic apparatus: *proposition, invocation,* division into books, etc. It was, I suppose, a remarkable achievement in its own way, just to have stuck with something of that magnitude long enough to complete it. Nor was it in any important sense 'fantasy.' I had, by and large, remained true to my original texts, with one important exception.

In order to make things work out dramatically, I 'invented' an angel. Instead of having Nephi simply be instructed to cut off Laban's head, I had two angels present, giving him contradictory advise—the 'Good Angel' argued that Nephi should kill Laban, and the 'Bad Angel' kept reminding him that murder was a sin.

The point of the alteration was purely artistic—and, to a degree, fantastic. I simply wanted to make an *internal* debate *external*; probably by that time in my schooling, I had already become engaged with Medieval morality plays, with Marlowe's *Dr. Faustus* and its configurations of 'Good Angel'/'Bad Angel' debates; and with Milton's own permutations on scriptures. My intent was innocent and, as it turned out, my assumptions were beyond naive.

The first responses I received were that I could never publish the poem. That turned out to be accurate, by the way, since the market for—as one early reader put it—"Seventeenth-Century *Iadic* poetry" had dried up about two and a half centuries earlier; strictly from a marketing standpoint, *The Nephiad* was and remains unpublishable.[*]

But that wasn't what the initial readers meant. They meant that I should not be *allowed* to publish the poem...for the simple reason that it diverged from the Book of Mormon account. In fact, one of the readers (whose scholarship I admire and whose books I still find fascinating) bluntly scolded me for having wasted my time by writing the poem in the first place: The Book of Mormon, he explained in great detail, had already said everything that could or should be

---

[*] It has, in fact been published in its entirety by Borgo/Wildside Press (2010), some thirty-five years after its initial draft.

said on the subject.

(I wonder, parenthetically, how that reader might respond to Orson Scott Card's *Homecoming* novels, to say nothing of *The Worthing Chronicle, Saints, The Folk of the Fringe,* and the Alvin Maker series.)

Having recovered somewhat from the exuberance and excesses of being a graduate student, I now understand a bit better what concerned those readers, even though I still do not quite agree with the vehemence or the absolutism of their rejections. True, it was possible that some hypothetical reader unfamiliar with the Church might assume *I* believed that there were two angels present at that crucial moment. True, it was possible that the same hypothetical reader might also assume that either the Book or Mormon or I was not accurate. True, it was possible—indeed probable—that the nature of the poem would make it unpublishable. And true, it was possible that I might have been wasting my time writing it (and, to be truthful, it did take nearly ten years for me to eliminate some lingering Miltonisms in my poetic style).

But both of those readers had missed the central point of *The Nephiad.*

It was a *poem.*

It was not a theological tract. It was not a re-writing of the Book of Mormon. It was certainly not an official statement of the Church of Jesus Christ of Latter-day Saints.

*It was a poem.* An artifact of the imagination. And nothing more.

In his edition of Charles Williams' Arthurian epic-fragment, *Taliessin Through Logres,* C. S. Lewis comments that one of Williams' greatest strengths as a poet was the simple fact that Williams always understood a single truth: ultimately, no poem is very important. In the theological terms Lewis uses, a poem might be interesting, but it will not in and of itself ensure one's salvation. [*]

That is how I felt about *The Nephiad.* It was an important poem for me to write, one that I still believe has specific strengths. It helped me understand critical points about poetry (After all, what better way to learn about the mechanics of an epic such as *Paradise Lost* than to write one.). It helped me endure some difficult and tedious times during graduate school. And it helped me understand a bit more completely what it might have *felt* like to be in Nephi's situation, to be faced with what seemed an impossibly complex moral

---

[*] Leon Surette's study of Pound, Eliot, Joyce, and Modernism makes essentially the same comment about Pound when it observes that Pound was a talented poet but not a prophet.

decision that required extraordinary courage to respond to. I believed—and still believe—in *The Nephiad* as a poem; but I have never felt the urge to cite it while teaching an Elders' quorum or High Priest' Group lesson.

Since then, I have written a number of LDS-oriented poems, and a number of Fantasy, Science Fiction, and Horror poems. At times the boundaries between the two approaches have blurred in odd ways. Perhaps the most successful Christmas program I have ever written, *The Gift of Christmastide*, was written during the early hours of a sleepless November night—with *Dracula Must Rise from the Grave* playing on the television in the background. And at least one of my favorite horror poems, "Black Dandelions," began as a black-ink doodle on the back of a Sacrament Meeting program several years ago, when my increasing deafness made it impossible for me to understand more than a fraction of what was being said during the meeting; since I was the organist and was sitting on the stand at the time, I had a choice of writing or sleeping—and chose the former as the least embarrassing.

### BLACK DANDELIONS

Black dandelions storm-heart black
Crowd the crumbling Commons wall.
Taproots crowned with grey-green
Toothy coils that curl upon themselves
Sink slowly Hellward....
Thirsty rootlets nose blindly for a draught
Of moistness where the Witchman
Lies amouldering.

They killed him first a month ago—
A blast of silver slicing lungs and heart
That blew life from his flesh.

They killed him next a fortnight past,
When flaming hawthorn pierced his skull
And crushed the convoluted grey within.

They burned his flesh until no thing remained
But ash and bone—then buried both
Two man-lengths deep beyond the Commons wall.

He waited yet another fortnight—
Buried deep, seed to Witchman seed in ashy crypt.
And now, with the full moon's lambent blast, grey
Ashes stir, burnt bones knit, moistness rises upward.
The Witchman rises...bringing with him
Lethal winds to scatter midnight Death-seeds
Among villagers beyond the Commons wall,
Where grow profusely in the darkness
Black dandelions, storm-heart black.

About twenty-five years ago, I wrote a poem that I considered an overtly religious poem, "The Blood Burns," an interior monologue spoken by the Roman soldier who had stood guard over Christ's tomb, some twenty years later. The speaker, mortally wounded in battle, is dying, yet all that he can hear is the sound of a large rock being rolled across the sand.

### THE BLOOD BURNS

The blood burns—
*Gods!* I had thought blood cold
but it burns down my side
between fingers once mine clutching vainly
at my wound.

The blood burns—
stripes of flame
growing from a tremor in my breath.
I once ran from threads of flame,
from quaking earth—
ran, and hid myself in shadowy groves,
and saw....

The blood burns
where I touched his corpse accidentally
before the stone rolled
across its opening. Then—that time—
my fingers froze with the chill of death.

But now....
The blood burns

and I dwindle to a hidden spark,
and the blood burns no more.
Rome's enemies exult at my death,
a fallen warrior.
The blood slows, crusts brown
upon sodden soil.

And there is nothing—
save the sound of sandstone rolling over sun-parched
    earth.

Initially, the poem was intended as part of a longer sequence of Easter meditations and monologues; as with so many ambitious projects, however, this one was never completed. Some months later, though, as I was finishing up a packet of poems for submission, I came across "The Blood Burns," and—more on a whim than anything else—included it with poems sent to the *San Fernando Poetry Journal.* At the time, the *SFPJ* was a highly political publication, so there was no compelling reason for me to send a religious poem there, but I did.

The surprise came later when I received a response—the editor had returned all of my 'political' poems but had *accepted* "The Blood Burns." An even greater surprise, bordering on shock, came when the issue arrived and I opened it to discover my 'Easter' poem listed on the contents pages with, among others, such works as "Ain't Enough Burn Unit Blues," by Judy Schravien; "Radioactive Rat Droppings found at Three Mile Island," by Pamela A. Malone; "Nuclear Tech Goes Mini" and "Nuclear Bombs Kill Whales," by the *SFPJ* editor Richard Cloke; "Under the Mushroom," by Margaret Key Biggs; "All Star Neutron Day," an Asian sonnet by Aaron Kramer commemorating the destruction of Nagasaki; and "Silent Screams," by Blair H. Allen.

Somehow my Easter meditation had blundered its way into a magazine dedicated to anti-nuclear poetry!

I read through the issue, from the first entry to "The Blood Burns," noting the movement and pacing that Cloke had established through his arrangement of poetry. When I read my poem, I was startled to discover that, with the exception of a single word, it legitimately *was* a Science-Fiction/Fantasy-verging-on-Horror poem about an unnamed but doomed victim of radiation sickness in the near future. Only the word "Rome" works against that reading, and even that one word can be made to fit metaphorically, symbolically, or imagistically.

So without knowing it, I had effectively bridged the abyss between religion and Science Fiction, theology and Horror.

Or at least the experience suggested how extraordinarily thin the actual distance between the two might be.

After that rather remarkable experience, it seemed only logical to explore the interface more consciously. A number of more recent poems have deliberately fused religion and the fantastic. In "Vampire," I wrote about a fragment of LDS history, a conflict over water-rights in an Idaho valley during the 1920s and 1930s that led to the excommunication or disfellowship of several members, including my great-grandfather. But that base-subject does not feature overtly in the poem:

### VAMPIRE

A vampire lives on the old homestead,
shadowing deep attic corners,
darkness in the light.

It lives there still—
but once it was threatened, I think,
when the Valley banded together

and built the new-brick church
on the corpse of the old-stone chapel
a generation old.

For a breath, it hesitated,
paled, faded into shadows cut in stone
above wheat fields thick with rattlesnakes.

For a breath...then it remembered:
water rights...arguments...disfellowships...
mindless faith that led

to numbness, stultifying
death.
And it returned to prey

as always on the living blood,
to suck hearts dry

that should have lived deep pools

irrigating souls. Instead the vampire rested,
roiled among the shadows,
emerged with glittering and thirsty fangs

It is a poem that I could not have been written without my background in LDS history, yet its first serial appearance, in *The Blood Review,* devoted exclusively to horror literature, clearly divorced the poem from any specific religious implications.

Most recently, I have been exploring the possibilities of merging Myth and LDS history in a series of poems modeled loosely on Williams' *Taliessin Through Logres.* Adopting a modified version of Williams' persona, the poet/priest Taliesin, as well as the larger framework of the Arthurian tradition, these poems consciously (perhaps self-consciously) weld LDS history and Arthurian imagery, creating a blend of religion and fantasy that I find particularly appealing—but that I will perhaps never be able to publish.

Each of the set assumes the presence of a poet/priest, who chooses to call himself Taliesin, at key events in the life of Joseph Smith, whom Taliesin images as an Arthur, with all of the mythic power that the figure entails. Of the six completed poems to date,[*] several are in a modified sonnet form invented specifically for this series—an attempt at connecting the poems even more tightly to literary tradition. Yet they can only be understood with reference to LDS backgrounds, as in the following:

### TALIESIN RECOUNTS THE
### WOUND TO ARTHUR'S LEG

It might have been an arm, a shoulder blade,
A rib (the thirteenth, harkening to its mate),
A hip-joint traitor-turned to cowled leg,
Or even an eye obscured by unseen mote;

It could have been any of these, his body
Turned against the man-soul inhabiting,
But it was his leg, infected badly,
Microscopic darkness orbiting

---

[*] *Taliesin* now numbers over twenty-five poems and will be included in a forthcoming collection.

Blood, destroying it—that simple—to kill
The King before his crown could be full forged.
But excised—*bone cut out with bloody skill*—
Removed, the sickness could no longer gorge

Itself on him, and died. But, wounded, lamed,
He bore its scars a lifetime, just the same.

Or, perhaps more explicitly:

### THE GRAIL

hidden beyond westward mists and sun-sleeps,
beyond waves of grasses green-brown ripe, and
hunched flanks of mountains, and roiled streams deep
with life, it sleeps also and dreams and sends

its dreams in dreams to Arthur where he lies
wide-eyed on a garret bed beneath rough
hand-hewn shingles that weep yet sticking tears
and glimmer lightness, dim but still enough

to catch his waking dreams and cast them high
as mountain pinnacles and reflect them
in six-spired elegance and draw from eyes
that see beyond rough shingles to the one

tears unspoken for the vessel and blood
of Christ, granite-encased for Galahad.

I am not sure how long this sequence will be when I finish it (or it finishes with me). Certainly I have no intention of creating a complete series of LDS/Arthurian analogues, in which each elements of the Arthurian tales has a specific parallel in LDS tradition. But at the moment it is a fascinating exercise in seeing to what extent I can expand the interface between the fantastic and the religious, between Myth and History, between poetic truth and theological truth.

What I have learned from the process, however, is that poetry claims for itself a variety of modes of knowing. The convention goes back well into the Medieval period and extends forward to effect some recent theories of fantasy. Readers of and audiences for poetry in the Middle Ages would have easily accepted the fact that poetry explored multiple levels of meaning—"Truth"—simultane-ously. They easily accepted an image as having literal, allegorical, analogical, and anagogical meanings—and just as easily accommo-dated to the fact that a single image could move gracefully from one level of interpretation to another without any difficulty.

Modern readers are often used to reading poetry on multiple, but different, levels:

- The poem as literal and meaning precisely what it says;
- The poem as metaphorical, apparently discussing one subject while actually dealing with a second, but still identifying at least indirectly with "truth";
- The poem as imagistic, in which the image might inherently be connected with factual "truth," but does not need to be so;
- And the poem as exercise of imagination, creating or re-creating images which may be unrelated to, separated from, even antithetical to factual "truths."

Even this rather simplistic listing suggests, in addition, that are sev-eral kinds of "Truth" that must be taken into account when evaluat-ing poetic versions of "Truths":

- Truth as fact (which fosters the illusion that we can share a common fund of agreed-upon "facts");
- Truth as that which transcends the surface nature of mere fact;
- That which speaks to eternal relationships uninflu-enced by transitory understandings and interpreta-tions;
- That which is revealed and stands eternally.

In addition to these complications, the role of poetry itself within the Fantastic has been hotly debated over the past several decades. A scholar as central to our varied definitions of Fantasy, Science Fic-tion, and Horror as Tzvetan Todorov has argued forcibly that "fan-tastic" poetry is scarcely even a possibility. By its very nature, po-etry opens the discourse on a figurative level:

Today, it is generally agreed that poetic images

are not descriptive, that they are to be read quite literally, on the level of the verbal chain they constitute,
not even on that of their reference. The poetic image
is a combination of words, not of things, and it is
pointless, even harmful, to translate this combination
into sensory terms.(60)

That is, poetry by its nature is essentially *non-representational*
(to use Todorov's term), it is inherently divorced from direct contact
with the 'real world,' it clearly opposes fiction (in which we antici-
pate/expect/demand connections with the world), and it requires that
the reader/auditor accept words as bearing meaning only within the
context of its own structure. Additionally, the Fantastic requires a
momentary hesitation on the part of the reader/audience, a hesitation
caused by the need to interpret an event as belonging either to the
Uncanny (consistent with unknown but real natural laws) or Supernatural (inconsistent with known natural laws). Since any line of poetry can be read figuratively, he argues, there can be no such authentic hesitation on the part of the reader; the reader automatically ac-
commodates both literal and figurative readings. Todorov's conclusion concerning poetry and the fantastic is quite direct:

...the poetic reading constitutes a danger for the fantastic. If as we read a text we reject all representation,
considering each sentence as a pure semantic combination, the fantastic *could not appear*; for the fantastic requires, it will be recalled, a reaction to events as
they occur in the world evoked. For this reason, the
fantastic can subsist only within fiction; poetry cannot be fantastic (though there may be anthologies of
"fantastic poetry"). (60)

The structural devices of poetry—rhythm, meter, rhyme, word
play—are all sufficient to alert the reader that the words read are *not*
to be taken as describing the 'real world' precisely; thus, there is no
opportunity for a fantastic 'reversal.'

As in other areas of his theoretical discourse, Todorov here
seems more restrictive than actual practice allows; there are, of
course, concerted efforts among poets to create Fantasy poetry, Science Fiction poetry, even Horror poetry—but he is correct in saying
that it is difficult to succeed. Too often, such poetry simply asserts
the surface elements of fantastic fictions, resulting in a general at-

mosphere of Horror, for example, but a lack of the sense that the work *is* Horror. After all, it is only a poem.

At the other extreme, it is equally possible to argue that ultimately there cannot be *religious* poetry…and for the same structural reasons. A line concerning 'god' or 'angels' or other such essentially religious elements can *also* be read as either literal (in which case the religious elements are simply asserted, not explored, and the poem runs the risk of failure *as poem*) or as figurative (in which case there need not be *any* religious meaning and, while the poem may succeed as a poem, it may not be at heart religious—or it may not be *perceived* as an inherently religious poem, a fate that seems increasingly to have befallen poems such as Milton's *Paradise Lost,* which, at the hands of a number of critics, becomes primarily political allegory, social commentary, historical affirmation, etc.

These general concerns (treated all too briefly here) are relevant to my intentionally and unabashedly personal discussion because even these cursory remarks (unsupported and unsubstantiated beyond the sketchiest level) suggest that poetry becomes as varied and as possible as the poets creating it—or the critics analyzing it. I cannot speak with authority on relationships between Poetry and Fantasy/Science Fiction, Poetry and Religion, and most certainly not Poetry, Religion, *and* Fantasy/Science Fiction except as far as my own writings have moved in and out of those categories over the past twenty-five years. My own experiences and the opportunity for evaluation presented by preparing this paper suggest that such boundaries seem unusually tenuous and fragile…as they should be. Religion and Science Fiction/Fantasy are not synonymous; they do not consist of perfectly overlapping circles. At times they touch; they may even overlap. And it is one of the roles of poetry to examine those overlays to see how one universe of discourse might illuminate the other.

# FANTASY, SCIENCE FICTION, AND HORROR IN *PARADISE LOST*:

## "AND ON HIS CREST SAT HORROR PLUM'D"

[This essay was presented as "'And On His Crest Sat Horror Plum'd': Some Elements of Science Fiction, Fantasy, and Horror in Milton's *Paradise Lost*" to Life, the Universe, and Everything" at Brigham Young University in 1995 and subsequently published in *Deep Thoughts: Proceedings of* Life, the Universe, & Everything XIII, *February 1-4, 1995,* edited by Steve Setzer and Marny K. Parkin, 1997. It has been revised lightly for this volume.]

In discussing the possibility of pre-Nineteenth-Century fantasy, including rudimentary science fiction and horror, it might at first seem idiosyncratic even to consider Milton's elegant and elevated religious epic, *Paradise Lost.* On the basis of genre, purpose, and treatment, it certainly touches on such equally elevated and traditionally related forms as Myth and (according to John M. Steadman) Tragedy, but it seems to lack many of the differentia that we would normally apply in defining Fantasy, Science Fiction, or Horror.

On the other hand, a number fantasy, science fiction, and horror scholars have included Milton (usually with references to *Paradise Lost*) into their discussions of the genres, either directly, indirectly, or inversely connecting Milton's epic with the fundamental impulses leading to the fantastic. The list of such scholars and theorists is extensive, indicating that there are indeed some important connections to be made. Among those who have used Milton to varying degrees of intensity as a touchstone in their discussions and/or definitions of the Fantastic (momentarily including all three genres under a single rubric) are:

- W. R. Irwin, *The Game of the Impossible: A Rhetoric of Fantasy* (1976);
- Rosemary Jackson, *Fantasy: The Literature of Subversion* (1981);

- •Colin Manlove, *Christian Fantasy from 1200 to the Present* (1992), in which he argues for *Paradise Lost* as perhaps the last major Christian fantasy of its kind;
- •David Ketterer, *New Worlds for Old: The Apocalyptic Imagination, Science Fiction and American Literature* (1974);
- •Eric S. Rabkin, *The Fantastic in Literature* (1976);
- •Robert Scholes and Eric S. Rabkin, *Science Fiction: History, Science Fiction* (1977);
- •Patrick Parrinder, *Science Fiction: Its Criticism and Teaching* (1980), with its chapter on the similar functions of Science Fiction and Epic;
- •Karl Guthke, *The Last Frontier: Imagining Other Worlds from the Copernican Revolution to Modern Science Fiction.* (1983; translated 1990);
- •James B. Twitchell, *The Living Dead: A Study of the Vampire in Romantic Literature* (1981) and *Dreadful Pleasures: An Anatomy of Modern Horror* (1985);
- •Victor Sage, *Horror Fiction in the Protestant Tradition* (1988);
- •Manuel Aguirre, *The Closed Space: Horror Literature and Western Symbolism* (1990).

As noted above, the intensity and the direction of their treatments of *Paradise Lost* necessarily differ widely. Rosemary Jackson discusses J. A. Symonds' perception of Milton's Satan as being "fantastic" in almost generic terms:

> One of the namings of otherness has been as "demonic" and it is important to recognize the semantic shifts of this term, since they indicate the progressive internalization of fantastic narrative in the post-Romantic period. J.A. Symonds saw all fantastic art as characterized by an obsession with the demonic. He referred to Shakespeare's Caliban, Milton's Death, and Goethe's Mephistopheles as "products of fantastic art." (54)

W. R. Irwin writes, on the other hand, that Milton specifically avoids the kind of treatment of Satan that might have resulted in modern Fantasy: "Let me start by saying what I believe most readers will intuitively accept, that fantasy cannot contain beings that are intrinsically heroic and those whose essence is either psychic, spiritual, or passional…" (74); therefore, he continues, while "Lucifer son of the morning" does not belong in a fantasy world,

> Satan, ultimately foolish and defeated despite the power he had through time owing to human folly, could be a character in a fantasy and does so appear in Mark Twain's *The Mysterious Stranger,* though here he is a nephew of the Enemy, little Satan. There is nothing intrinsically heroic, psychic, spiritual, or passional, and there is no mystery, no evil. The quality itself and those who embody it may be plumbed to the depth by reason. Milton understood this routine principle of moral theology, and this was part of what moved him to portray Satan objectively. In *Paradise Lost* he made no such attempt to objectify God, and little to portray the Son of God, who in *Paradise Regained* is properly shown because he has become the incarnate Christ. (74-75).

In other words, given his epical treatment of character and fable, Milton precludes any sense of the poem as fantasy. When those characters are treated in a different manner, and the setting is altered from mythic Eden to C. S. Lewis's equally mythic but simultaneously fantastical Perelandra, the result is fantasy (Irwin, *Game* 140)—or, the result may *be* fantasy, since scholars such as Scholes and Rabkin refer to Lewis's Perelandra novels as religious parable or anti-science-fiction, rather than fantasy.

In considering the possibility of *Paradise Lost as* science fiction, Karl Guthke tacitly argues against *Paradise Lost* as even proto-science-fictional because of Milton's obvious theological emphasis:

> Milton is another writer whose piety makes him respond less than enthusiastically to the new ideas [of science], and in the manner of his response he too is representative of his time. In 1638/39 Milton had visited Galileo, the prisoner of the Inquisition, at his house at Arcetri, near Florence. One can picture him reacting to Galileo's beliefs about cosmology, the ba-

sis of the modern concept of plurality, with a polite shrug of the shoulders.... He is moderately interested, but basically it does not matter to him whether or not God created living beings in other worlds. His convictions as a Protestant...cause him to focus his attention solely on the centrality of man in God's view—man as descended from its first ancestors in the Garden of Eden and redeemed by Christ. (127)

Robert Scholes and Eric S. Rabkin go further, finally questioning whether works such as *Paradise Lost* are even to be discussed as progenitors to modern Science Fiction:

Even the literary ancestry sometimes claimed for science fiction itself might better be called, in part at least, religious fantasy. Dante, Thomas More, and Milton all ventured beyond the limits of normal terrestrial experience to generate fictions, and if to venture beyond known worlds or to leave the terrestrial globe were enough to make a work science fiction, it would be reasonable and proper to call Dante's *Commedia,* More's *Utopia,* and Milton's *Paradise Lost* works of science fiction. Yet of all these only More's, which is the least adventurous in its voyaging, even begins to approach the mental territory of modern science fiction. The worlds of Dante and Milton remain separate from science fiction because they are constructed on a plan derived from religious tradition rather than scientific speculation or imagination based, however loosely, on science.... They are religious fictions, and to read them rightly we must suspend any disbelief in the religious tradition that supports them. (43-44)

Still, it has been argued for at least thirty years that *Paradise Lost* contains some elements of science fiction because, as Colin Manlove states (echoing Marjorie Hope Nicholson), "Satan is one of the first space-travellers" (*Christian,* 106). Manlove further argues that, while there are mentions of travel through space previous to Milton's, most, if not all, paid "scant attention to the experience of the voyage itself and its distances" (*Christian,* 318n). He also cites Nicolson's assessment of this passage from the poem:

Nowhere in poetry do we find more majestic conceptions of the vastness of space than in the work of this blind poet, in those scenes of cosmic perspective in which we, like Satan on the one hand, God on the other, look up and down to discover a universe majestic in its vastness. (*Christian,* 318n)

Yet while Milton does indeed portray Satan flying through space (*PL* III 560-571), Guthke argues that the poet consciously ignores any of the potentials for what we might see as science fiction. In Book VIII (1-178), when Adam and Raphael discuss cosmology and the universe, Milton uses the opportunity to "put all such cosmic speculation, whether for or against the plurality of worlds and of humankinds, firmly in its place" (130); according to Raphael,

> To ask or search I blame thee not, for Heav'n
> Is as the Book of God before thee set,
> Wherein to read his wondrous Works, and learne
> His Seasons, Hours, or Dayes, or Months, or Yeares:
> This to attain, whether Heav'n move or Earth,
> Imports not, if thou reck'n right, the rest
> From Man or Angel the great Architect
> Did wisely to conceal, and not divulge
> His secrets to be scann'd by them who ought
> Rather admire; or if they list to try
> Conjecture, he his Fabric of the Heav'ns
> Hath left to thir disputes, perhaps to move
> His laughter at thir quaint Opinions wide
> Hereafter, when they come to model Heav'n
> And calculate the Starrs, how they will weild
> The mightie frame, how build, unbuild, contrive
> To save appearances, how gird the Sphear
> With Centric and Eccentric scribl'd o're,
> Cycle and Epicycle, Orb in Orb... (VIII.66-84)

Thus, although the Paradise of Fools episode in Book III (ll. 440-465) touches on science fiction/fantasy—particularly the Cosmic Voyage and the possibility of life on other planets—there is a strong sense that Milton's intentions in creating his poem would militate against the kind of speculation that would suggest science fiction, and the kind of cognitive indeterminacy that would allow for fantasy.

As far as Horror as genre goes, the case is similar. Some critics find reason to exclude even the possibility of Literary Horror in *Paradise Lost,* while others see in the poem, and particularly in Milton's treatment of Satan in Books I and II, seminal images and motifs of contemporary Dark Fantasy and Horror. Twitchell differentiates between "old horror" and "modern horror" in ways that reflect directly on the ambiguities of *Paradise Lost:*

> The invocation of horror, the fabrication of fright, has always been present in the English tradition from *Beowulf* on. But what separates "old" horror from what I call "modern" horror is that, prior to romanticism, horror monsters were usually the means by which the artist held his audience's attention while he prepared his protagonist for heroism. The monster was there to be destroyed, and if it could scare the readers first that was fine, because they would then appreciate the hero even more. Pre-romantic monsters were in the text, much as Sidney prescribed, to show by their destruction the power of *virtú.* (*Dreadful,* 25)

While this description may seem apt for many early "horrors," it does not quite describe what one finds in *Paradise Lost.* If Satan is considered as an "old" horror, who then serves as the protagonist-in-waiting who will destroy him? Not even in *Paradise Regained* can Satan be literally destroyed, and certainly within the confines of the longer epic, he is imprisoned and restrained but not destroyed. If, on the other hand, Sin and Death are "old" monsters, the same is true—they cannot be destroyed, at least not within the boundaries of *either* epic. In fact, it seems, Satan, Sin, and Death may share more with "modern" monsters than with "old" ones:

> In modern versions we forget the victims and even the hero, but we remember the monster. Who, for instance, kills Dracula? How is the Frankenstein monster destroyed? Are we sure the werewolf is dead? Monsters have become bogeymen, and as the child in *Halloween* says, "Ya can't ever kill the bogeyman." Also curious is that now the monsters have become aristocrats (Count Dracula, Baron Frankenstein, Doc-

tor Moreau, Doctor Jekyll, and so forth), and the victims are no longer "ladies in distress," but buxom
young girls of the bourgeoisie. The hero is still a
young man, but without much personality and with
precious little *virtú*. (25)

Perhaps even more instructive is the extent to which much of this
paragraph can be applied to Satan in *Paradise Lost*. We remember
him; we admire and remember the magnificent rhetoric of his
speeches, even when God's or the Son's words have faded. Satan is
an aristocrat, one of the elevated orders of angels. His victim is more
closely allied to "buxom young girl" than "lady in distress"; her hero
is a young man (chronologically, at least) whose single most important act is to *disobey* God's commandment; and both have even been
described as resembling nothing so much as a pair of English shop-
keepers, albeit without trousers or gown.

In an earlier study, Twitchell explicitly connected Milton's Satan
with the development of the Byronic/Gothic hero, itself an early
stage of contemporary Horror. Milton's Satan is the precursor to a
"growing artistic concern with the demonic and perhaps vampiric"
and the Byronic/Gothic hero is "Milton's Satan reborn..." (*Living
Dead*, 75). Even more specifically, Brontë's Heathcliffe, acting as
pseudo-vampire, is "a lineal descendant of the Gothic antihero who
has as his grand progenitor Milton's Satan"; indeed, the first generation of readers and critics of *Wuthering Heights* saw Heathcliffe as
an unredeemed "'fiend,' 'an incarnation of evil qualities,' filled with
'implacable hate,' as well as 'ingratitude, cruelty, falsehood, selfish-
ness and revenge.' He was a devil, 'impelled to evil by supernatural
forces'" (*Living Dead*, 116).

Certainly these descriptions suggest the concerns of contemporary literary horror as well as Milton's theological concerns in creating the figure of Satan. And equally certainly, it would be a wrench-
ing of form and purpose to suggest that *Paradise Lost* should be removed from the "Epic" category and take its place on the bookshelf
labeled "Horror" beside Stephen King, Robert McCammon, Dan
Simmons, or Dean R. Koontz. Even so, there are a number of suggestions that the poem does in fact approach "horror" from an essentially modern perspective, sufficiently so that passages occasionally
do elicit the same sorts of responses that King and others expect
from their readers.

Milton seems to have been aware of the implications of "horror,"
both as word and as concept. As early as the Nativity Ode, permuta-

tions on the word appear, but generally in a context that communicates verbal rather than visceral horror. That is, in stanza twenty-seven of the Ode, Milton wants to communicate the *sense* of horror, but restrains himself from attempting to make his readers feel or experience the visceral, physiological symptoms of horror, of what King refers to as the "gross out." Instead, the Nativity Ode *asserts* horror, using the word descriptively:

> With such a horrid clang
> As on mount Sinai rang
> While the red fire, and smouldring clouds out brake
>     ... (157-160)

Yet within a few lines, he reiterates the word, this time infusing it with a more substantive sense; we are invited not just to *know* that something elicits horror, but to *see* horror personified in that thing: "Wrath to see his Kingdom fail," Satan "Swindges the scaly Horrour of his foulded tail" (171-172). Additional references in "L'Allegro" (ll. 1-4), *Comus* (ll. 36-39), *Lycidas* (ll. 75-76) and the paraphrase of Psalm 138 (ll. 27-28) indicate that the word was a functional part of Milton's poetic vocabulary, although almost always at the level of assertion—a thing is *horrid* or a *horror* not because the reader immediately perceives it as such, but because Milton overtly claims it to be so.

When we reach *Paradise Lost,* however, the sheer numerical incidence of the word increases dramatically. Variants on *Horror* (not to mention words such as *terror* and *fear*, which are also associated with Horror literature) occur no fewer than eight times in Book I, thirteen times in Book II, three times in Book IV, two times in Book V, seven in Book VI, two in Book IX and four in Book X (most describing the consequences of the fall), and one each in Books XI and XII; not coincidentally, the references cluster primarily at those points in the narrative that focus on Satan, the archetype of evil.[*]

At two points, Milton even puns on the etymology of the word (as he does so often throughout his poetry). *Horror* is derived from the Latin *horrere*, meaning 'to tremble, to bristle, to be in horror.'

---

[*] Book I, 51, 61, 83, 137, 224, 250, 392, 563; Book II, 63, 87, 178, 220, 513, 577, 616, 644, 659, 676, 703, 710, 846; Book IV, 18, 392, 989; Book V, 65, 120; Book VI, 210, 252, 305, 307, 607, 668, 863; Book VIX, 185, 890; Book X, 472, 539, 789, 843; Book XI, 465 (twice); Book XII, 79

Most of its variants continue that sense of "bristling":

> Horrendous—from Latin *horrendus*, gerundive of *horrere*
> Horrent—from Latin *horrens*, present participle of *horrere*.
> Horrible—from Latin *horribilis*
> Horrid—from Latin, *horridus*
> Horrific—from Latin *horrificus*
> Horrify—from Latin *horrificare*, to bristle
> Horripilation—from Latin *horripilatus*, past participle of *horripilare*, to bristle with hairs

Similarly, Milton would have been aware of the etymology of *comet*, coming from both Greek and Latin as meaning 'long-haired star'. Thus it is surely intentional when Milton asserts in Book I that the arrogant Satan stood

> Unterrifi'd, and like a Comet burn'd
> That fires the length of Ophiucus huge
> In th'Arctic Sky, and from his horrid hair
> Shakes pestilence and Warr. (707-710)

Satan's hair is *horrid* because it is comet-like, bristling and streaming out from his head; but it is also *horrid* because it is Satanic, evil, capable of inspiring depths of terror and fear. In a subsequent reference, Milton compounds the pun and moves his definition of *horror* a step further when he again uses the word in two senses simultaneously—the first, its etymological one; and the second, its moral one. As Satan and Gabriel square off for heroic battle at the end of Book IV, Milton describes Satan:

> On th'other side *Satan* alarm'd
> Collecting all his might dilated stood,
> Like *Teneriff* or *Atlas* unremov'd;
> His stature reacht the Skie, and on his Crest
> Sat horror Plum'd... (IV. 985-989)

In these two references, Milton has both indicated his interest in the possibilities inherent in the word and suggested that as he uses it he is subtly altering its meaning. The first reference is assertive; Satan's hair horrifies because it is horrible. Essentially, in spite of the pun, the line is a tautology, ignoring the possibility of description to elicit a horrified *response* in favor of instructing the reader simply to *be* horrified. In the second, however, *horror* is now external to Satan, an entity of some sort, plumed and prepared for battle, that the reader is invited, however vaguely, to envision.

Essentially, such a differentiation suggests the two primary modes of communicating horror in contemporary literatures. Assertive horror *instructs* the reader. Often, specific writers depend on a key word to signal the approach of Horror; with H. P. Lovecraft, for example, the touchstone word is "eldritch." Although the word merely means 'strange,' 'unearthly,' or 'weird,' with a possible link to an Anglo-Saxon word meaning 'fairyland,' in Lovecraft's fictions it frequently functions as a trigger, alerting readers that they are supposed to be horrified at this point. When he couples *eldritch* with *horror* itself, the expected responses are even stronger.

At a very different level, however, writers may attempt to re-create the physical symptoms of horror through description and narration—what King (in his typical under-rating of his own work) frequently refers to as the "gross-out." In such scenes the reader is asked to *image* horror, to visualize it so completely that the body responds appropriately. In this context, Horror as genre could be defined in the same terms that Irwin uses to differentiate pornography from Fantasy: Fantasy is essentially an intellectual game of "what-if"; pornography, on the other hand, incorporates an entirely different sort of "fantasizing" and has as its intended outcome a purely physical—not an intellectual—response (*Game* 90-91). Without suggesting any further connections between Horror and pornography, it seems clear from King's definitions (and other horror writers') that Horror as genre similarly intends to elicit a physical, rather than an intellectual, response—a shiver along the spine, the gathering of flesh into goose bumps, even small fluctuations in bodily rhythms of heartbeat and respiration.

While asserted horror may occur in literatures of all eras, visceral horror seems more closely linked to post-Romantic, post-Gothic works. Thus, it should come as no surprise that the majority of references in *Paradise Lost* are essentially assertive; Milton identifies something as "horrible" or "horrid" simply because it is. The references do not impact in any significant way on the elevation, the dignity, the elegance of the epic surrounding them. Thus, we find references to Satan's "horrid crew" (I.51), to Hell as a "Dungeon horrible" (I.61) and a "horrid Vale" (I. 224), to the "horrid silence" of Hell (I. 83), to Moloch as "horrid King" (I.392), and so forth.

Only once in Book I does Milton seem to depart from verbal, assertive horror, as Satan embraces his new realm and, for the moment, comes close to personifying the word:

> Farewel happy Fields
> Where Joy for ever dwells: Hail horrours, hail
> Infernal world, and thou profoundest Hell
> Receive thy new Possessor.... (I.250)

Even here, however, the effect is ephemeral at best, so highly generalized as to suggest the entirety of Hell rather than any specific, physical, visual focus for a physiological reaction.

The transition from asserted horror to visceral and visual horror becomes more explicit in Book II, however, in which Satan confronts Sin and Death at Hell's Gate. In a poem that makes conscious use of supernatural characters and mythic actions elevated beyond the realms of mortality, the appearance of two abstractions *as allegorical characters* has elicited much comment and controversy. Is it not enough, critics argue, that Milton shows us God, the Son, Satan, and the various concourses of angels; isn't it straining even the credibility of epic to *show* Sin and Death as concretions? In addition, during the opening lines of the Book, *horror* retains its largely assertive function: weaponry is described as "horrid" (II.63) and "horrent" (II.513); Hell and the River Styx are "abhorred" (II. 87, 577), and so forth.

This sense alters, however, as the Book progresses. First we see groups of fallen angels

> Thus roving on
> in confus'd march forlorn, th'adventrous Bands
> With shudd'ring horror pale, and eyes agast
> View'd first their lamentable lot.... (II.614-617)

The visual sense of pale flesh and eyes wide-opened with shock (*Aghast* is derived from the Anglo-Saxon *gasten*, 'to frighten,' intensified by the prefixed *a-*) momentarily replaces assertive with imaginative horror; readers are invited to *see* rather than merely to accept.

When Satan approaches the "horrid Roof/And thrice threefold Gates" (II. 644), however, an interesting transition occurs. Earlier, *horror* had been used to describe Satan himself, his cohorts, his new realm. In a sense, even though Satan is himself a supernatural character, he has become the norm by which things and events are judged. Now, for the first time, he approaches something new, something which is *horrid* not so much because it reflects Satan's inherent evil but because it is now external to him (apparently). Milton's description of Sin does not use the word *horror*; instead, he attempts to re-create the *experience* of horror—visceral repugnance, disgust, revulsion, loathing. In images reminiscent of Spenser's Error in *The Faerie Queene*, Milton depicts Sin:

> Before the Gates there sat
> On either side a formidable shape;
> The one seem'd Woman to the waste, and fair,
> But ended foul in many a scaly fould
> Voluminous and vast, a Serpent arm'd
> With mortal sting: about her middle round
> A cry of Hell Hounds never ceasing bark'd
> With wide Cerberian mouths full loud, and rung
> A hideous Peal: yet, when they list, would creep,
> If aught disturb'd thir noyse, into her woomb,
> And kennel there, yet there still bark'd and howl'd,
> Within unseen. (II. 648-659)

Milton's description is intended to elicit a horrified response, amplified in part by his audience's familiarity with Spenser and with visual representations of Sin and Death in paintings of the period (See Roland Frye, 111-124). The next lines place that horror in an equally familiar context, comparing Sin's Hell-hounds to other mythic images:

> Farr less abhorrd than these
> Vex'd Scylla bathing in the Sea that parts
> Calabria from the hoarce Trinacrian shore:
> Nor uglier follow the Night-Hag, when call'd
> In secret, riding through the Air she comes
> Lur'd with the smell of infant blood, to dance
> With Lapland Witches, while the labouring Moon
> Eclipses at thir charms. (II.659-666)

Nor is Death any less startling as seen through Satan's perspective:
> The other shape,
> If shape it might be call'd that shape had none
> Distinguishable in member, joynt, or limb,

Or substance might be call'd that shadow seem'd,
For each seem'd either; black it stood as Night,
Fierce as ten Furies, terrible as Hell,
And shook a dreadful Dart; what seem'd his head
The likeness of a Kingly Crown had on. (II.666-673)

From Satan's point of view, the confrontation is as unexpected, as potentially horrifying as recognition/confrontation scenes in Bram Stoker's *Dracula,* Stephen King's *Salem's Lot,* Robert McCammon's *Stinger,* or any number of other contemporary Horror novels. A character abruptly encounters something that is, given his or her understanding of "reality," clearly beyond expectation, almost beyond belief. While Satan does not respond with overt *horror* to the "grieslie terrour" or the images presented (II. 677-679), Milton's audience could be expected to. At this single point in the poem, Milton seems to cease *asserting* horror and attempts to present it.

It does not seem coincidental, either, that this passage has generated as much controversy as it has. Read from a modern perspective, it seems to signal a momentary shift from the distanced, almost objective stance that Milton establishes for his Epic Voice, into something darker, deeper—something with more connections to the neurological system than to the intellect. The abrupt intrusion of abstractions-made-flesh alters at least temporarily the direction the poem follows; and for the duration of the confrontation at Hell's Gates, the reader is invited into a universe where Horror is not only asserted verbally, but experienced/envisioned physically.

# RETHINKING "LEWIS AFTER MILTON":

## SUGGESTIONS CONCERNING RELIGION, SCIENCE FICTION, AND POETRY

[Portions of this essay first appeared in *Star\*Line* (Science Fiction Poetry Association) Vol. 6, No. 6 (November-December 1983): 6-8. It was subsequently revised and expanded for presentation at "Life, the Universe, and Everything," the Brigham Young University Symposium on Science Fiction and Fantasy, February 19, 2004.]

A little over twenty years ago, in November of 1983—and just twenty years after C. S. Lewis's death—one of my early literary notes appeared in *Star\*Line,* the newsletter of the Science Fiction Poetry Association. Entitled "Lewis After Milton: A Sense of Direction in Science Fiction Poetry," this rudimentary excursion into defining the genre concentrated on two figures that had by then become crucial to my own poetry and poetics. John Milton's Renaissance epic, *Paradise Lost,* had provided the focus for my doctoral dissertation four years previously; and I had just completed several years tenure as editor of *The Lamp-Post of the Southern California C. S. Lewis Society*. Steeped in the works of both men, it seemed logical to look to them for some sense of definition...or, as I wrote at the time, some sense of direction in my chosen genre, Science Fiction Poetry.

Since then, much has changed. The world has moved on. Lewis, not to mention Milton, has receded in some ways, replaced by more contemporary and (to the minds of some) more relevant authors. But the basic ideas I had explored in that early note remained with me.

It thus seemed a likely prospect to revisit that essay, bringing with me the weight of two subsequent decades of thought, practice, and exploration. Both Milton and Lewis remain keys to my understanding of poetry—indeed, *Paradise Lost* provided the model for my own epic poem, *The Nephiad,* in process for over a third of a century before its final manifestation in 2010. And Lewis keeps a persistent place in the periphery of my vision (especially as his works suggest directions from which to approach the writings of Orson Scott Card).

I still agree with Steve Rasnic Tem's comments in *The Umbral Anthology*, one of the early seminal collections of Science Fiction Poetry, that Science Fiction Poetry (rather like Science Fiction itself) is unusually difficult to define, even though we each believe that we can recognize it when we read it. His conclusion was that, at least as far as his anthology was concerned, such poems have a distinctly science-fictional theme. That such a qualification begs the question was clear to both Tem and his readers; that such a definition may be the best we can come up with was equally clear. Yet two poems—both overtly Christian in scope and purpose, both dealing with the same fundamental content, yet ultimately vastly differing in effect—might well illuminate some landmarks on the road toward a definition of intersections between religion and Science-Fiction poetry.

The poems are by Christian poets who have—with greater and lesser justification—been included in various lists of science fiction writers. Several critics mention Milton's *Paradise Lost* as containing suggestively science-fictional elements; and even more include portions of C. S. Lewis's Ransom trilogy as classic science fiction. An equal number of critics and readers—and in Milton's case, substantially more—might dispute these claims, yet the fact remains that both authors seem linked in one way or another with the genre. Of more importance, I think, Lewis knew Milton's work and responded to it in his own fiction, as in *Perelandra*. And, since both wrote Nativity poems, it is not surprising to find similarities between Milton's "On the Morning of Christ's Nativity" and Lewis's "The Turn of the Tide," reprinted in 1981 in Chad Walsh's *The Visionary Christian: 131 Readings from C. S. Lewis* (186-188).

Both poems begin at the same point, using mainstream forms and rhymes to evoke visions of Bethlehem. Yet these visions are not smoothly conventional images of Christmas. Sound patterns in such lines as Milton's "All meanly wrapt in the rude manger lies" largely contradict the tone anticipated in Christmas verse, while Lewis's opening lines grate even more harshly, sharply, vigorously: "Black and bare/Were the fields, hard as granite the clods;/Hedges stiff with ice; the sedge in the vice/Of the pool, like pointed iron rods..." (1-4). Far from reflecting the soft-edged world of Christmas cards, Lewis's lines strongly evoke an observed, observable world—a world in which sound and sense reflect fact.

Lewis parallels Milton for ten lines or so, creating a silence over the earth similar to Milton's; in fact, Lewis virtually repeats Milton's "The oracles are dumb" in his own "The oracles were dumb" (12)...while simultaneously creating an intriguing spin on relevance by shifting verb tense from present (narrator as participant) to past (narrator as commentator). Lewis and Milton both follow the movement of that silence as it spreads through the Earth. But there the similarities cease. Milton moves consciously inward with his Ode; the pagan gods—neatly listed and categorized—retreat from the silence of the Child, retreat internally, into a hell *encompassed* by the world. The Child becomes, in metaphorical (almost metaphysical) terms, larger than the gods of the earth as they withdraw from...and into...Him:

> Nor all the gods beside,
> Longer dare abide,
>          Nor Typhon huge ending in snaky twine:
> Our Babe, to show his Godhead true,
> Can in his swaddling bands control the damned crew.
>          (Stanza XXV)

This movement parallels the early Seventeenth-Century worldview—pre-scientific, overtly theological, only tangentially accepting rudimentary efforts toward externalized, objectified science and technology.

Lewis was familiar with, and to a large extent sympathetic to, Milton's attitudes; so much so, that in his own nativity poem, he repeats Milton's sense of movement as silence spreads inevitably out from the child. But Lewis belonged to a time which viewed the earth from a cosmic perspective, as a miniscule part of an unimaginably immense structure. The subject of his poem, then, may seem traditional—the Nativity and Incarnation of Christ—but his treatment is anything but. He departs radically from Milton by turning outward, transforming what began as a main-stream Nativity poem into what might most satisfactorily be considered theological science fiction. The silence accompanying the birth of Christ sweeps through the Near East, touches "Caesar on Palatine," continues on "Through Carthage and the Gauls, past Parthia and the Falls/of Nile and Mount Amara" in lines that echo Milton's visions of human kingdoms in his second great epic, *Paradise Regained*; the sense of geography is careful, evocative and stridently earth-bound, yet it almost immediately assumes a more precise, scientific, science-fictional tone:

From the Earth
A signal, a warning, went out
And away behind the air. Her neighbours were aware
Of change. They were troubled with a doubt.
(ll. 26-29)

After conjuring "Salamanders in the sun" and astrological references to "Houses and Signs," then coupling the latter to "Ousiarchs divine," Lewis refers to "Great Galactal lords" and to a recurring theme in contemporary secular science fiction, the inevitable winding-down of the universe:

And a whisper among them passed, 'Is this perhaps the last
Of our story and the glories of our crown?
—The entropy worked out?—The central redoubt
Abandoned? The world-spring running down?'
(ll. 38-41)

In both poems, the harmonies of celestial music soon supplant the other-worldly silence. Milton, as is appropriate for his age, invokes the mystically powerful Music of the Spheres. In Lewis, however, the description of the music becomes almost analytical, medical, clinical: "Then pulsing into space with delicate, dulcet pace/Came a music, infinitely small/And clear" (ll. 54-56). This music spreads outward to embrace all worlds, then collapses in on itself, returning the reader to the Nativity. As it works backward through the solar system, the music narrows its cosmic perspective until the poem again concentrates on Terran geography, culminating in the mythic and Christic image of the phoenix.

The final stanzas in both poems re-create peace and silence, but again there is an essential difference between them. Milton's peace incorporates overtly supernatural beings—"Bright-harness'd Angels...in order serviceable," reflecting his Christian universe. Lewis, while just as intimately committed to the Christian universe, chooses instead to conclude his Nativity poem with a return to sharpness, to the naturalistic imagery that characterized the opening lines of "The Turn of the Tide":

So death lay in arrest. But at Bethlehem the bless'd
Nothing greater could be heard
Than a dry wind in the thorn, the cry of the One new-

born,
>                And cattle in stall as they stirred. (82-85)

If nothing else, the use of "thorn," sets up the internal rhyme in the line while simultaneously returning us to the harsh, sharp sense of Lewis's opening lines.

Comparing Lewis's performance with Milton's reveals an underlying difference between the mainstream world view and the science-fictional one. Milton's poem is placed firmly within a traditional Christian universe, geo-centric and inwardly oriented. In his outward movement, however, Lewis confirms what may be considered an essential element in science fiction poetry: this Earth is no longer central—the vast spaces beyond it have taken on physical reality and become inhabitable and inhabited. True, Christianity underlies Lewis's poem, but the fact that the content is overtly Christian, is, in this narrow sense, largely irrelevant. The poem shows an awareness of scientific knowledge—a willingness to explore imaginatively the limitless expanses beyond the earth (and at the same time to connect those expanses back to the earth) that seems fundamental to science fiction, no matter what the content might be.

Since first examining these two poems in light of defining Science Fiction Poetry, I have not only considered the points suggested but written a number of my own poems that consciously or unconsciously respond to Milton and Lewis. In doing so, I have refined slightly the essential differentia between traditional and SF poets— the movement from inward to outward—to incorporate two more elements. Religious SF poetry can also respond to situational or contextual stimuli. By this I mean that poems can be science-fictional in *treatment* or in *essence*. The difference between the two approaches relates primarily to the degree of speculative imagination involved in each.

To give an example: At about the same time I was reading Lewis's "The Turn of the Tide" and working rather intensively with Milton's poetry, I decided to *write* a Science Fiction poem, one that would, rather as do Lewis's and Milton's, incorporate religious thought in a speculative form. The impulse behind this poem was essentially *situational*; that is, the over-riding concept is strictly according to my religious belief, but the less crucial landscape within which that belief is incarnated is equally obviously science-fictional…other worlds and other peoples. The result was *"Ad Astra*

*perFidem"* (1980)<sup>*</sup>

> *And I heard a great voice bearing re-*
> *cord from Heav'n*
> *He's the Savior, and only Begotten of*
> *God—*
> *By him, of him, and through him, the*
> *worlds were all made,*
> *Even all that career in the heavens so*
> *broad.*
>
> *Whose inhabitants, too, from the first*
> *to the last,*
> *Are saved by the very same Savior of*
> *ours;*
> *And are, of course, begotten God's*
> *daughters and sons,*
> *By the very same truths and the very*
> *same powers.*
> —Joseph Smith

The totem of their god was marred;
Stigmata starred its palms and wrists
And feet. The Elder waited patiently
While through wrenched teeth I hissed

As

If a single questing sound. He spoke:
"Not here. Not we. Another world
In darkness dressed." He broke
A choking sigh. "Another people

One

Has told us of." I swallowed stone
And would not speak. "Another world
Where bentness dwells, where droned
A hideous strength against our God

Who

Straightened him that first had warred
To bend all life from wide infinity.

---

<sup>*</sup> The poem originally appeared in *LDSF2*, edited by Ben Urrutia (Ludlow MA: Parables, 1985): 112; it has since been reprinted several times.

A world of stupid men, bored
With life, experimenting with

Sin

As if they knew not what would come
Of it." I looked around: a world
Like mine, unlike my distant home
In never having suffered war

And

Futile strife. A distant world where God
Had come—one time—in glory-light,
And spoken thoughts that blossomed awe
And echo, though their legends

Fault

Fouled history. They waited One.
He came.
      That was all.
            That simple.
That wonder-full.
            Here, on the rim
Of our extension into space,

Has

(On the first inhabitable world)
Humankind found humanoids—like us—
Enough like to be brothers. Birth
Of our new universe! Yet spirit-deaths

Overcome

Pretentiousness. For our God,
Our Lord of worlds innumerable,
Stood here. And on the planet that I trod
As child...only there, on one

Home

In all the Universe, did man—
God's progeny—crucify
And scourge His Son.
          Our simple plan,
To proselyte for Humankind,

Seek

Equals on the seedling planets far,
Is come to nothingness. Ashes heaped
Upon base pride.
      And so we turn to go,
Return to Earth, the only world

We

           Know to kill the Christ,
           The only needing desperately
           His birth with us—as Man—to heal
           Our error and to cauterize our hearts
    Now!

The poem certainly reflects Lewis's works—witness 'bent,' 'bentness,' and 'hideous strength'—and possibly suggests the ambitious-
ness of some of Milton's early poetry. But even though it is clearly
Science Fiction and was recognized as such by editors and publishers of three SF-oriented books and journals, it is so primarily
through its situation. The ideas—the 'theology'—does not necessarily require Science Fiction. As the head note from Joseph Smith indicates, "*Ad Astra perFidem*" embodies a specific religious tenet by
using an SF framework. It is Science Fiction Poetry only to the extent that Mormonism, to paraphrase Orson Scott Card, is a science-
fictional religion: we believe in other planets, in other worlds, in
faster-than-light travel … *and* in the effects of Christ's sacrifice here
on Earth and throughout the universe.

    Four years later—having matured somewhat in years as well as
(one hopes) in poetry, I tried again. This time I selected the same
topic as had Milton and Lewis: the Nativity. Again, situation dictated much of the SF apparatus the poem required: another world,
another culture, but linked to ours by a common belief in Christ. The
result was "Celebration" (1984).[*]

           On that night—
           that night of all solemn nights—
           a thousand million faces blossomed skyward
           like moonflowers (silvered
           by the light of one moon,
           touched with shadow
           by the second)—
           eye-trajectories
           to the Wing.

           In worship, yes. But not

_____

[*] The poem first appeared in my collection *Naked to the Sun: Dark Visions of
Apocalypse* (Mercer Island WA: Starmont House, 1985): 26. It has subsequently
been reprinted several times.

in lush idolatry.
The Wing held no sacred hopes
itself;
its arc of stars
pinioned planets
opening into other quadrants
of their Galaxy.

They could count the Twelve Suns
and see the darkness
ripe beneath the Wing,
darkness where—when the night
was still, just so—and eyes
squinted to tight lines
crossing faces lost in awe—
then, perhaps, one in a thousand
could see that blot of light
that was The Galaxy.

And on that night,
a thousand million faces
two thousand million eyes
celebrated
The Coming on a distant world
too many thousand years ago to count—
A Coming,
and an End.

Each dweller on the planet—
each on myriads of worlds—
Knew of Him, spoke of Him,
saw Him, felt Him,
loved Him.

But on that night,
with faces glowing as bright buds
and eyes like slits of deep black faith,
they saw—perhaps—a smudge that was
the Galaxy that bore hidden in its womb

the yellow Star
that saw Him born.

Unlike "*Ad Astra*," however, "Celebration" attempted to cross the divide between situation and concept; it essayed to view a conventional Christian event—the Nativity—from a new perspective in time and place. It was, to that extent, more strictly Science Fiction Poetry than was the earlier poem.

A third poem, "One With Him" (1983), however, tried to move as far from simple situational SF as possible. Instead of beginning from a specific theological point, the poem reversed the process and worked from science-fictional speculation back to theology.

In 1967, Brian W. Aldiss published an extraordinary novel titled *An Age* (the next year it appeared in the U.S. as *Cryptozoic!*). As unfair as it is to reduce a complex novel to a single sentence, *Cryptozoic!* explored the possibilities for human society—and for individuals—if we in fact had been reading time *backward*, from a dimly remembered 'future' back to a fully realized but prescient 'past.' Aldiss's novel was secular, but in the process of writing a study of his works for Starmont House (published in 1986), I found the idea increasingly intriguing. Ultimately, I applied his SF speculation to religion: if we do indeed read time backward, what then would become of the Plan of Salvation? Starting from this imaginative 'what if?' I wrote the poem:

### ONE WITH HIM[*]
#### For Brian W. Aldiss

"And time run back and fetch the Age of Gold."—John Milton, "On the Morning of Christ's Nativity"

"...what we regard as the flow of time in fact moves in the opposite direction to its apparent one....Energy accumulates from less organised to more highly organised bodies: piles of rust can integrate into iron rods."—Brian W. Aldiss, *Cryptozoic!*

Immortal Christ wraithes through
Eastern twilight, entering

---

[*] This poem first appeared in *Star*Line* [Science Fiction Poetry Association] Vol. 6, No. 6 (November-December 1983): 5; it was subsequently reprinted in *Naked to the Sun* (Mercer Island: Starmont) 1985: 31; and reprinted elsewhere.

The Cave of Birth. Cold flesh
Awaits agony and birth upon the Cross—
Birth remembered by prophets
Through the future to Adam's time.

Three days flee—sunrise on Friday
Evening. Spirit invests waiting
Flesh. Shattered legs knit. Blood
Spurts blindness from the soldier's eye—
Ascends the wooden shaft to thrust
Warmth into Christ's pale breast and
Make whole a broken heart.

Time moves: suffering of trial,
Betrayal's pain, glory in Jerusalem,
Wonder of discipleship—arriving
At peaceful death in the stable.
The God-child returns to his mother
And his God.

Eons wander—humanity assembles.
Demons sweltering in Milton's Hell
Surge into Heaven, gradually forget
Rebellious thoughts until at last
Christ and Lucifer meet—and Lucifer
Restored.

Civil war forgotten,
And at the End, all children
Of the great immortal God
Gather unto Him
Eternal and unchanging.

The plan fulfilled.
Creation gathered at the foot
Of God—and none are lost,
And none are left behind.

The result was, I think, conceptual Science Fiction poetry, poetry
focused on SF as genre, on its structures and lexicon, on its extrapolative potential, while using as content not religious doctrine but religious *speculation*. Like the other poems discussed—Milton's,
Lewis's, my own—it fulfils basic requirements for Science Fiction.

At the same time, it incorporates other elements as well, including the subjective, inward movement of religion and the outward, objective thrust of science.

The movement toward speculation and imagination proved worthwhile. My other two poems were well received, each being reprinted at least once. But "One with Him" received the strongest responses of the three. In addition to a first-ballot nomination for the Nebula Award in 1986, it appeared in Orson Scott Card's *Short Form* listing of the four strongest SF poems of the year.

Looking back twenty years to the original version of "Lewis after Milton," I find that I still agree in large measure with what I wrote. At the same time, the division between inward and outward seems unnecessarily simplistic, given my own explorations in religious SF poetry.

*NOTE: Some years after completing this essay, I took it in hand to attempt a pastiche of Milton's Nativity Ode, imitating his stanzaic and metrical patterns but applying them to my own frame of reference. The result, which in good seventeenth-century manner uses Milton's title to emphasize the fact that this is homage rather than plagiarism, is another version of a science-fiction Christmas poem:*

### ON THE MORNING OF CHRIST'S NATIVITY

I

It's dark and drear today,
The sky a numbing gray,
    With cloud-banks bowing near to brush the ground;
The wan white snow is gone,
Absorbed into the lawn
    That stretches in brown desolation 'round,
While in the barren garden beds
The first brave tulips break, to raise their gladsome heads.

II

And in my heart I yearn
For Spring's rainbowed return,
    And wish that I were now in Other-When;
That darkness veiled the land
And in a starry Band
    Bright Angel courses, far as eye could ken,

Proclaim in verses pure, and call
The advent of Good Will and Peace on Earth to All.


### III

If I were Other-Where
And heard that holy Air
      Resounding over shepherds' eager ears,
Then might I join the throng
And know that I belong
      With hosts of worshippers who shed all fears,
Might joyfully meld my song with them
And journey through dark vales to distant Bethlehem;


### IV

Where Mary enfolds her Son,
Her strenuous labors done,
      Near Joseph, steward of the mortal Maker
Chosen from before
Wild oceans voiced their roar
      Or whispered in a world-wide, blue-froth breaker;
Or eagles soared through tumbled skies,
Or spirit shone through lion's, tiger's, lynx's eyes.


### V

Elected ere each world
In cosmic order whirled
      About a thousand thousand thousand stars;
A simple child, to grow
And know both joy and woe
That mark His trail of days like shadow bars;
Though Son withal of Father-God,
Content to bear His pall of needful flesh-façade.


### VI

In that Other-Where
A rough-hewn manger, bare
      Of all but fragrant golden straw,
Would serve as cynosure
Within the night obscure,
      And silent eyes—now moist with tearstains—draw
From Heaven to long-expectant Earth
As simple shepherds greet an Infant's Holy Birth.

VII

The Child with eyes tight-closed,
His fragileness exposed
      To all the vagaries of mortal life,
Sleeps peacefully and dreams
Perhaps—or so it seems—
      Of Heaven's rest exchanged for earth-bound strife,
Of praises formed on every tongue,
And crystal anthems by hosts of Angels freely sung.


VIII

Or should we still extend
Beginnings without End
      And see Him in divinest Councils speaking;
Where two exalting Plans
Are offered forth, for Man's
      Eternal Destiny and Fate both seeking;
Intelligences without start,
As Spirits clothed, hear that each must soon depart;


IX

And whether yet impelled,
By One's strong will compelled
      To troop in irons back to Heaven's cell;
Or if by faith return
And endless honors earn,
      Or fail, and through their choices merit Hell—
The lot is theirs—no vote sustained;
Each heart is free, and thus, strict agency maintained.


X

Some seek the safest way,
That in stolen freedom lay,
      Where One will force each Spirit's right decision,
And joined in gleeful mirth
At those whose trial on Earth
      Might end with them soul-bound by Sin's derision,
While they who chose in fear this plan
Were guaranteed safe-conduct back to God, as man.


XI

But more were stirred by Him

Whose Plan at first seemed grim,
     Since it retained the chance that some might fail;
But those whose true Will spoke
Would break Perdition's yoke,
     And after trials endured in bodies frail
Might through the Son's unending Light
Thus prove themselves full worth Celestial Worlds bright;

XII

And sing forevermore
Creation's mighty score
     From worlds unnumbered through perpetual Space,
And hymn with one accord
The Glories of their Lord,
     Whose life and death rang greatness for their race;
While every note to Him thus sung
Trebles but the praise of God from every tongue.

XIII

But would that be too much
Encumbrance laid on such
     A sweet and tender Babe as this here sleeping?
Would the jading weight
Of untold worlds' fate
     Disturb his pleasant rest with weary weeping?
Is this too great a burden still
For One so tiny, weak, and helpless to fulfill?

XIV

If aye, then we must turn
To future years to learn
     How His Plan's fruition might unfold;
But oh! that leads to fears
And terrifying tears
     Upon a high and lonely Mountain cold,
Where He alone must suffer woe,
And He, of all God's Sons, alone to Death must go;

XV

And so conclude His Word
By countless Spirits heard
     That He thus takes upon Him Mankind's sins,
And by that selfless Act

Completes the Eternal Pact,
      And Heaven's approbation fully wins;
While millions taste their pented breath—
In awe, regard on High the instant of His Death.


XVI

To tarry at that sight,
Or marvel at His plight,
      Would prove too much for mortal heart to bear;
To look beyond were wise,
A respite for frail eyes
      And solace to all hearts worn thin with care;
For through His death he works a change
And fashions thus a vessel for our souls' exchange.


XVII

For after three dark days
He our full forfeit pays,
      With broken heart and blood for Mankind shed;
And with the morning dew
Arises—Lives!—anew
      And walks this Earth with simple footsteps' tread;
'Mid lilies white and diamond pure
He works for us forever deadly Sin's last cure.


XVIII

But now the Infant sleeps,
While Mary softly weeps
      In joy and sorrow for the coming years;
And falters, filled with awe!
At Mercy wedding Law
      And treasures up great promise mixed with fears;
And in His face, composed and fine,
She sees the coming Judgment of great Adam's line.


XIX

For the bright Son dawns with Power,
Whose Might and Grandeur flower
      With full achievement of His chosen Task,
And mounts above wide throngs
Repentant of their wrongs,
      Content in His great Presence now to bask;

While he with Wisdom's somber grace
Consigns each spirit to its well-appointed Place;


XX

Until each Heavenly Sphere
Bides, eager to draw near
   The seat of Radiance and ethereal Throne;
Across the cosmic waste
Each planet waits firm-placed
   To feel the sear of flame that each must own
Before they wheel through reverend skies
And humbly bow before their loving Sovereign's eyes.


XXI

And He will judge each kind,
Each Making of His Mind
   On counted Worlds that whirl without End;
From them accept His Crown
Of Honor and Renown,
   And every knee in every Where shall bend
In recognition of His power
Foretold, and now encompassed by this final hour.


XXII

Then the Creator-Son
His mortal conflict done,
   Will fold all Cosmos in His firm embrace,
Where vast Intelligence
Uncounted Eons hence
   Will praise His Name and magnify His grace;
And each, enrobed in flesh and bone
Renew the Plan and seek progression as His own.


XXIII

But no! it is not so;
For us there can be no
   Other-Where or Other-When than here;
Let us softly leave
While day-larks gently weave
   Their lullabies to fall on Infant ear;
And let Him, as we found Him, sleep
Surrounded by poor shepherds, with their lowly sheep.

## XXIV

The sullen clouds have fled,
By day's sweet brightness led;
      And in my heart I find a welcomed bliss;
For while the Infant dreams,
The nooning Sun now beams
      And on my burgeoning garden leans to kiss
The warming earth and interpose
With crowning Iris spears, the Lily, and the Rose.

# "TO BE STILL A MAN":

## ABSTRACTION AND CONCRETION IN C. S. LEWIS

[This essay first appeared in *The Lamp-Post of the Southern California C. S. Lewis Society* Vol. 6, No. 1 (January 1982): 1-6 and is reprinted with their permission. It was subsequently presented in a slightly longer format to the Western Regional Conference on Christianity and Literature, held at Pepperdine University, February 6, 1982. It has here been further edited for clarity.]

C. S. Lewis is recognized as a master stylist by his detractors as well as by his admirers. His prose is invariably—and enviably—clear and easily understood. Margaret Hannay has in fact suggested that his stylistic clarity occasionally does perhaps as much harm as good, by implying that his content is equally simplistic:

> When I was a college student, I was much drawn to *Mere Christianity*; it set out the Christian faith neatly, in a comprehensible fashion. Now I find it too shallow for my needs, wondering, with others, if anything so clear and simple could possibly be true. (265)

Lewis's style was carefully crafted to enhance his message, his ideas; and in this narrow, literary sense, he succeeded admirably.

As with so many other elements in his prose, however, his emphasis of stylistic clarity was important beyond merely allowing for easy communication between writer and reader. In several essential ways, it related directly to his Christian commitment, to his view of literature as a means of demonstrating religious truths.

In his quest for ways to educate twentieth-century readers—many of them woefully ignorant of the complex issues with which Lewis had to deal—he used straightforward, often simple techniques as tools by which to make clear intricate statements. His attitudes toward style, therefore, range far beyond its being merely artistic and artificial decisions about sentence length or paragraph development. For Lewis, style was intimately related to reality, to the extent that his stylistic decisions often reflected his Christian beliefs and the universe he was dedicated to exploring.

This relationship between style and reality can best be demonstrated by concentrating on a single element of his style—his use of abstractions and concretions. His writing is consistently concrete—this technique is perhaps more than any other responsible for the clarity of his prose. Yet at the same time, concretions are more than merely stylistic for Lewis. He enhances the simple literary device, embedding significance within it, until the differences between abstractions and concretions take on structural and moral overtones.

Usually the choice between abstraction and concretion is primarily stylistic. Some writers elect to manipulate the potentials of each, subtly altering the effects of sentences or paragraphs on readers. Grammarians most frequently approve of concretions, while warning against the dangers of abstraction: lulling the readers with interminable "strings of prepositional phrases, those monotonous adjective-noun pairs, and those uniformly colorless terms"; failing to define relationships clearly; and confusing sentence elements. And, one writer concludes:

> Worst of all, once you've actually written such a sentence, you may imagine that you've actually said something, and thus lose contact with your reader. (Crews, 114)

When considered in a grammatical sense, the words *abstraction* and *concretion* present few problems. They are strictly defined, and in most instances, easy to identify, even when the same word is capable of fitting either definition. *Automobile*, for example, is obviously more abstract than *Ford*; *transportation* is similarly more abstract than *automobile.* In a broader sense, however, they are more complex. The decision between using abstractions and using concretions potentially transcends the level of style to become a serious method of developing fictions. The concretion may exist in the stylistic level to aid in clarity and precision, as a visualizing tool enabling readers to become more involved with the work; and it may simultaneously represent the abstraction itself, standing for the larger entity without losing any of its individualizing force or vigor. In the process, the *universal*, the abstraction, is defined more fully than would otherwise be possible. John Gardner alludes to this tendency when he defines the critic's role as one of explanation and evaluation, which means he must make use of his analytic powers to translate the concrete to the abstract. (8)

In other words, the artist deals on the level of the concretion; the critic (and the critical reader)extrapolates from it relevant abstractions. The principle of abstraction/concretion thus becomes essential to the role and functions of art.

There is in addition a third use of abstractions and concretions, beyond the grammatical and the structural. And this use is of particular interest in Lewis's writings. The techniques become inextricably associated with his Christian outlook, and with his assessment of the moral state of his characters and situations. They become shorthand statements of truthfulness and trustworthiness.

On the level of style, *Out of the Silent Planet*, for example, could not begin with a firmer sense of the concrete, of the specific:

> The last drops of the thunderstorm had hardly ceased falling when the Pedestrian stuffed his map into his pocket, settled his pack comfortably on his tired shoulders, and stepped out from the shelter of a large chestnut-tree into the middle of the road. A violent yellow sunset was pouring through a rift in the clouds to westward, but straight ahead over the hills the sky was the colour of dark slate. Every tree was dripping, and the road shone like a river.

One might experiment interminably with the multiplication of adjectives and adverbs to make the description seem even more specific, but as Lewis wrote it, the scene is set precisely and meticulously, and the reader moves easily into the world of the novel. Even the most abstract element of the passage—the intentionally vague "Pedestrian"—is not as generalized as it initially appears. In addition to the suggestion supplied by the capital *P* that this is in fact *the* pedestrian, a specific individual with a particular function in the story, there is the additional resonance of its Wellsian character. The hero is here conceptualized as a function, much like the characters in the opening pages of H. G. Wells' *The Time Machine*: the Time Traveller, the Psychologist, the Provincial Mayor, the Medical Man.

Lewis's continuous awareness of the concrete is critical because it allows him to manipulate concretions and abstractions on the more important levels of application and meaning. In this sense, his use of the elements becomes more fundamental, less a superficially stylistic choice.

He frequently endows a single character with sufficient particular development for the reader to empathize; yet at the same time, he seems almost to rely on stereotypes (Walsh, "Critic," 76; Hannay, 97). In both *Out of the Silent Planet* and *Perelandra*, for example, he seems not so much to draw characters as to create caricatures. There is, however, a strong sense of purpose in this method of characterization. He shows the reader a single village of *hrossa*, concentrating on a description of a single inhabitant of that village. Ransom meets two *sorns*, who virtually stand for their entire race, and a single *pfifltrigg*. On the basis of these few individuals, he constructs a full picture of Malacandrian life.

The situation in *Perelandra* is even more extreme. The Malacandrians at least had personal names. On Perelandra, there are only the Green Lady and the King, as much titles as names, yet more than enough of both. Only at the conclusion of the novel do either receive individual names.

Superficially, this trait suggests that Lewis depended upon stereotypes, refusing to exert more care than was necessary in developing his characters. Yet he seems to have done so consciously. Ransom, for instance, understands the narrowness of his observations, almost scorning the superficiality of his experience of the Malacandrian landscape and its peoples: "It was as if a *sorn* had journeyed forty million miles to the Earth and spent his stay there between Worthing and Brighton" (*OSP* 144). Yet he is wrong. He *does* understand Malacandra—not, to be sure, the almost irrelevant details, the accidents of form and structure that might be eternally convoluted, but he does understand the *essence* of Malacandra. The individuals he meets are individuals—irascible and abrupt or cold and clinical—but they are simultaneously representatives of their world. As such, they give Ransom all of the information he needs to understand them and their relation to Maleldil.

In *Perelandra*, characters even more overtly blend the abstract and the concrete. Ransom, the Green Lady, Weston, and the King—all represent individuals yet at the same time stands for larger groupings. The Green Lady, for example, comes to life, grows and develops during the course of the novel, engaging the reader in the process of her growth and the possibility of her degradation. Lewis carefully points out that even to herself she "grows older" through her interchanges with Ransom and Weston.

She is, however, also a complex of abstractions. Martha Sammons refers several times to Lewis's fears that he was attempting the impossible in *Perelandra*: to represent both a virgin and a pagan goddess in a single figure, even though such characters were poles apart in human experience, after the Fall (23, 96, 157). The lady is recognizably individual, yet she is also the mythic, archetypal mother-Eve figure, both to Ransom and to the reader.

The same holds true for the other characters: Ransom, Weston, and the King. Ransom is a rather sedentary Oxford don (although admittedly somewhat altered by his experiences on Malacandra). But at the same time, he is *The Ransom, Elwin Ransom*, 'beloved of God,' an almost allegorical abstraction by whose actions the Lady's fall is to be averted. He is both individual and function, concretion and abstraction (147). At first, he consciously dissociates his two roles in the novel—his surface role as character and his underlying, more important role as representative of a process. He finally unites the two, however, with a single act of consciousness, accepting himself as both concretion and abstraction. He realizes that there is no large distinction between myth and fact, except from a terrestrial perspective, and that he has been forced out of the smaller pattern into the larger. Even before the world was made, he had been incorporated into Maleldil's framework:

> And he bowed his head and groaned and repined against his fate—to be still a man and yet to be forced up into the metaphysical world, to enact what philosophy only thinks.
> "My name also is Ransom," said the Voice. (148-149)

Lewis uses different phrasing—fact versus myth, accident versus essence, mortal versus metaphysical—but the import is the same. Ransom is at once a concretion of humanity and an abstraction for the process by which humanity (in any of its physical manifestations) might be saved from the consequences of the Fall, through the consequences of the Incarnation.

As important as stylistic and structural concretions are for Lewis, however, he moves beyond these concerns to incorporate into his fictions an awareness of abstractions and concretions that is infused with Christian significance. The dichotomy between the two becomes a means of delivering moral judgments on characters and situations. In general, moral statements are expressed concretely. Throughout *Perelandra,* for example, the extent of characters' levels of abstraction parallels their distance from the Eldila and Maleldil.

The positive extremes of God, heaven, and the Good are represented by statements firmly grounded in concrete imagery and definition. Pure joy is represented by eating a particular fruit from a particular tree. The opposite extremes of Devil, hell, and Evil are released from such constraints, and often become so generalized as to lack any coherent meaning. The epitome of Evil in *Perelandra* is so far distanced from its earlier, specific Weston-self that it becomes not *a man* but the *Un-man*, something that allows for neither description or explanation.

Of course, not every utterance Lewis gives to Weston is an abstraction. But Weston's use and abuse of concrete language do not suggest that Lewis accepts Weston's views. On the contrary, when Weston is conspicuously concrete, Lewis is at some pains to identify those statements as distortions of the positive to serve evil ends. In fact, Weston's use of concretions parallels his use of intelligence itself—both are weapons, to be employed when necessary and then set aside as irrelevant (128). He speaks in concretions most frequently during the early stages of the Lady's temptations, when she is so closely linked to the memory of the King's wishes and to the will of Maleldil that she is almost incapable of thinking in any terms other than immediacy and specificity.

When Weston first meets Ransom, he launches into a long speech that relies heavily on abstractions:

> [S]pirit—mind—freedom—spontaneity—that is what I'm talking about.... The final disengagement of that freedom, that spirituality, is the work to which I dedicate my own life and the life of humanity. The goal, Ransom, the goal: think of it! *Pure* spirit: the final vortex of self-thinking, self-originating activity. (92)

During the course of that interchange, Weston condemns Ransom for "relapsing on to the popular level," that is, for forcing Weston to pin his generalizations down to demonstrable fact. The dialogue climaxes with Weston's absurd accusation that Ransom is "still wedded to…conventionalities…still dealing with abstractions" (95). He fails to see the irony in this statement or his later comment that "There is no possible distinction in concrete thought between me and the universe" (96).

However, when Weston first meets the Green Lady, he uses a different approach. He uses extreme simplicity and concreteness. His language is carefully streamlined and direct. When the Lady asks, for example, why he is so interested in the commandment that she and the King not spend night on the Fixed Land, he directs her away from the question and suggests that she merely *think* about dwelling there. He emphasizes the "sole command" and urges the Lady to consider it. But in doing so he is also urging her to think beyond her experience and contemplate abstractions for their own sake: "I had thought I was to be always Queen and Lady," she says in response. "But I see now that I may be as the Eldila" (106).

Later, however, Weston alters his approach, using grand abstractions to disguise the fundamental—and essentially concrete—choice between obedience and disobedience: "It was at this stage that [the Un-man] began to teach her many new words: words like Creative and Intuition and Spiritual" (132). Ransom despairs, urging the Lady to recognize the fact that Weston is making her see "words that mean nothing" (132). He rightly perceives the essence of this temptation— the substitution of a glittering generalization for thought and meaning. And when the Lady answers, not with equally abstract words but with laughter, Ransom is relieved and retains some hope that she will withstand the Un-man. More than anything, however, Ransom fears Weston's primary weapon, the "turgid swell of distinctly splendid images" (134). As the temptations progress, the Un-man relies more and more on generalizations and abstractions, on the systematic dissociation of words from experiential reality.

Ransom, on the other hand, moves in the opposite direction. In Chapter 11, he passes through a series of crises, from inaction to action. Lewis defines this fluctuation by allowing Ransom to flutter from concretions to abstractions to concretions. The chapter begins with a solid basis in experiential perception, as Ransom feels the presence of Maleldil (140). From this position within the concrete, he wavers toward grand theological abstractions, and back again to insistent concretions, from doubts to faith, until finally he refuses even to contemplate abstractions. As he accepts the inevitability of a physical confrontation with the Un-man, he "emerged into unassailable freedom" (149). To indulge in the false freedom of abstractions is to be bound, morally and spiritually, to falsehoods and emptiness. To submit to the concrete, however, is paradoxically to become free, an image Lewis uses frequently in his fictions, particularly in *The Last Battle.*

Lewis subsequently confirms the rightness of Ransom's choice. The confirmation is initially experiential, concrete, and direct. Considered in the abstract, the Un-man/Weston had seemed unbeatable, virtually unassailable. In the concrete, however, he/it is vulnerable:

...the very taste of its strength in their grapples had altered Ransom's state of mind completely. He had been astonished to find it no stronger. He had all along, despite what reason told him, expected that the strength of its body would be superhuman, diabolical. He had reckoned on arms that could no more be caught and stopped than the blades of an aero-plane propeller. But now he knew, by actual experience, that its bodily strength was merely that of Weston. (154-155)

Later Lewis affirms the appropriateness of Ransom's decision to attack the Un-man. The prose describing the battle becomes more specific, depending more upon concrete imagery for its force:

The joy came from finding at last what hatred was made for. As a boy with an axe rejoices on finding a tree, or a boy with a box of coloured chalks rejoices on finding a pile of perfectly white paper, so he rejoiced in the perfect congruity between his emotion and its object. (156)

From this point on, Ransom relies less and less on abstractions and, instead, expresses himself and his perceptions almost entirely in concrete images and language.

What has been said here about the Lady, Weston, the Un-man, and Ransom, in the context of *Perelandra*, applies equally throughout Lewis's writings. As a stylist he knew the power of concrete statements and images and incorporated such structures into his arguments whenever possible. In his characterizations, he parallels this tendency, making single individuals simultaneously function as representatives of entire races, or nations, or—as with the Lady—planets. Yet rarely does he allow his characters to become abstractions or stereotypes. They retain a strong sense of the concrete.

And finally, on a moral level, he uses concretions to define moral standards. Concretions are consistently associated with those statements and characters who most fully define Lewis's Christian worldview; abstractions most frequently are reserved for viewpoints with which he disagrees and against which he is arguing. His Christian commitment parallels his technique as a stylist, just as his stylistic expertise allows him to express his Christian commitment with greater energy than might otherwise be possible. For some writers, the choice between abstraction and concretion might seem essentially simplistic; for C. S. Lewis it is implicit in his concern for both the functions and ends of literature and for his Christian worldview.

# C. S. LEWIS AND THE
# MUSIC OF CREATION

[This essay first appeared in *The Lamp-post of the Southern California C. S. Lewis Society* Vol. 3, Nos. 3-4 (July-October 1979): 1-3 and is reprinted with their permission. It has here been slightly edited for clarity.]

Music has long provided images for the order man has seen—or at the least hoped to see—operant in the Universe. In the Book of Job, for example, the Creation occurs as "the morning stars [sing] together, and all the sons of God [shout] for joy…" (38:7). Similarly, Milton developed the image of music as an adjunct of Creation; Merritt Y. Hughes simply states—with considerable justification from the account of Creation in *Paradise Lost*—that "It was as music that Milton imagined the Creation." (184). Yet traditionally and conventionally, music remained an *image* for Creation, a way by which the creative impulses of a God beyond mortal comprehension might be expressed and perceived by men. In C. S. Lewis' creation-fable, *The Magician's Nephew,* however, music is treated as the *mode* of Creation, as Narnia is brought into being as a result of Aslan's song.*

When Digory and company first arrive in the darkness that is to become Narnia, they are literally and figuratively encased within a Void, a pre-existent Nothingness which would emerge as Narnia through the vitalizing power of the Lion. All are convinced that they have *not* merely landed on another planet, perhaps during the dark of night. The Witch, Jadis, feels the difference immediately: "'This

---

* Lewis' use of music as a means of creation has an interesting parallel in J. R. R. Tolkien's mythology of Middle-Earth. In the *Ainulindalë*, for example, Tolkien refers to the Ilúvatar "propounding to [the Ainur] themes of music…. But when they were come into the Void, Ilúvatar said to them: 'Behold your music!' And he showed to them a vision, giving them sight where before was only hearing." (*The Silmarillion*, ed. Christopher Tolkien [Boston: Houghton Miflin, 1977], pp. 15, 17).

is not Charn,' came the witch's voice. 'This is an empty world. This is Nothing.'" (96) Yet almost immediately the Nothingness is given form, although a tentative one. The Cabbie reassures his fellow travelers, then suggests that "the best thing we could to do pass the time is sing a 'ymn" (97). His experiences on Narnia begin with a Hymn of Thanksgiving. The narrator comments that it was not very suitable to a place which felt as if nothing had ever grown there since the beginning of time; yet in a larger sense, the Hymn was eminently suitable. The purpose of Narnia, as finally revealed in *The Last Battle*, is to provide a place for the Harvest, just as Charn perhaps might have but was prevented from doing so by the pride and self-destructiveness of Jadis and her immediate forebears. Narnia begins with music, just as Charn is ended by a single note from the gong, which brings the ancient ruins to dust. And significantly, two of the intruders into the Nothingness that would become Narnia refuse to sing: Uncle Andrew and Jadis, the two most tainted with the evil of older worlds.

The human music is, however, only a prelude. "In the darkness, something was happening at last. A voice had begun to sing" (98). The voice is initially sourceless, directionless, all-pervasive. The song is wordless, not even recognizable yet to human ears as music. Indeed, Lewis refers to it as "noise" (a nicely ambiguous term that suggests both meaningless clatter and meaningful harmony, as in "Make a joyful noise unto the LORD [Psalm 98:4; 100:1]). Above the limits of human understanding, however, there are meanings, perhaps analogous to those comprehended by Milton's angels as they witness the Creation in *Paradise Lost*. The only response from the group of travelers is appropriate and simultaneously unusual: "'Gawd!' said the Cabby, 'Ain't it lovely?'" (99). Lewis does not often allow his characters to indulge in profanity, yet in this context the single utterance "Gawd!" is less a profanation than an instinctive recognition of the identity of the Singer, as yet unseen and, to mortal senses at least, unknown.

Suddenly, the voice is joined by uncountable others. The stars (which we already know from *The Voyage of the "Dawn Treader"* are sentient beings) in essence recognize their individual melodies in the song of the Creator.[*] Digory "felt quite certain that it was the stars themselves who were singing, and that it was the First Voice,

---

[*] Similarly, the Ainur in the *Ainulindalë* recognize and respond to their own individual melodies in the greater music of Ilúvatar; Melkor's great sin, in fact, lies in his desire to interweave his own themes into Ilúvatar's song.

the deep one, which had made them appear and made them sing" (99). The celestial worlds which (as Lewis suggests in *The Discarded Image* as well as in the Ransom trilogy) exist outside the earth have broken through the Nothingness to shed their light on the song of Creation.

Again, the Cabby responds to these new experiences more wisely than he knows. "Glory be! ... I'd ha' been a better man all my life if I'd known there were things like this" (100). *Glory be!*: the hackneyed phrase is infused with truth, with the wonder of Creation. It is again a tacit recognition of the importance of the event and of the identity of the Singer. The Cabby understands, but still on an unconscious level. The cliché hides the truth.

With the arrival of the stars, Light comes to Narnia. The important responses—those of the watchers—reflect the moral statures of Digory and the others. The children are rapt, their eyes shining, their mouths open. The Cabby joins them, already displaying some of the childlike wonder that will ultimately help to transform him into King Frank. Andrew's mouth also opens, but not in joy; as we later discover, he has convinced himself that the song is not a song, but merely ungoverned sounds, and he finds it increasingly to his distaste. The Witch, however, understands the "noise" better than any of the others. She understands it, but cannot countenance it. Like the devils in *The Screwtape Letters*, who can never forget "that ghastly luminosity, that stabbing and searing glare which makes the background of permanent pain to our lives," the Witch responds to the celestial music with violence and pain, recognizing it and hating it (*Screwtape*, 26).

As the sun rises, a conspicuously different sun from the bloated, sanguine sun of Charn, the watchers see the Singer for the first time: Aslan the Lion. The Lion is, of course, an appropriate form in which the Singer might appear. In the traditional Renaissance Scale of Beings, the Lion is the noblest of beasts; and we must never forget that Narnia is essentially the land of, by, and for beasts. Its Creator is the first among them, the Lion—yet simultaneously, again as we have discovered in *The Voyage of the "Dawn Treader,"* the least among them, the Lamb. If, in our world, the lamb shall lie down with the lion, in Narnia, the Lamb and the Lion are one.

As soon as the identity of the Singer is known, Jadis and Andrew renew their efforts to steal the children's rings, and again, a verbal exchange ensues, cut off (as usual) by the Cabby: "'Old your noise, everyone,' said the Cabby. 'I want to listen to the moosic'"(103). For the first time, Lewis allows one of his characters to identify the

Song as "music"; until now, it had been simply referred to as a "song."[*] And equally important, the mortals present at the Creation of Narnia now differentiate between the undisciplined "noise" of their own utterances and the music of the Creation. The Cabby's desire to listen is significant; the altered song brings forth the first indigenous life of Narnia, the plants. He wants to understand the music, and of the five present, he is the only one able to do so. Andrew and Jadis are too busy conniving to gain possession of the rings, and Digory and Polly are too busy trying to avoid Andrew and Jadis. Finally, however, the Cabby speaks again, reinforcing with words of command his desire to watch and listen to the spectacle: "'Oh stow it, Guv'nor, do stow it,' said the Cabby. 'Watchin' and Listenin' 's the thing at present; not talking'" (106). Polly is finally allowed to listen to the music and begins to unravel its intricate patterns, responding to them and interpreting them. And, more importantly, she defines the source of them:

> When a line of dark fire sprang up on a ridge about a hundred yards away she felt that they were connected with a series of deep, prolonged notes which the Lion had sung a second before. And when he burst into a rapid series of lighter notes she was not surprised to see primroses suddenly appearing in every direction. (107)

Like a symphony conductor, the Lion is seconds before the orchestra; unlike with the conductor (as Polly realizes), "all the things were coming…'out of the lion's head.' When you listened to his song you heard the things he was making up when you looked round you, you saw them" (107).

As the music becomes more intelligible, the listeners respond to it, dividing themselves again according to their natures. After an abortive attempt at destroying the Lion, the Witch shrieks and runs, recognizing (with the pagan deities in Milton's Nativity Ode) the power implicit in her opponent. Uncle Andrew, a lesser evil than Jadis, attempts to run but fails even in that, becoming a ludicrous figure as he topples into a streambed. But the children cannot move; they are entranced with the beast, "terribly afraid it would turn and look at them, yet in some queer way [wishing] it would" (108). The

---

[*] One is reminded here of Milton's elevation of *music* to an eternal conduit between sinning humanity and God's celestial world, as in "At a Solemn Music."

children have begun to participate willingly in the music and to understand, however rudimentarily, the nature of the Lion. Andrew and Jadis are impelled by their own evil—in a rather Augustinian way—to withdraw from the source of the music, the source of good.

Again the song changes, and the animals of Narnia are brought forth. The humans are affected, as far as they are able to be so. Digory feels hot and flushed, and even Uncle Andrew finds some reserves of strength. The land, however, responds even more violently than do the listeners. With great heaves, it disgorges the animals, each responding immediately and instinctively to a particular strain in the Lion's song, matching their harmonies to that of their Creator.* And as they do, they overwhelm the celestial music, generating a mundane music recognizable to mortal ears.

And with that, the celestial music stops. Creation is achieved, at least physically. The Lion falls silent, then begins selecting his chosen animals. Those not selected leave, to fulfill the measure of their creation as beasts; those selected remain, clustering about the Lion. And with a final burst of "pure, cold, difficult music" accompanied by a "swift flash like fire," the music is completed. The Lion no longer sings. He speaks, uttering words easily understood by Digory, Polly, and the Cabby:

> Narnia, Narnia, Narnia, awake. Love. Think.
> Speak. Be walking trees. Be talking beasts. Be divine
> waters. (116)

The words are understandable on a human level; the mystery of Creation is finished. In its place is the arduous yet ultimately rewarding task of making that Creation achieve the ends for which it was called into being. Aslan's music has descended from celestial unintelligibility to become the mundane speech of a new world.

---

* Again, note the similarity between Lewis' conception of the animals harmonizing with their Creator and Tolkien's of the Ainur singing in concert with Ilúvatar.

# THE MECHANISMS OF FANTASY

[This essay first appeared in *The Lamp-Post of the Southern California C. S. Lewis Society* (Vol. 4, Nos. 3-4 [August-November 1980]: 13-14, 16) and is here reprinted with permission. It has been revised slightly for this volume.]

C. S. Lewis himself admits that his Space Trilogy begins rather peculiarly—mundanely, in fact—when compared to other works. Ultimately, he defends himself on grounds largely defined by the traditions of the fairy tale. What for us seems exotic and unique, for example a knight on horseback encountering a castle, complete with ogre and damsel in distress, was a commonplace for the original storytellers, who might have seen knights and castles, at least, frequently. Hence he sets his own "fairy tale" in a commonplace contemporary setting. In *Out of the Silent Planet,* a rather undistinguished university embarks upon a quiet walking trip.

In some respects, however, Lewis's explanation (while valid) seems incomplete, or perhaps one-sided. His conception of the universe, coupled with his Christian orientation, seems as influential as the literary conventions of the fairy tale in his structuring of the beginning of the trilogy. Within the context of the three novels, he had to confront a fantasy universe (in which events are well beyond the explanations of accepted science) as well as a science-fictional one (in which science provides all needed explanations). And his attitudes toward science and scientists, at least as they appear in the trilogy, were for the most part negative. As L. Sprague De Camp and Thomas D. Clareson note in their discussion of image of the scientist in science fiction:

> Occasionally, even in science fiction, [the scientist] has been bitterly attacked, simply because he is a scientist and holds scientific/materialistic views, as perhaps most notably in C. S. Lewis's *The Hideous Strength*.... (198)

As a result, the connections between the scientific, objective universe and Lewis's fantasy universe are unusual, when compared to similar treatments written by other, less overtly Christian-oriented writers.

In a writer such as Tanith Lee, a definite abyss forms between the objective and the fantasy universes, so definite that there is little or no interchange between the two. In *Night's Master* and *Death's Master*, for example, the reader is thrust immediately into the realms of Death and Night, worlds which have no apparent connections to the worlds of the reader's experience.[*] Physical laws function differently, allowing for unicorns and spirits, demi-urges and changelings wholly impossible in the reader's "reality." The fantasy world may reflect our world, but it does not share substance with it.

Alternatively, the fantasy writer may allow for interactions between the two universes, but those interactions are strictly governed by immutable laws, usually laws derived from the fantasy universe and requiring magic for their fulfillment. In Stephen Donaldson's Illearth trilogy, the hero (anti-hero, actually, since he is leprous, unwilling to act, and essentially amoral within the context of the alternate Earth) moves through the boundaries between the real and the fantastical, but not of his own volition. His white-gold wedding band is a source of "wild magic" in the fantasy world and provides the ultimate motive force for Thomas Covenant. He and he alone of all men enters the parallel universe to communicate with giants, lords, and other creatures which inhabit the land.

Piers Anthony similarly invites intersections between the two universes while simultaneously dividing them. In the Xanth trilogy, the magical land of Xanth is protected from mundane penetration by a magical shield; the two frames exist side by side but, with few exceptions, with no interaction. And those exceptions are, again, governed by the laws of the magical universe, not of the mundane. In his novel, *Split Infinity*, Anthony locates the two parallel frames—the science-fictional and the fantastical—on the same planet. The physical features are basically the same, although man has nearly destroyed the science-fictional Photon, while the fantastical Phaze retains its virginal lushness. However, any interactions between the two frames are determined by the laws of Phaze, the magical planet. Stile, the hero passes through the curtain from Photon into Phaze, but only *after* his Phaze analogue has been killed. And artifacts, among them the robot Sheen, cannot pass through the curtain at all.

---

[*] The specific mechanisms by which Lee establishes the viability of her fantasy universe are discussed in Collings, "Words and Worlds."

For most men, the division between the two worlds is absolute; when that division is in fact broached, it is through accordance to the laws of Phaze (fantasy), not of Photon (science).

In a writer such as Roger Zelazny, the division begins to fade. In Zelazny's Chronicles of Amber, the objective universe is in fact part of a larger framework, the magical, fantastical universe of Amber. But travel from this Earth to any of the other shadow worlds is again strictly controlled by the laws operant in Amber. The hero, Corwin, awakes in the opening paragraphs of the series amnesiac and confined to a hospital ward in our world. He has no name, no identity. Only gradually does he become aware that he is not of Earth, that he is in fact a Prince of Amber. When he finally does move from this shadow back to the all-encompassing universe of Amber, he can do so only through the mediation of his brother who, according to the laws of the fantasy universe, imagines subtle alterations in the earthly landscape. As these alterations take substance, the travelers move through time and space; the more the imagined landscape approximates Amber, the closer the two come to the Castle of King Oberon. Later in the series, when Corwin has recovered his memory and his powers, he may wander at will through innumerable shadow worlds, but the power of interaction remain essentially the prerogative of Amber. Men of Earth not only cannot move from the objective universe to the fantasy universe at will, in most cases, they are totally unaware of the existence of Amber.

In most fantasies, then, there is a division between the objective universe (the reader's experiential universe) and the fantasy universe. In some novels the gap is not bridged; the author merely thrusts the reader into an alien setting, with no indication that any world other than the fantasy world exists. In others, the author provides for interaction between objective and fantasy worlds, but those interactions are almost invariably controlled by the laws of the fantasy universe. There are bridges between the two frames, but they remain essentially separate and isolated, manifestations of totally different realities which happen to coincide sufficiently for a minimal interrelationship.

In C. S. Lewis, however, a different pattern emerges. On the surface, it would seem that he, too, separates his fantasy world from the objective world, allowing interchanges only when initiated in the former. In the Chronicles of Narnia, for example, there does appear to be a definite gap between Earth and Narnia (or any of the other worlds reached through the Wood between the Worlds). The children cannot *go* to Narnia; they are *taken* there. In *The Silver Chair,* Eustace and Jill discuss this limitation. Eustace has heard that his cousins, the Pevensies, have "had their share" and can't return to Narnia, but he hopes that he and Jill can, perhaps on their own initiative. "You mean we might draw a circle on the ground—and write things…and recite charms and spells?" asks Jill.

> "Well," said Eustace after he had thought hard for a bit. "I believe that was the sort of thing I was thinking of, though I never did it. But now when it comes to the point, I've an idea that all those circles and things are rather rot. I don't think he'd like them. It would look as if we thought we could make him do things. But really, we can only ask him. (6)

Narnia seems to be one with Xanth, or Photon, or Amber—a world which impinges upon ours but is not truly congruent with it.

This appearance is misleading, however. In fact, there is an essential difference in the handling of Lewis's fantasy universes (both in the Chronicles of Narnia and in the space trilogy) which sets him apart from most other writers of fantasy. For Lewis, there are no actual barriers between the world we know and the world we share through his imagination. True, for the most part humans enter Narnia through forces not their own. The wardrobe and the "Picture in the Bedroom" in the early volumes of the Chronicles are prime examples of means of involuntary entrance into Narnia. The wardrobe functions according to the rules of Narnia, not of Earth; it is not an eternally open doorway into a fantasy world. In this sense, Narnia often chooses who will enter, and when.

There is another mechanisms in the Chronicles, however, which functions more constantly and more consistently. In *The Magician's Nephew,* Uncle Andrew may misunderstand the precise nature of the rings, mistaking the functions of the greens and the yellows, but he is correct on one crucial point. The rings are a physical device to facilitate transfer from one world to another, i.e., from the objective universe of the reader to the fantasy universe of Narnia. And they function consistently, regardless of who invokes their power by touching them; in *The Last Battle,* Edmund and Peter recognize the power of the rings as a mode of entering Narnia. They are not actually used, but Lewis nowhere casts doubt on the possibility of their use.

The initiative rests with the individual rather than with his awareness of the exotic laws governing a world of magic. The rings represent a physical connection between worlds, making Narnia equivalent with our world rather than superior to it. This equivalence is stated directly in *The Voyage of the "Dawn Treader"* as the Lamb speaks to Lucy:

> "Not for you," said the Lamb. "For you the door into Aslan's country is from your own world."
> "What!" said Edmund. "Is there a way into Aslan's country from our world too?"
> "There is a way into my country from all the worlds," said the Lamb.

And later:

> "…I have another name. You must learn to know me by that name. This was the very reason you were brought to Narnia, that by knowing me here for a little, you may know me better there." (208-209)

Narnia and Earth co-exist within the same plane. The interactions between the two are free-flowing. Anyone, even one as skeptical, arrogant, greedy, and essentially un-Christian as Uncle Andrew, may stimulate the rings into action. Narnia may on occasion reach into Earth and draw individuals to her; but she is ultimately open to any, not merely the few who understand the physical laws of both realms.

The space trilogy illustrates this direction in Lewis's thinking even more clearly, In *Perelandra*, Ransom suggests that the interactions between Earth and the fantasy worlds of Perelandra and Malacandra are dependant initially upon actions within our world (22). The heroes of Perelandra and Malacandra—indeed Maleldil himself—cannot interfere with the internal worlds of Earth/Thulcandra until the barriers have been broken from within. We find no magic wardrobes or pictures that come to life in the space trilogy. Instead, interfacing between the two universes is accomplished by means of mechanisms created by humans. Weston's spacecraft does more than merely carry men to Mars; it simultaneously opens Earth to the influence of the eldila of unfallen planets and ultimately to their presence on Earth itself.

This element in the trilogy establishes the parity between the world which Lewis (and his readers) knows experientially and that which exists within his imagination. Unlike most other fantasies, in which either the objective world or the fantasy world finally defines a true "reality," Lewis's fantasies offer an image of a universe in which both the objective and the fantastical co-exist. There is no sharp distinction between the two, as between Xanth and Mundania or between Photon and Phaze; nor is the Earth merely a manifestation of a larger fantasy universe, as in the Chronicles of Amber. Instead, Lewis visualizes the universe as a unity, comprehending both those elements which are best described as scientific (although those elements are often presented as controlled by evil minds, as, for example, the ship in *Out of the Silent Planet* and *Perelandra* and the oracular, mechanically preserves head in *That Hideous Strength*) and those which are non-rational, mystical, magical, or fantastical. And over all presides a single figure of a Deity who Himself comprehends both. Aslan/Christ moves at will through either world; Maleldil/Christ can turn to good both the flawed impulses toward righteousness of the inhabitants of Malacandra and Perelandra and the machinations of the "bent" Weston, Devine and the staff of N.I.C.E. Ultimately for Lewis the differentiation between the fantasy universe of the novel and the objective universe known by the reader dissipates. The terms become identifying tags for portions of the same reality, viewed from different perspectives but both nonetheless parts of a unified whole under the control of God.

# BEYOND DEEP HEAVEN:

## GENERIC STRUCTURE AND CHRISTIAN MESSAGE IN C. S. LEWIS'S RANSOM NOVELS

[This essay was presented to the Conference on Christianity and Literature, Biola University, Los Angeles CA, April 1985; and subsequently published in *The Lamp-Post of the Southern California C. S. Lewis Society* (December 1986): 17-22, 33. It has been slightly revised for this volume.]

In *The Achievement of C. S. Lewis*, Thomas Howard asks one of the most difficult and pertinent questions concerning Lewis's Ransom novels—"What are they?" (53). In varying forms this question occurs in most criticism of the books, either overtly or implicitly as writers attempt to fit them neatly (and sometimes not so neatly) into generic classifications.

The novels have proven difficult to classify, however. Possible definitions of genre include Chad Walsh's quest tale (*Literary Legacy*, 121); Humphrey Carpenter's "series of children's books in disguise" (220); Martha Sammon's "planetary romance" (14); and Lewis's own reference to "three science fiction novels." Unfortunately, Lewis's defining them as science fiction does not resolve the problem. If anything, his comment encourages even more diversity. Many critics who concentrate on Lewis consider the trilogy science fiction, often without stating clearly what that classification entails. Critics of science fiction, on the other hand, frequently refer to Lewis but deny him a place in the genre. Patrick G. Hogan argues that Lewis's fictions do not "fit comfortably either the classification of science fiction or fantasy" (266), while James Gunn, Eric S. Rabkin, Robert Scholes, Robert A. Heinlein and others consider the books more parable than science fiction. The elements of science fiction embedded in the books tantalize but do not warrant a clear generic classification.

In addition to this definitional confusion, many of the critics who discuss the Ransom novels treat the three as a unified trilogy within one genre. There are historical precedents for such an assumption since the trilogy as form is intimately connected to science fiction and fantasy, from Tolkien's *Lord of the Rings*, to Asimov's Foundation Trilogy, to Brian Aldiss' Helliconia volumes. Yet most of the difficulty a reader encounters in the Ransom novels stems from their responding best to separate approaches. Arguments for or against the trilogy as science fiction, mythopoeic fantasy, or anything else, usually concentrate on one or two volumes, while apologizing for the third (most frequently *That Hideous Strength*) and implying that things would have been much neater had Lewis not written it. This confusion is largely unnecessary, however, since Lewis seems not to have intended the volumes as a trilogy at all, as evidence both by his own comments (Hooper 8) and by the fragment of a fourth Ransom narrative, *The Dark Tower*.

Finally, then, we are left with a series of contradictory and unenlightening assertions. Lewis wrote science fiction—and he did not; he wrote anti-science-fiction, or Wellsian and Stapledonian speculation, or Asimovian social fiction, or quest epic, or children's tales, or simply religious propaganda. A more helpful approach is perhaps suggested in Samuel R. Delany's discussion of "reading protocols"—generic assumptions readers make while interpreting an individual text (234-236). If we apply Delany's theory and approach the three Ransom novels as separate entities, tied by common characters and themes but generically disparate, we discover a number of fruitful possibilities for interpretation.

Underlying the three, of course, is Lewis's Christianity. Ransom as Christ-surrogate and mediator links the books thematically and theologically, to the extent that several critics have used Ransom as a crux in interpreting the novels. In spite of these connections, however, the novels remain vigorously individual—so much so that they virtually require readers to develop three separate sets of reading protocols. While each might fit into Lewis's generalized definition of science fiction as mythopoeic, the individual treatments do not necessarily coincide.

*Out of the Silent Planet* is superficially the most science-fictional, the most frequently adduced as evidence for that classification. Donald Glover considers it the closest to traditional science fiction, "giving considerable attention to the journey through Malacandra (though using little technical paraphernalia)" (77). Glover's disclaimer identifies the most serious flaw in such a classification; in spite of having a space ship and a scientist, *Out of the Silent Planet* is virtually devoid of any interest in scientific developments. The ship transports Ransom to Malacandra; later, in *Perelandra*, Lewis similarly whisks Ransom to Venus but simply does through the non-scientific mediation of eldila/angels. *Out of the Silent Planet* does indeed incorporate many of the trappings of conventional science fiction, including Lewis's version of "little green Martians," the batrachian Pfiffltriggi; but those components remain vague, undeveloped, and subordinated to Lewis's Christian purposes. If we approach the novel with reading protocols appropriate for traditional science fiction, *Out of the Silent Planet* sadly disappoints.

Marjorie Hope Nicolson and Mark Hillegas, however, have capably argued that precisely those elements which militate against the novel as science fiction most clearly work to define it as a sub-genre of *fantasy*, a Cosmic Voyage. As Hillegas details in his discussion of the internal and external structure of the Cosmic Voyage, *Out of the Silent Planet* is inherently more philosophical and less technical than straightforward science fiction. The few science-fictional elements are subordinated to Lewis's larger purposes of removing a representative human from the Earth, introducing him to an "alien" world, and through his reactions and interactions deriving conclusions about the nature and state of humanity. Like Lucian's *True History*, *Out of the Silent Planet* becomes a vehicle for social satire.

Moreover, if we consider the novel as a fantasy, many presumed weaknesses diminish. The flaws in Lewis's "scientific" representation of Mars disappear, since Lewis is now accountable only to the Malacandra of imagination, not to the Mars of scientific fact. Bringing the reading protocols of fantasy to bear upon *Out of the Silent Planet* also highlights critical points in the narrative— episodes in which Ransom shows the hesitation or amazement that critics such as Tzvetan Todorov, Erik S. Rabkin, and W. S. Irwin have related to fantasy. Throughout his time on Malacandra, Ransom forms expectations, only to have them inverted, resulting in astonishment and culminating in the final reversals, such as Ransom's perception of humans from the "alien" point of view (125); and his discovery that the Malacandrians are not in fact true "aliens" but co-creations with humans of Maleldil the Elder. The ostensibly alien society on Malacandra is thus constructed to counterpoint the society Lewis knew so well on this planet.

To consider *Out of the Silent Planet* as fantasy—either through the narrow definition of Cosmic Voyage or through fuller explorations into theories of the fantastic—resolves most of the difficulties in the text while raising a minimum of new ones. Glover notes that Lewis himself suggested an element of the fantastic in *Out of the Silent Planet* in his reply to Haldane—the attack on Weston, for example, was "farce as well as fantasy" (78). To be sure, there are elements of science fiction—and of myth—but they diminish the more completely we immerse ourselves in the story, leaving the fantastic: talking animals, spirits, reversal and astonishment, and an intuition of the marvelous and the awesome that is central to Lewis's Christian commitment.

Of the three novels, *Perelandra* is perhaps the most easily classified and creates the least critical dissent. It does not read like science fiction in any acknowledged sense; nor does it bear the distinguishing characteristics of the Cosmic Voyage. Simply by having Ransom reach Perelandra through the intervention of the eldila rather than by spaceship, Lewis indicates a generic shift. The rudimentary sense of science fiction suggested by Weston's ship in *Out of the Silent Planet* disappears almost immediately, as do the characteristics of Cosmic Voyage, leaving us free to interpret the narrative through protocols appropriate to myth.

The relationships between myth as genre and the claim that the novels are science fiction is not necessarily contradictory. A number of critics, including Gary Wolfe, Patricia Warrick, Casey Fredericks, and Ursula K. Le Guin have noted an affinity between science fiction and myth. Wolfe and Warrick would agree with Le Guin that

> science fiction is the mythology of the modern world —or one of its mythologies.... For science fiction does use the mythmaking faculty to apprehend the world we live in, a world profoundly shaped and changed by science and technology: and its originality is that it uses the mythmaking faculty on new material. (64)

In *Perelandra*, Lewis re-creates the Myth of the Fall in space, on a planet that has not yet fallen and never will. The science-fictional elements—alien worlds, spacecraft, non-terrestrial humanoids, (the Lady is, after all, green)—blend with Christian mythic traditions Lewis inherited through Milton to expand both myth and science fiction; traditional form weds speculative content, traditional Christian motifs are transplanted into space.

Since *Out of the Silent Planet* relies heavily on the patterns of fantasy, Lewis's transition to myth in the subsequent volume becomes logical. David Leeming notes that "the final step in the peeling away of the layers of fantasy [takes] us to myth itself, where the quest of all of us for total being is expressed in the adventures of the hero" (*Flights,* 261). To lead the reader from the fantasy Mars of *Out of the Silent Planet* to an unknown world on the verge of temptation, Lewis structured *Perelandra* as myth, a choice partially dictated by his subject, with its Miltonic echoes. Since Lewis addressed temptation and sin rather than the role of humanity within the Christian cosmos, he logically elected to work within the framework of the Myth of the Fall. The mythic element is so strong, in fact, that Sammons defines Lewis's purpose as "to give the Christian story fresh excitement by retelling it as a new myth" (23). Or, to cite Nicholson, "Lewis has created myth itself, myth woven of the desires and aspirations deep-seated in some, at least, of the human race" (*Voyages,* 254).

The third Ransom volume, *That Hideous Strength*, generates the most confusion, with its blend of science (or rather *scientism*—Lewis's term for the ethical abuse of scientific knowledge), fervent faith, and myth. The key to the novel lies in a structural principle already addressed—inversion of expectation. In *Out of the Silent Planet*, the inversion was overt, creating a repeating sense of amazement in Ransom. In *Perelandra*, it is more subtle; the Green Lady is tempted to understand the nature of good and evil, ignorance and knowledge. She does—but through a fundamental inversion. She grows by obedience, not disobedience. There is no need for a *felix culpa* on Perelandra, Lewis points out, since there is no Fall. Through her relationship with Maleldil and her assessment of arguments presented by Ransom and the Un-Man, the Green Lady stands, thereby inverting human (i.e., Thulcandran or terrestrial) history. In *That Hideous Strength*, however, Lewis attempts a more fundamental generic inversion, literally standing science fiction on its head, by intruding elements inimical to its objective, scientific frame-work—that is, the overtly theological implications of Maleldil, eldila, demons (Macrobes) and the Merlin-figure.

The novel is unquestionably ambiguous. Lewis calls it "A Modern Fairy-Tale for Grownups," although it lacks most traditional "fairy-tale" techniques. On the other hand, Lewis is interested in examining scientific and technological change within human society—one goal of science fiction. One of the focal points in the narrative, after all, is the N.I.C.E.—the National Institute for Co-ordinated Experimentation. Nor does the book simply condemn science; Hingest is a chemist as well as one of the admirable characters in the book. He leaves the Institute when it is clear that its purposes are political, not scientific.

In spite of this, there remain anomalous elements which might militate against *That Hideous Strength* as science fiction—gods, angels, and magicians. Here, I think, Lewis explores possibilities, expands definitions, and restructures a genre to make it appropriate to his Christian concerns. Arthur C. Clarke has argued that a science-fictional narrative is allowed one "miracle"—one technological advance that seems, from our state of knowledge, improbable but possible. A writer may posit FTL (faster-than-light travel) or time travel, but not both. To do the latter would strain the reader's ability to accept the premises of the narrative.

When one analyzes *That Hideous Strength*, it is difficult to determine which technological "wonder" provides its foundation. There are few scientific developments in the text; Lewis notes that most were already possibilities when he wrote the novel. Not even the re-animation of Alcasan's head is as "scientific" as it seems, since all of the apparatus involved in the procedure is ultimately shown to be irrelevant.

Yet there *is* a basic assumption in the novel. Lewis posits as fact—not article of faith—the existence of God, and proceeds to explore the impact of technology in a universe in which God demonstrably exists. From that single point, he constructs every facet of the narrative, including excursions into scientific philosophizing, episodes hinging upon scientific (or pseudo-scientific) jargon common in science fiction, and characters who pride themselves upon their objectivity and pragmatism. In a phrase, Lewis constructs "Christian science fiction."[*] Characters use the scientific method to verify their perceptions, something missing in both *Out of the Silent Planet* and *Perelandra*. Mark Studdock first hears of the bent eldila through Frost's quasi-scientific explanation of the macrobes (256-257); the Objectivity Room at Belbury juxtaposes Christianity and science—and Frost himself admits that those subjected to the room might turn in either direction. Even more significantly, Ransom and Dimble define Merlin in scientific rather than mythic or fantastic terms; instead of saying that Merlin was enchanted, ensorcelled, or entranced, Ransom says simply that Merlin "went out of time, into a parachronic state" (226) —in effect, Merlin is a time-traveler.

Language in *That Hideous Strength* similarly strives toward the objective. The confusion of tongues at Belbury draws on biblical patterning but more importantly suggests Lewis's concern for language as objective phenomenon. The primal language, Old Solar, creates an identity between the thing represented and the sounds rep-

---

[*] In a like manner, Milton redefined and inverted traditional, classical epic conventions to create something new, the Christian epic.

resenting it—an idea also developed in a science-fiction novel by Samuel R. Delany, *Babel-17*. Language is important in all three novels; as evil develops, it becomes abstract in form (Wither acts like a zombie) and in expression, as in Weston's philosophical abstractions in *Out of the Silent Planet*, the Un-Man's in *Perelandra*, or the scientists' in *That Hideous Strength*. Conversely, as one approaches the Good, language becomes more concrete, tied to things and people. The cataclysm at Belbury is thus less a miraculous mingling of tongues than the working out of the inevitable, "scientific" functions of language in Lewis's Christian universe.

In *That Hideous Strength*, then, Lewis makes a single assumption about the universe and assesses scientific observation and experimentation in that universe. Belbury allies itself less with demons and devils than with a rebellious faction of a coexistent suprahuman species. The eldila are understandable through rational, experiential knowledge rather than through faith. Ransom is released from his earlier dependence on faith; his knowledge of the various beings is as "scientific" as Withers' or Frost's knowledge of macrobes.

In the Ransom novels, then, Lewis creates something more complex than a trilogy about an on-going character. He explores the possibilities of Christian beliefs by expanding literacy genres—fantasy, myth, and science fiction—to discover how fully each might bear the meanings he wished to communicate. The results is a trilogy which is not a trilogy but three novels pressing beyond traditional genres to discover the best mode of presenting Lewis's Christian message.

# OF BOOKS AND REPUTATIONS:

## THE CONFUSING CASES OF KING, KOONTZ, AND OTHERS

[This essay first appeared in *Demon-Driven: Stephen King and the Art of Writing.* Edited by George Beahm. Williamsburg VA: GB Publishing Ink, 1994. It has been slightly revised for this volume.]

Several years ago, my then-teenaged son came home from high school chuckling—itself an odd enough circumstance to merit remembering. But the reason for his laughter was even more intriguing than the fact of it, particularly as it bore directly on my own efforts in Science Fiction, Fantasy, and Horror criticism.

His junior English class was preparing to face the great unmentionable, the horror of the year—the dreaded TERM PAPER. His teacher had handed out a long list of possible topics, all American authors, and the students were required to submit proposals for a paper that would discuss at least three works by a single author, or one work by three authors, combining the students' perceptions with relevant outside sources.

During the discussion, one student noted that his favorite author, Stephen King, was not included on the list. No, the teacher answered solemnly, King was not included. Another student noted that several other contemporary popular writers were missing from the list also, and asked why.

In response the teacher said that such writers were only of interest to readers unable to handle the sophisticated expression of the "classics."

"In other words," the second student shot back, defending himself and his friends who read King and others, "we read them because we're too stupid to understand the classics?"

"Uh, no," the teacher answered, obviously backpedaling. She continued to talk in generalities about the lack of sophistication in contemporary popular writers, noting in passing that most students hadn't even considered using King as a topic for the paper until a few years before, when a professor from Pepperdine began publishing books about him.

At this point, my son sat up and began paying more attention.

Then, the teacher continued, the professor made things worse by holding discussion groups at the local library, actually talking with groups of high-school students about King and his works as if they had literary merit.

Now my son was *really* paying attention, wondering if he should raise his hand and say "That's my father," or wait it out and see what else the teacher would say.

He decided to wait it out.

And discovered that in spite of such odd behavior (fortunately isolated) in a college professor, there really wasn't enough criticism on Stephen King or writers like him to merit including them on the list of possibilities for the TERM PAPER.

End of discussion.

* * * * * * *

When my son reported this experience—grinning the whole while and (I'm sure) wondering how I would take this implied slur on my reputation (such as it is)—I was struck again by the short-sightedness of academic establishments that continue to exclude King, Koontz, and others like them from the lists of "approved" materials.

While Hawthorne and *The Scarlet Letter,* Melville and *Moby Dick,* and Dickens and *A Tale of Two Cities* are certainly central literary achievements in our culture, even fascinating topics for further research and discussion by adult readers, I am less convinced now than I was as a high-school student that they are necessarily appropriate for freshmen, sophomores, and juniors in high school, many of whom are barely beyond being functionally literate, many of whom lack even the slimmest backgrounds or historical perspectives for assessing such novels, and many of whom are explicitly more interested in Poe, Bradbury, and King. Yet instructors are forced in turn to force high-school students to read works that probably even most teachers would be unlikely to read for pleasure.

On the other hand, the opposite approach seems to be requiring contemporary, written-for-the-occasion texts that are themselves less literary artifacts than exercises in political correctness, sociological conditioning, and artificially induced diversity. Either way, the established programs often simply ignore the fact that kids like to read (and watch) things by Stephen King.

There are, of course, strong arguments against allowing King into curriculums, even as tangentially as letting students use his works for an out-of-class term paper.

His writing is often violent. It is often gross and explicit, both sexually and linguistically. It is often fantastic. It is often highly critical of accepted institutions, including home, family, politics, and education.

But the kids *read* him. Based on my experiences leading discussion groups about his books, high-school-aged readers often *devour* his books, memorize his books, know more about what he has written than I do.

And then they are told by teachers that he is too unsophisticated, too peripheral to what is really important in the universe, too *common* for students to waste their time on, when it would seem that teachers would welcome the opportunity to confront a writer who perhaps more than any other is molding the imaginations and minds of contemporary adolescents. After all, if so many students read him, and he is so awful, so damaging to the social fabric, so utterly without redeeming social value, it would seem even more important to discover what it is that draws younger readers to him. To refer back to my son's experience, the teacher stated to the class that anyone who read more than two or three King novels had to be warped, perverted, highly disturbed. At that point my son couldn't help laughing out loud—and was tempted to put the teacher even more on the spot by noting that he (my son) had read about thirty King novels and that his father had read *everything* that King had published. If two or three relegated a reader to warp-dom, where would thirty, forty, or fifty books put someone? Perhaps wisely, my son restrained his impulse, and the teacher was free to continue her defense of the *status quo* reading list.

No, King is not sufficiently elevated, not sufficiently elegant, not sufficiently a part of the teachers' own university backgrounds (implying that they might actually have to read him and study him themselves in order to lecture to classes) that he is simply inappropriate as the subject for a research project.

And to prove their point, they pound the final nail into the coffin of any would-be term-paperist: *There's just not enough criticism written about him to make the effort worthwhile.*

Again and again I have heard this comment and been stunned at the ignorance it betrays. Certainly for many Science Fiction, Fantasy, and Horror writers, the claim is unfortunately true. Some of the finest writers in the genres have been ignored by traditional critics and scholars, to the point that accurate bibliographies are not even available for many, if not most. In spite of the valiant efforts of publishers like the late Ted Dikty of Starmont House and his series editor, Roger Schlobin, who between the two of them saw to the publication of several dozen introductory monographs; or Rob Reginald at Borgo Press, with his continuing series of definitive bibliographies—in spite of the work of dozens of scholars and critics approaching such monumental tasks as the life works of Isaac Asimov and Robert Heinlein and others almost as prolific and as central to our reading heritage—in spite of all of this effort, it is still too easy for teachers to issue lists of term-paper topics that ignore some of the most popular and influential writers of our times.

But to make that claim for Stephen King?

I glance at my bookshelf and see the three-inch-thick manuscript that represents my work on a Stephen King bibliography (scheduled for publication by Borgo Press in December 1993), and I wonder. Woefully out-of-date already since its completion in 1991, ready to be updated with hundred more items before it has even been published, the manuscript nevertheless includes over *3,000* items, both primary and secondary, including titles of several dozen books exclusively about King (a number of them from prestigious university presses), more dozens of articles in scholarly and popular journals and magazines, and hundreds of reviews ranging from the *New York Times Book Review* to localized fan presses—but this is not enough to allow students sufficient exercise in the fine and ancient art of literary research.

Granted, not all of the criticism and scholarship available on King is first class. I think of one article that discovers Vietnam allegories in a King story, when King himself has stated publicly that he sees (or intended) no such subtext himself. Or another critic who, after publishing three very expensive specialty editions of interviews and criticism notes that he considers King little more than a literary hack (although presumably a source of no little income).

Nevertheless, it seems important to recognize that much of the criticism is solid and, more important yet, that Horror writers are an intrinsic and essential part of understanding late twentieth-century American culture. Writers like Stephen King, Dean R. Koontz, Robert McCammon, Dan Simmons, and others have written works that transcend narrow genre classifications, that have grappled with the fundamental social problems we face today, and have explored them through the *metaphor* of the monstrous and the horrific—as if AIDS, molestation, homelessness, and *-isms* of various sorts were not already monstrous and horrific enough. These writers have described *us* in the clearest and broadest of terms—not pessimistically or nihilistically but often with an undercurrent of true hope. On the surface, their images may be frightening, but then so is our world. The "pre-millennial cotillion" that Koontz depicts graphically in *Dragon Tears* is not just a figment of his imagination. The worldwide plague that wipes out most of humanity in King's *The Stand* is only a few degrees beyond the plagues—diseases, social unrest, political threats—that we presently face. The fictional disintegration of society in McCammon's *Swan Song* or *Mine* or *Stinger* reflects the real disintegrations we see around us. Their unique visions of what it is to live here, to live now, is captured in these and other novels and stories in ways that no alternate form can legitimately duplicate.

And our children read those novels and stories.

Our children see the world in terms of the visions these novels and stories create.

Our children need to understand more completely what it is that these writers are working to achieve.

# THE RADIATING PENCILS OF HIS BONES:

## THE POETRY OF STEPHEN KING

[This essay first appeared in *The Shape Under the Sheet: The Complete Stephen King Encyclopedia,* ed. Stephen Spignesi (Ann Arbor MI: Popular Culture, Ink., May 1991), 627-632. It is here reprinted by permission].

As a writer, Stephen King is not well-known for his poetry; virtually lost among the million-copy novels, the short stories, the reviews and interviews and articles King's readers read, discuss, and anatomize are eight short published poems, most dating from his college years and appearing in esoteric arts magazines published by the University of Maine, Orono. More recently, two poems were included in his 1985 collection, *Skeleton Crew.* Although difficult to find, the early poems are nonetheless worth the effort, if for no other reason than that they provide interesting and valuable insights into the development of King's imagination and his art.

Poetry is a precise form. The limitations of line length, stanza form, rhythmical and verbal patterning all lend a sense of focus to poetry. It is characterized by compression of idea and image, by exploration of the possibilities of language. More than any other literary genre—short fiction, screenplay, especially the diffuse bulk of the novel (to say nothing of the long novel, a form that King has frequent recourse to)—poetry requires careful control of every element. A single false word in a 150,000-word novel may not even be noticed; a single false word, even a false sound pattern, however, may destroy the cumulative effect of a ten-line poem.

In addition, poetry lays additional constraints on the writer in terms of coherence, development, and the ability to communicate elliptically. The single image succinctly described must be capable of unfolding, of inviting the reader into the experience of the poem, and of repaying with continual depth and expressiveness as the reader returns to the poem again and again.

Poetry, then, is a difficult form. A number of major novelists began their careers intending to be poets. C. S. Lewis's first books were collections of poetry; Faulkner had aspirations to being a poet; more recently—and in an allied form to King's—Orson Scott Card worked extensively with poetry and poetic drama before turning to science fiction and fantasy. In each case, forays into poetry became part of the writers' apprenticeship, providing opportunities to develop linguistic skills, imagery, rhythms, and discipline that would prove invaluable in later works.

In addition, of course, early poems frequently incorporate ideas and images that will recur in more extended forms later in a writer's career. This is particularly true with King, whose handful of published poems are often of interest less for their inherent value as poems than as indices to King's development. Although the poems may demonstrate what King's critics might consider unusual perceptivity and sensitivity in a writer whose fiction has earned him a reputation as the "king of horror," the poems do not rivet the reader's attention to the same extent as his stories and novels, in part simply because King's many strengths are most apparent in longer forms—particularly his unique narrative stance, that half-familiar colloquial voice that engages readers' imaginations and makes it almost impossible for them to break away from the stories he tells. The more formal distancing and verbal texture of poetry often comes between King as poet and his audience.

By virtue of their form, his poems work against King's colloquial narrative approach. Rather than encompassing the fate of the world, or even the fate of a complex cast of intriguing characters whose stories are told over the expanse of three hundred, or five hundred, or eight hundred pages or more, the poems concentrate on the small, on the minute. They are not themselves trivial, but they carry an implicit sense of triviality when considered next to the bulk of *The Stand* or *IT*, for example, or even the lesser weight of *Carrie, Salem's Lot,* and the other novels. Yet the poems—especially the earliest of them—fascinate because of the light they shed on King's interests and imagination.

In fact, his earliest published poem, when viewed through the superior vision of hindsight, becomes virtually a catalogue of themes and techniques that will become increasingly important.

By 1968, King had already professionally published four stories and completed the manuscript for *The Long Walk* (published essentially unrevised eleven years later). In the fall of that year, "Harrison State Park '68" appeared under King's name in *Ubris,* a publication of the University of Maine at Orono. It is a long elliptical poem of 100 free verse lines, with stanzas scattered across the page, incorporating white space as well as text into the visual effect of the poetry. "Harrison State Park '68" is, at first glance, obviously experimental and exploratory, as befits the time and situation of its composition—the work of a socially- and literarily-aware college students in the late sixties. The subject is a murder in Harrison State Park, a location in Maine mentioned in several of King's later novels.

As a poem, "Harrison State Park '68" is not particularly strong. It relies on verbal clichés ("If you can't be an athlete,/be an athletic supporter"), on overt puns ("call me Ishmael/i am a semen") that sometimes establish only marginal connections with the remainder of the poem, and on elliptical images that disintegrate rather than integrate the communication. Even by the time the poem was written, the use of fragmented white space to create poetic texture had become a visual cliché, while the text often shifts from full, conventional use of capitals to erratic use of lower case *i* for the first person pronoun. In addition, it is equally erratic in ignoring punctuational devices: "can't" appears conventionally spelled in one stanza, while "dont"—without the apostrophe—appears in another. Such inconsistencies of usage occasionally impede the movement of the poem.

However, in spite of those difficulties—which should not be considered surprising in the work of a twenty-year-old neophyte poet—"Harrison State Park '68" repays reading. It begins with what will become a trademark in King's fictions: headnote quotations to suggest the direction of the story to follow. In this case—as with *It*, which pairs a quotation from William Carlos Williams' *Patterson* with a line from Bruce Springsteen—the passages are carefully juxtaposed to create a sense of internal tension: Thomas Szasz's "All mental disorders are simply defective strategies for handling difficult life situations" collides in context, vocabulary, structure, and meaning, with Ed Sanders' "And I feel like homemade shit."

Yet the headnotes—and their conscious juxtaposition—are effective and appropriate. The poem deals with tension, with conflict, with juxtaposition of images. The early lines "*Modern Screen Romances* is a tent on the grass/Over a dozen condoms/in a quiet box," with their quiescent evocation of sexuality and illusion, clash with the poem's horrific conclusion:

> oh
> dont
> please touch me

> but dont
> dont
> and i reach for your hand
> but touch only the radiating five pencils
> of your bones:
> —Can you do it?

In addition, throughout the poem there are suggestions of devices that will become vintage King. The repetition of "—Can you do it?" throughout the poem adumbrates the incessant "Do you love?" that helps establish atmosphere and texture in "The Raft" and "Do the Dead Sing?" (later published as "The Reach"). Several stanzas in "Harrison State Park '68" include brand-name references—Sony, Westinghouse, Playtex living bras, Fig Newtons—as well as references to cultural icons such as the Doors and Sonny and Cher. Even the topic, with its implied social criticism and obvious connections to fear, terror, and horror, foreshadows King's later preoccupation with death in its multifarious manifestations. The sense of isolation, fragmentation, and disintegration that the form, structure, and content of the poem communicate will find themselves repeated and expanded in virtually every story King will tell.

More successful as an independent poem and more indicative of the directions King's imagination will follow, however, is "The Dark Man," published in the Spring 1969 issue of *Ubris* and the 1970 issue of *Moth* (also a publication of UMO, with Burton Hatlen as advisor). The differences between "Harrison State Park '68" and "The Dark Man" are striking. The earlier poem is verbally and visually diffuse, lacks a clear focus in its elliptical and imagistic approach to violence, and echoes content through its explicit visual arrangement of seemingly unrelated stanzas. The later poem, on the other hand, is from first glance more tightly focused, with its lines and stanzas shaped into a conventional format that is clearly a poem. It begins with a strong, almost stridently abrupt image:

> i have stridden the fuming way
> of sun-hammered tracks and
> smashed cinders....

Subsequent stanzas repeat the initial syntactical structure, "i have...i have...i have," using that repetition to create an undercurrent of rhythm and power. King's images are implicitly and explicitly violent, rough, often verging on the horrific: "desperate houses with counterfeit chimneys"; "glaring swamps/where musk-reek rose/to mix with the sex smell of rotting cypress stumps..."; and

> i forced a girl in a field of wheat
> and left her sprawled with the virgin bread
> a savage sacrifice.

The poem concludes with a simple, understated assertion of the speaker's ultimate identity: "i am a dark man."

To King's later readers, of course, that phrase will resonate with meaning that far exceeds the confines of a single poem. The "dark man" is nearly as consistent a motif in King's fictions as the "monstrous woman." One dark man, Roland Deschain, is the key figure in the Dark Tower cycle who pursues the Man in Black, while another, Randall Flagg, forms the evil center of *The Stand* and *Eyes of the Dragon*. More specifically—and more interestingly in terms of "The Dark Man" as suggestive of King's later works—his initial description of Flagg in *The Stand* echoes the atmosphere and feeling, and at times even the specific rhythms and vocabulary, of the poem. In the five pages of Chapter 17, King's paragraphs incessantly repeat similar syntactical openings: "Randall Flagg, the dark man, strode south..."; "He walked rapidly...," "He walked south...," "He moved on...," "He moved on...," "He hammered along...," "He rocked along...," "The dark man walked and smiled," "He strode on...," and "He stopped." Only in the final three paragraphs does King shift to another structural form—and the shift is significant because Flagg suddenly becomes aware that "His time of transfiguration was at hand. He was going to be born for the second time...." He becomes, as does the speaker of the final line of the poem, the archetypal Dark Man.

In addition, the images in *The Stand* echo those sketched in the poem. In a sequence that builds on the rape imagery of the final stanza of the poem, King writes of Flagg that

> The women he took to bed with him, even if they had reduced intercourse to something as casual as getting a snack from the refrigerator, accepted him with a stiffening of the body, a turning away of the countenance. Sometimes they accepted him with tears. They took him the way they might take a ram with golden eyes or a black dog—and when it was done they were *cold*, so *cold*, it seemed impossible they could ever be warm again. (Ch. 17)

And, as with the speaker of the poem, Randall Flagg's world is replete with violence and terror:

> He hammered along, arms swinging by his sides. He was known, well known, along the highways in hiding that are traveled by the poor and the mad, by the professional revolutionaries and by those who have been taught to hate so well that their hate shows on their faces like harelips and they are unwelcome except by others like them who welcome them to cheap rooms with slogans and posters on the walls, to basements where lengths of sawed-off pipe are held in padded vises while they are stuffed with high explosives, to back rooms where lunatic plans are laid: to kill a cabinet member, to kidnap the child of a visiting dignitary, or to break into a boardroom meeting of Standard oil with grenades and machines guns and murder in the name of the people. (Ch. 17)

Even in the rhythms, alliterations, and periods of that final extended sentence, one can hear echoes of similar lines in "The Dark Man," down to and including portions that virtually scan as iambic/dactylic units. The poem is 42 lines long, divided into five stanzas of increasingly dark imagery that ultimately have required portions of more than five novels for King to explore more fully.

The other two poems published in *Moth* have less impact and are less relevant to his later career, perhaps because they are substantially narrower in focus. "Silence" is a twelve-line monologue, superficially suggestive of King's later poem "Paranoid: A Chant" in its obsession with "the feary silence of fury." Other than that single line, there is little in the poem that is memorable or suggestive. "Donovan's Brain," as the title indicates, reflects the horror film by that title and is again an exercise in obsession and terror—the latter signaled by typographical placement of a single word in the center of the page between lines of asterisks:

*********

horror

*********

In its combination of filmic echoes and strident imagery—
"warped and sucked by desert wine/raped by the brain of that mon-

strous man"—the poem moves King a step closer to devices that will help form the texture of his subsequent fictions (and is, as King notes, an early exercise toward the novel that would become *The Dark Half*).

A year later, another short poem appeared, an untitled work in the January 1971 issue of *Onan*, also published in Orono. There is even less here that looks forward to King's enormous impact as a novelist, in part perhaps because of the subject: fishing. At a time when King was involved in writing not only tales of horror and terror for *Cavalier* and *Startling Mystery Stories* but also more generally mainstream and mostly unpublishable novels—the opening chapters of *Rage, The Long Walk, Sword in the Darkness* (an unpublished race-riot novel), and *Blaze* (an unpublished reworking of Steinbeck's *Of Mice and Men*)—it should not surprise that his poetic imagination might turn to mainstream images as well. Beginning "In the key-chords of dawn," the poem is a 24 line meditation on sport and responsibility; it concludes with the awareness that when the second overwhelms the first, it is time to "put away our poles." Even in a work as insubstantial as this, however, there are indications of growth and maturity through an increasing sense of verbal and visual control in the lines. The images are less violent, less vigorous, but more disciplined than those in "Harrison State Park '68," for example.

The sense of maturity continues in the next poem, a paean to baseball called "Brooklyn August." Dedicated to Jim Bishop, one of King's instructors at UMO, it appeared in *Io* in 1971. Again, the subject vitiates any sense of direct influence on King's major novels, except that baseball touches the lives of later characters in *IT* and elsewhere. Of some interest, however, is the overt structure of the piece, a blend of traditional poetry and the rhythms of prose. Three rhyming sequences of lines (all with terminal long-*O* rhymes) are interrupted by free-verse descriptive stanzas that move baseball from an idealized national pastime to a sometimes dark reality. The lines snap back from prosaic texture to carefully rhyming couplets reminiscent of Eliot's famous

> In the room the women come and go
> Talking of Michelangelo

from "The Love Song of J. Alfred Prufrock" (and in fact using the same terminal rhyme sound) suggests a dissociation of perception as the poem shifts from repetitive, formalistic statements couched in rhyming couplets to the minutiae of observation expressed through free verse and the rhythms of prose. The poet's vision is expanding, incorporating not only his own observations and interests but also tags of literary heritage as well, a tendency already suggested by echoes of Poe in "The Glass Floor" (1967) and "The Blue Air Compressor" (1971). In later works, King's use of literary allusions and structures would become increasingly complex and important, from the multiple literary references in *The Shining,* to the assertion of an essentially Lovecraftian universe in *IT,* to the unabashed assumption of the guise of genre-romance in *Misery.* King's arsenal of direct allusions would ultimately incorporate Melville, Lovecraft, Yeats, Frost, Hemingway, Faulkner, Milton, Orwell, Tolkien, Wells, Stoker, Dickens, Shakespeare, Golding, Coleridge, O'Casey, and others—a tempering of classical and traditional literary elements to counter stridently contemporary and pop-culture references to Bob Dylan, The Who, John Jakes, Bruce Springsteen. "Brooklyn August" lies a long way from the focus of King's major works, but even in its distancing, the poem demonstrates one of his fundamental structural devices.

Following the appearance of "Brooklyn August," King seemed to have abandoned poetry for the less restrictive, freer, more expansive (and—to be honest—more profitable) possibilities of short story and novel. His list of publications during the next fourteen years includes dozens of short stories; every novel through *The Talisman, The Eyes of the Dragon,* and the final Bachman novel, *Thinner;* and his non-fiction study of horror in film and television, *Danse Macabre.* During the same period, over a dozen films based on his works appeared, many of which he had a hand in developing. Then, when *Skeleton Crew* appeared in 1985, King surprised many of his readers by including two more poems: "Paranoid: A Chant" and "For Owen." Both differ radically from the earlier poems; both show advances in tone and voice that might be expected from a novelist of King's stature.

"Paranoid: A Chant" is an internal monologue, told in colloquial vocabulary and rhythms through the perceptions of a speaker whose own grasp on reality and truth is at best shaky. The speaker is presented as marginally uneducated ("I can't go out no more"), obsessed by fear, and communicating that fear in staccato bursts of accusation and self-revelation. Verbal and syntactical structures collapse onto themselves; punctuation and other conventional means of establishing order and coherence are absent. The reader is forced to question the narrator's sanity, while the speaker continually, obsessively asserts that he is sane: *these things are happening,* he says, *believe me, I know.* In the warped perceptions of the narrator, luncheonette salt becomes arsenic, "greeting cards are letter-bombs," scholars are suborned by the FBI, and "a dark man with no face" crawls "through nine miles/of sewer to surface in my toilet, listening...."

With the inexorable inner logic-not-logic of madness, the poem ends where it began, with an offer of coffee to the unnamed listener (an offer anyone with any intelligence would refuse) and a return to the opening stanza of the poem. Nothing has changed. Nothing more is known about reality or truth. The circle of madness is closed and the chant resumes.

"For Owen" is less threatening, in part because the narrative voice more closely approximates King's own. The poem is apparently directed toward King's younger son, focusing on the fears and frustrations of a child attending school. Both poems are written in the first person, but where "Paranoid: A Chant" generates an increasing sense of unease and discomfort as the reader discovers what lies in the speaker's mind, "For Owen" soothes and expands metaphorically to suggests the universal experience of death, not in terms of the terror defined in the more horrific stories in *Skeleton Crew*—"The Mist," "Gramma," "The Raft," or "Nona"—but rather in terms of the gentle awakening and understanding that Stella Flanders attains in "The Reach." The poem is admittedly cryptic, reaching for meaning through references to school children as fruit: watermelons, bananas, plums. But by the final lines, the speaker penetrates the metaphors and deals with death, noting that just as a school child must learn to write, he also must learn the art of dying. In the context of *Skeleton Crew*, "For Owen" seems unusually gentle.

Almost lost in the millions of words that comprise King's thirty-three book-length publications and his nearly two hundred published stories, articles, and reviews; virtually buried in university archives and special-collections rooms; reviving echoes of a young King self-consciously exploring the power of words—in spite of the circumstances militating against easy access and easy reading, these eight short poems nonetheless suggest, foreshadow, resonate. Each represents a small fragment of King's imagination; each expands that fragment into something larger, more complex than it had been. As poems, none will probably endure as acknowledged master-works of twentieth-century literature; as integral elements in King's development and growth, however, each retains both interest and importance.

# ON KUBRICK'S *THE SHINING*

[The original version of this essay appeared as "On *The Shining*" in George Be-ahm's *Phantasmagoria* (#5 [April 1997]: 7-12). It has been edited and amended. Over a decade old, it does not address the intriguing question of comparisons be-tween King's novel, Kubrick's film, and King's own film version, released as a television mini-series shortly after this essay was written.]

Stephen King's *The Shining* remains among his most teachable novels. In an informal discussion at the International Conference on the Fantastic in the Arts (1984), King in fact noted that when his works find their ways into university-level literature courses, *The Shining* is the most likely to appear.

Several points account for the novel's popularity as a class-room text. It is consciously (and often self-consciously) literary in its allu-siveness, with references ranging from Shakespeare and Samuel Johnson to Arthur Miller and Truman Capote, with frequent stops along the way for brief nods to Emily Dickinson, T. S. Eliot, Wil-liam Carlos Williams, Peter Straub, and a host of other literary lu-minaries, including, not coincidentally, Edgar Allan Poe. It becomes in some senses a compendium of the literature which has preceded it, summarizing and transforming multiple themes, techniques and movements through its own narrative of hauntings and madness.

In addition, the novel is equally consciously an artifact con-cerned with the creation of artifacts—a metafiction of sorts. Jack Torrance stands not only at the center of King's narrative but at the creative center of his own literary work, his play-in-progress. The relationships between Torrance's life and his attitudes toward litera-ture become an important motif in *The Shining*, until life and art eventually merge as Jack creates his own imagined realities.

And finally, *The Shining* is unique among King's fictions for the strong thread of conscious symbol-making that functions as a corol-lary to Torrance's literary pretensions. Throughout, Torrance trans-lates his experiences into symbolic statements, most obviously when he encounters the wasps while repairing the Overlook roof. For pages at a time, Torrance indulges in symbol making, explaining his life, with the wasps, the roof, and the Overlook itself as metaphors. From this perspective, *The Shining* is an ideal vehicle in itself to introduce and discuss the literary dimensions of contemporary dark fantasy and horror.

Perhaps these inherent qualities in the novel stimulated Stanley Kubrick's initial interest in filming *The Shining*; at the least, they contribute to the unique texture of the completed film, since Kubrick attempted to translate into film many of the literary characteristics of King's novel. The result is, as one might expect, certainly the most controversial film version of any King work to date; only *The Stand* and *Pet Sematary*, both now in production [1997], might lead to more difficulties in representation than did *The Shining*.

Initially, of course, the coupling of King and Kubrick seemed ideal—the most popular writer of horror fiction and the most prestigious director of science-fiction/fantasy films. Many looked to Kubrick's work on the novel to become a crucial statement (if not the *definitive* statement) on the nature of horror film. Dan Christensen's "Stephen King: Living in 'Constant, Deadly Terror'" noted that none of the projects relating to filming King's work was as "promising or intriguing" as what Kubrick was doing with *The Shining*. David Schow's "Return of the Curse of the Son of Mr. King: Book Two" went even further. The clear failure *Salem's Lot* to do justice to King on the television screen brought audiences, with trembling anticipation, into theaters to catch *The Shining*, whose attendant production mythology was enough to suggest a classic film at the very least, at the most a milestone in cinematic horror or something to justify the reactionary plaudits given the film by critics who, though zealous, were conspicuously few in number.

Even after production, King remained publicly enthusiastic about the film. In "Horrors," an article in *TV Guide* identifying the ten scariest films on videocassettes and discs, King listed *The Shining* as his fifth choice, commenting that while the film diverges greatly from his novel, it nonetheless "builds a claustrophobic terror in a relentless way" into the narrative. "Could it have been done better?" he asks, then responds: "Over the years I've come to believe that it probably could not. The film is cold and disappointingly loveless—but chilling."

Originally, Kubrick apparently intended to follow King's plot closely, although rumors circulated for some time that the film would probably diverge widely from King's text. In fact, when Christensen questioned King about the persistent rumors, King said that he had asked Stanley how close he was following the plot and he said extremely closely. There are going to be some minor changes, but nothing substantial. In terms of plot, it's going to follow the book very closely; whether or not it's going to follow the book in spirit is something else again.

In terms of Kubrick's diverging from the original text, however, in an interview published in 1978, Peter S. Perakos elicited the following comment from King:

> From the beginning, when I first talked to Kubrick some months ago, he wanted to change the ending. He asked me for my opinion on Halloran [sic] becoming possessed, and then finishing the job that Torrance started, killing Danny, Wendy, and lastly himself. Then, the scene would shift to the spring, with a new caretaker and his family arriving. However, the audience would see Jack, Wendy, and Danny in an idyllic family scene—as ghosts—sitting together, laughing and talking. And I saw a parallel between this peaceful setting at the end of the picture and the end of *2001* where the astronaut is transported to the Louis XIV bedroom. To me, the two endings seemed to tie together.

After further discussions with Kubrick, King apparently (and accurately) believed that Kubrick had abandoned that highly unlikely conclusion; such an overly optimistic treatment of the idea that spirit continues beyond life would contradict too strongly what had gone on before in the film. Kubrick's conclusion avoided that difficulty while raising a number of others.

If King had any immediate reservation about the project at that point, they apparently lay more with casting than with the screenplay. King's Wendy Torrance is strong, beautiful, and intelligent; Shelley Duvall, he noted, "just looks sort of nervous and overbred." Jack Torrance, on the other hand, was not "the Jack Nicholson type at all; not flamboyant, almost withdrawn. I had someone like Martin Sheen in mind. But nobody will talk about that sort of thing in pre-production. What they want to talk about is someone who's bankable—and Nicholson is that."

Certain elements of initial production led to odd parallels between King and Kubrick. One of the most daring divergences in the film is Kubrick's use of a hedge maze rather than a topiary garden—and a subsequent re-writing of major portions of the narrative. In an interview, King noted that it was

> very funny to me that he chose a hedge maze, because my original concept was to create a hedge maze. And the reason that I rejected the idea in favor of the topiary animals was because of an old Richard Carlson film, *The Maze*. The story was about a maze, of course, but in the middle of the maze was a pond. And in the middle of the pond, on a lily pad, was the grandfather who was a frog. Every night, grandpa turned into a frog and so they had to put him into the pond. To me that was ludicrous. So I abandoned the idea of a hedge.

Kubrick's decision to replace the topiary animals with the hedge maze seems appropriate in the context of the film as completed. The maze as image is central to Kubrick—witness the subtitle of Thomas Allen Nelson's full-length of Kubrick's films, "Inside a Film Artist's Maze," as well as mazes and puzzles in films such as *2001* and *A Clockwork Orange*. In addition, trying to animate hedge animals might have led to the added difficulty of creatures that resembled Disney characters.

In her review of the film prior to its release as a network film, Judith Crist noted that it "provides us with the ultimate in horror." Although she is aware of the changes Kubrick introduced into the structure of the narrative—particularly Kubrick's emphasis on family relationships rather than setting—Crist states that

> As the sense of menace unreels in the brightly lit and handsomely furbished public rooms, in the mysteries behind a locked door, the echoing footfalls and the flashes of horrifying hallucination, the child becomes our medium, the father our menace. The film's triumph is Nicholson's in his minutely portrayed transition from ordinary householder to Mephisthophelean madman: his is the true tool of terror.

Thus far, we have been concentrating on the film as reflecting (however variously or skewed) Stephen King. More than any other of the films based on King's novels, however, *The Shining* requires more. Kubrick is, after all, responsible for several of the most successful—and most controversial—films over several decades. From the beginning of his career, Kubrick attempted to incorporate his personal vision into every film he made; and, with few exceptions, he succeeded in this attempt. His earliest films were experimental or documentary shorts: *Day of the Fight* (1951); *Flying Padre* (1951); *The Seafarers* (1953). In 1953 he produced, directed, photographed, and edited *Fear and Desire*; two years later, he co-produced, directed, photographed, edited, and scripted *Killer's Kiss*. The next two films, *The Killing* (1956) and *Paths of Glory* (1957), were products of Harris-Kubrick Productions, with Kubrick directing and participating in writing the screenplay.

With *Spartacus* (1960), Kubrick's role was radically limited. Stepping in to replace director Anthony Mann, Kubrick was restricted from many of the freedoms he had enjoyed; he found himself instead in the position of a typical Hollywood studio director: responsible for directing the actors, composing shots, and supervising editing. "What is missing from the list," Nelson points out, "is that script control which was crucial to the artistry of *The Killing* and *Paths of Glory*, and which has lent distinction to all his films since *Paths* with the lone exception of *Spartacus*." The result was less Kubrick-on-film that Kirk Douglas and Dalton Trumbo.

Following *Spartacus,* Kubrick reasserted his particular vision on his films by retaining greater control over the finished products. He directed *Lolita* (1962) and co-produced, directed, and partially scripted *Dr. Strangelove, or How I Learned to Stop Worrying and Love the Bomb* (1964). With *2001: A Space Odyssey* (1968), Kubrick's hand became even more apparent. He produced and directed the film, working with Arthur C. Clarke in writing the screenplay (as an interesting sidelight, Clarke frequently watched the day's rushes before writing portions of the novel; in a sense, novel and film were produced simultaneously, a daring oddity in this day of novelizations from commercially successful films). In addition, Kubrick received screen credits for designing and directing special photographic effects and, given the increasingly complex and sophisticated integration of classical music into the backgrounds of Kubrick's subsequent films, it might be assumed that he played a major role in selecting the music as well—by Richard Strauss, Johann Strauss, Aram Khachaturian, and Gyorgy Ligeti.

In one of Kubrick's most powerful, impressive, and artistically designed films, *A Clockwork Orange* (1971), Kubrick again retained control by producing, directing, writing the screenplay from Burgess's novel, and setting the visual image to music from Beethoven, Edward Elgar, Rossini, Purcell, Rimsky-Korsakov, and others.

Kubrick's 1975 version of *Barry Lindon*, while not a commercial success, continued his exploration of a specific vision. He again acted as producer, director, and screenplay writer, with John Alcott in charge of photography for a second time (the first time had been in *Clockwork*)—he would also direct photography for Kubrick's next film, *The Shining*. Music, as before, was drawn from a variety of sources: Bach, Frederick the Great, Handel, Mozart, Schubert, Vivaldi.

By the time we arrive at *The Shining*, then, several patterns had become apparent in Kubrick's work, most critically his determination to retain control of a film's final form. By doing so, he was able to stamp the text—whether original or based on well-known novels—with his own particular trademark. His choice of John Alcott for a third film suggests that he found Alcott's work especially appropriate in expressing visually what Kubrick saw as the underlying conceptions of a film. And the background music for *The Shining*, while not as intrusively present or inextricably connected with the narrative as was Beethoven's to *A Clockwork Orange*, nonetheless furthers Kubrick's explorations: the eerie sounds of Bartok, Ligeti, Krzystof Penderecki, Wendy Carlos, and Rachel Elkin develop almost an independent existence within the context of the film.

It is not surprising, then (or rather, should not have been surprising, since many viewers of the film *claimed* surprise) that *The Shining* should turn out to be as much Stanley Kubrick as Stephen King, if not more so. Nor is it surprising that viewers expecting "Stephen King" should react angrily, often venomously, when given a different "SK": Stanley Kubrick. Schow's vigorous conclusion is simply that Kubrick proved himself incapable of handling King's material: "And if *The Shining* is really that American Gothic portrait of the death of a family relationship, just what is Kubrick—an American expatriate—doing filming it?" The film is, in a word, "boring."

Nevertheless, the film and its director-producer-screenwriter were not without their supporters. F. Anthony Macklin begins his "Understanding Kubrick: *The Shining*" by acknowledging that most viewers dislike the film. There are, however, good reasons for that dislike—and, he contends, for ultimately appreciating the film, in spite of the fact that it diverged from King's text and that it did not use conventional treatments to create terror or horror. Instead, one must approach the film from a different perspective, namely, that the film represents not King, not horror as a genre, but the unique vision of Stanley Kubrick. To do so brings five main points in focus.

First, the characters in the film seem flat and banal because Kubrick wants them to; the texture of the film is in fact carefully constructed, resulting not from miscasting but from Kubrick's underlying philosophy. In this sense, the film should be compared to Kubrick's own *2001* instead of to King's novel. The interview with Ullman, Macklin points out, owes more to the intentionally uncommunicative briefing scene in *2001* than to King's crisp, precise dialogue.

Second, Kubrick's films continually explore outlets for aggression—most specifically the apes in *2001*, Alex in *A Clockwork Orange*, and certainly Jack Torrance in *The Shining*. Jack's aimless wanderings in the Overlook, his pointless one-man games of catch, his obsessive typing of a single line indicate his lack of outlet. The point is underscored, Macklin notes, by Kubrick's recurrent use of Roadrunner cartoons as background. Danny watches one at the beginning of the film; Larry Durkin's television shows one when Hallorann arrives to rent a Snowcat; and Danny is again watching one when Wendy goes downstairs and sees Jack's manuscript. The explicit violence in the relationship between the Roadrunner and Wile E. Coyote has specific analogues throughout the film.

Third, for Kubrick, objects and machines are almost more important than people. Certainly in *Dr. Strangelove* and *2001* that sense emerges; in *The Shining*, Kubrick focuses on the maze, for example, as an external object that reveals Jack's inner nature, as well as Wendy's and Danny's.

Fourth, the problems most viewers had with characterization in the film are in fact responses to Kubrick's intentions. Nicholson has been accused of "everything from being boring to overacting," Macklin notes. More accurately, however, Nicholson is responding to a difficult task. He must blend the banality and the absurdity of Kubrick's vision of the character, constantly destroying his own chances to rise above either. Consequently, he "changes from the banal would-be writer in the interview to the absurd, impulsive extrovert at the bar to the lively, vicious killer at the end." To do so requires that he not give a coherent, polished performance—and viewers disparage him for not doing so.

And fifth, Kubrick's *The Shining* is satirical in ways that King's novel is not. Kubrick sees American culture as "a cartoon and a caricature," Macklin concludes, intruding parodies of Nixon and Johnny Carson at seemingly inappropriate moments. Even the concluding photograph implicitly critiques contemporary American society by juxtaposing it with an image of a 1921, postwar, celebratory America which no longer exists. Given these five points, Macklin argues, viewers are almost bound to misinterpret Kubrick's intentions. The film is complex but repays careful attention. Visual techniques impel interest, and, "with the added awareness that banality, aggression, objects, ordinary characters, and satire often play a meaningful part in a Kubrick film, we should be able to deal with it."

Approaching Kubrick from another perspective, Greg Keeler refers briefly to King's article in the January 1981 issue of *Playboy,* citing the comment that horror films are like "lifting a trap door in the civilized forebrain and throwing a basket of raw meat to the hungry alligators swimming around in the subterranean river beneath." He then compares several mainstream films about the disintegration of the family—*Ordinary People, Tribute, Kramer vs. Kramer*—to such films as *Burnt Offerings, The Amityville Horror,* and *The Shining.* "Though they all ostensibly deal with uppity houses," he says, they "are also about families going to pieces. They are gatorland's answer to the touching melodramas of the forebrain." Point by point, Keeler analyzes *Kramer vs. Kramer,* identifying theme, plot, characterization, language, and episode. For each, he finds horrific analogues in *The Shining,* a dark counterpoint focusing on the nightmare rather than the melodrama. The comparisons lead to the conclusion that "no matter how one views the differences between these films, there is no doubt that the family has to disintegrate for the characters to survive, either physically or psychologically."

Yet another approach to *The Shining* concentrates on its place in Kubrick's oeuvre. Nelson's "Remembrance of Things Forgotten: *The Shining*" forms the final chapter in *Kubrick: Inside a Film Artist's Maze.* As such, it suggests ways in which the film culminates much that had gone on before in Kubrick's work. Nelson carefully details themes, images, cinematic details of set, characterization, casting, and editing—all pointing to Kubrick's control over the final film. Additionally, Nelson casts back to suggest references throughout *The Shining* to Kubrick's earlier films, including a half-facetious discussion of the number 21 in interpreting Kubrick's maze/puzzle images. "Numerically speaking," he concludes, "*The Shining* is 2001 in reverse gear."

All of this is to argue that perhaps the best approach to Kubrick's *The Shining* is to divorce it from connections with Stephen King—not because Kubrick failed to do justice to King's narrative but simply because it has ceased to be King's. While the film's opening panorama effectively sets the mood for both the novel and the film, the first shots of the Torrances suggest how radically Kubrick has in fact departed from King's original. Casting does create serious problems if one insists upon King's Torrances; yet Kubrick's Wendy is appropriately dissociated from romantic love. There is nothing in Duvall's performance to suggest the relationship between King's Wendy and Jack. Instead, she clearly represents an exclusively maternal figure, standing between husband and son as protector for the latter, antagonist to the former. For her to do so alienates the viewer expecting King's Wendy; her stance is, however, critical to Kubrick's.

Similarly, Nicholson's performance remains ambivalent. He is not King's Jack Torrance. King makes it clear that the evil in his novel is centered in the Overlook itself. The manta-shaped shadow that escapes from the shattered window of the Presidential Suite is an external evil that has dominated the hotel; once it escapes, the Overlook becomes merely an empty hull, justifiably destroyed in cleansing flames. Evil has not been defeated, merely displaced; in fact, not until *It* will King allow a clear and permanent defeat of an evil force.

This sense disappears in Kubrick's film. Nicholson's Jack Torrance in large part replaces the Overlook as focus of evil. From the opening scenes, he is clearly dissociated from his family—and from himself. There is no emotional connection between him, Wendy, or Danny. His progress in the film details increasing fragmentation and degeneration. Yet in an important way, he stands at the center of the tragedy, displacing Danny in crucial scenes. The film-Danny escapes, not through Hallorann's aid as in the novel, but by luring his own father into the frozen maze and abandoning him—effectively killing his father and rescuing his mother in what may be an oddly Oedipal image. And since the film-Jack has also largely supplanted the Overlook as well, there is no need to destroy the structure; given Kubrick's re-interpretation of the narrative, to do so would be to resort to stereotypic pyrotechnic special effects for a climax. Instead, he literally focuses on Jack Torrance, on the photograph in the empty hotel.

Again and again, Kubrick replaces critical points in the novel, constructing his own narrative that touches only tangentially on King's. The wasps disappear, and along with them Jack's opportunity for conscious image-making; Kubrick's Jack is incapable of such depth of perception. For him, the replacement image of the maze is doubly appropriate—visually as Jack loses himself in the maze-like corridors of the hotel (which he never leaves until the final scene; leaving it means death for Jack), and psychologically in the mazes of his own madness. The roque mallet also disappears, replaced by the more overtly violent axe, which in turn juxtaposes nicely with Nicholson's insane "Here's Johnny!" parody as he breaks into the apartment. Even the animated fire hose—which King notes actually formed the initial image for writing the novel—disappears.

In exchange, Kubrick adds his own imagistic complexity to the film. Mazes appear and recur...in the carpeting, in the intricate angles of corridors and rooms, in the model inside the hotel, in the actual maze outside. In an interesting cut-shot, Jack stares down at the model; as the camera draws nearer and nearer, the viewer discovers Wendy and Danny walking at the center of the maze, and Kubrick has neatly bridged inner and outer, Jack's inability to solve mazes with Wendy and Danny's need for experience outside the hotel.

Similarly, Danny's incessant riding through corridors on his big-wheel not only touches on the maze image but reflects Kubrick's treatment of sound and silence in *2001*. As the big-wheel crosses from wooden floor to carpet (usually with an intricate maze-like pattern), the abrasive sound ceases, creating an irregular regularity in sound and silence reminiscent of the astronauts' breathing in the earlier film. And, also reminiscent of *2001*, Kubrick consistently frames shots through stark, angular, geometrically precise openings, with organic movement and shape caught within unmoving, artificial regularity.

Throughout the film, at every level from script to casting to set design, Kubrick imbues *The Shining* with his own personality, his own vision. And his images work. They are not King's, but they do work. To that extent, Kubrick's film does resemble King's novel. Both are eminently "teachable," self-consciously literary/artistic manifestations of theme, imagery, symbolism. Both demonstrate creative talents focused on a single narrative, exploring the possibilities of verbal and visual representation, of novel into film.

# INTERVIEW WITH SHUEI SAI:

## THE FILMS OF STEPHEN KING

**From:** Shuei Sai
**Sent:** Friday, March 14, 2003 1:27 PM
**To:** Collings, Michael
**Subject:** Interview Questions Request by Japanese Newspaper

Dear Dr. Collings:
    Thank you so much for taking the time to speak with me this morning. I have contacted you on behalf of Kikuma Morikita, a staff writer of *Asahi Shimbun* in Tokyo. *Asahi Shimbun* is one of Japan's leading dailies with a circulation of 8.3 million (See www.asahi.com; Click on "English").
    The reporter is delighted that you agreed to do the interview via e-mail. The following are the background and specific questions by the reporter.

**[Background]**
    In late February, Mr. Morikita and a photographer visited the Bangor region to prepare a story for a feature series entitled, "Journey to the World's Memorable Quotations," that will be carried in the Sunday editions of the newspaper. In the series, a reporter would introduce a certain saying, or a paragraph from literary works, or a poetry passage, and then tell how it was born and/or its meaning today. For example, if Galileo's "The earth moves," were the selected one, the reporter might visit the Leaning Tower of Pisa and the Vatican, and describe the relationship between religion and science in Medieval Europe. NASA scientists might be also interviewed.
    Mr. Morikita decided to select a paragraph from Stephen King's works, one that gives readers courage and hope—for now, a line from *It*. The reason is simple—he is one of Stephen King's "addicts". He has read more than twenty of his books (albeit the Japanese translation). The main focus of the visit to Bangor was to ex-

plore why Mr. King's work touch the heartstrings of so many people, not only in the US, but elsewhere, and why the Kings remain in the small town despite his fame and wealth. He interviewed more than a dozen individuals in Bangor, most of whom got to know Mr. King in various settings, and learned a great deal about the relationship between the town and the writer.

Many Japanese readers are more familiar with Mr. King's films than his novels themselves, and the reporter was looking for someone who can talk about Mr. King's films with authority. He learned of you in a Japanese book on Stephen King, and also one of the interviewees in Bangor told him that you are one of the few people who actually worked with Mr. King. For your information, before the reporter's visit to Bangor, Mr. King's assistant informed the reporter saying, "Stephen has let me know that he has no objection if anyone on your list agrees to being interviewed for this project."

**[Questions by the reporter - translated from Japanese]**
Please note that the questions may be redundant. If so, please ignore ones already answered in other questions.

*Q1. What would be your "King's Best 5" movies, including TV mini series. Why?*

I would probably list the following as among my favorites, although it is difficult to identify only five 'best' from the many that I have enjoyed:

> *Stand By Me*
> *The Stand*
> *It*
> *The Green Mile*
> *Shawshank Redemption*

There are really two reasons for the films on this list. First, several of them represent King's writing through images other than horror; and second, several of them incorporate horror but remain true to King's vision, ideas, and effects.

*Stand by Me* was the first adaptation of a King property that fully succeeded for me, in part because both the director, Rob Reiner, and I grew up at the same time King, so much of what King had to say in "The Body" impacted me strongly. The film reflected the utter simplicity of King's story, yet enriched it with Reiner's own visual imagery. Everything in the film—landscape, characters (and the actors who played them), dialogue—fit together perfectly, so that I had the sense that I was not just seeing an adaptation of the story but living within the story. It was intense, emotional, cathartic, powerful. And to this day I still consider it among the best adaptations.

The same can be said for *The Green Mile* and *Shawshank Redemption*, again at least in part because of the director/screenwriter for both, Frank Darabont. Darabont has been a fan of King's for many years, studying his works (as well as enjoying them), and imagining how they might be translated into another medium, film. Darabont's first attempt, *The Woman in the Room*, demonstrated how a filmmaker could alter King's text, even in important ways, and still adhere absolutely to what the story meant. In the longer films, Darabont applied all that he had learned, restraining and refining the elements of horror in both stories so that they gave the films an edge but did not overwhelm the sheer interest in human actions and reactions. They are believable, and (I think) enduring films.

*The Stand* and *It* are among my favorites because they come closest to suggesting King's amazing skill at drawing complex figures and setting them in complex environments. Both miniseries were based on what I consider his strongest novels; both reflect King's storytelling powers directly through his involvement with the films; and both again restrain the sense of horror. Because they were intended for television, the films could not go into the graphic horror that occurs in both novels; instead, they create their tension through indirection and suggestion. In addition, the actors in both fit King's characters remarkably well.

*Q2. It seems that the films with less horror elements such as "Stand By Me," "The Shawshank Redemption" and "The Green Mile" have been more successful than others. Why do you think it is?*

I agree. I think the reason is that King's kind of horror works best internally. That is, we read a passage and imagine what is happening...and that internal image provokes much greater terror/horror/fear than any film image can. When we read we can make the horror our own—when we watch a film, we are forced to watch the things that someone else (director, special effects director, etc.) *thinks* will terrify us. And since the films' images can never top our own imaginations, the filmmakers are forced to rely on more and more blood, more gruesome monsters, flatter characters (about whom we often don't really care). The films simply become too much, as in *Pet Sematary* or the innumerable *Children of the Corn* sequels.

In the ones listed, King's characters show through. They are believable, convincing, and empathetic. We *want* to care about them; and therefore when we leave the theater after watching *Stand By Me*, for example, we are more aware of the tragedies and glories of childhood than we are of any monsters or horrors. Those films touch us directly because they can use images we are familiar with and through those images change us. The films you listed are successful because they are superlative films based on superlative stories, not because they are film version of King's words. Story and film work together to attain something greater.

The horror films can be fun—there is something enthralling about the sheer mayhem in *Maximum Overdrive*, for example. But the non-horror films draw connections between us and the characters that increase every minute.

*Q3. It is said that the movies based on Stephen Kings novels often failed. My view on this is that a movie that emphasizes "bloody bodies and fearful monsters" would express only half of what Stephen King wants to appeal. What do you think?*

Again I agree. King is perhaps one of the most misunderstood authors of our time. Even he likes to talk about himself as a purveyor of blood and horror...if he can't scare us, he will try to gross us out. But beneath that level, I think King cares deeply about the world around him, about culture and society, about the roles of family and education, about children and the dangers that threaten them—not just monsters but things like cancer and evil people and speeding trucks. In almost all of his novels, certainly in his best ones, the monsters are there less for their own selves than as images of those things we fear in the real world. When a film concentrates too much on the "bloody bodies and fearful monsters," it ignores the substance that supports the story. The monsters come across as the focus of the film and viewers are not shown the depth of character that King wants us to see.

King has said that no film can alter his words—no matter how good or bad a film version is, his book still sits on the shelf, exactly as he wrote it. Unfortunately, many people only know King's work from the films, however, and they therefore assume that all he is good for is to tell mindless stories full of blood and guts. He's right, of course, that his real stories are still out there, available to any reader, but too often film-goers never get that far. So the filmmakers must try to outdo each other. The next "King" film has to have more blood and monsters than the last. And the next has to outdo that one. And so on, until all that we get are rather stale repetitions of the same thing.

As I suggested earlier, the 'best' King adaptations are the ones that recognize that his monsters are metaphors for our own world, our own lives, our own evils, and concentrate on people instead.

*Q4. As you know better than I do, while "The Shining" by Stanley Kubrick attracted some attention, Mr. King did not like it and later came up with a mini series using his own screenplay. Would you cite your "King's Worst 5" movies in terms of failing to help the audience understand Stephen King, regardless of the quality as a film per se? Why?*

This is an interesting question. It's easy to come up with a list of really-really-bad-films made from King's stories: *Children of the Corn* and *Graveyard Shift* come readily to mind. In both cases, the filmmakers tried to pad out what should have remained short stories…emphasis on "short." The films add too much, concentrate on horror and violence, stretch it out over too long a period. And what we get almost bores us. It certainly doesn't send us back to King's books to read the story itself.

*Firestarter*, on the other hand, erred by being too literal. It followed King's words almost exactly; it was reasonably true to his characters; and it restricted itself pretty much to the actions his novel described. But it didn't capture the spirit, the life, the vitality of the book. Someone watching the film would, again, probably have little interest in reading anything by King, and would miss some exciting and important literature.

What others? Well, most of the earlier versions seem marginally related to King, and some are out-of-date. *Dead Zone*, for example, would probably would probably seem dated, jaded, even though when it was first shown it was quite exceptional. But probably the award for capitalizing on King's name without even trying to capture the essence of his work should go to *Lawnmower Man*. It wasn't a particularly bad film—it just had nothing (except the title) to do with anything Stephen King ever wrote.

Finally, I am wary of any films that are sequels of earlier films. *Salem's Lot II*; *Lawnmower Man II*; *Children of the Corn II, III, III,*

*V* and so on. They claim to represent King's words but don't; they capitalize on his name, his popularity, his drawing ability. They hope to make money but often don't seem to worry much about being good films on any level.

*Q5. It looks that films based on King's books continue to be made. Why do you think the movie industry is so much interested in Stephen King's work?*

There are probably two levels of interest.

The first is commercial. His books sell. By the millions. Around the world. Therefore movies made from those books should sell just as well. And since King has written dozens of novels and stories, there is a huge potential for making money by making films.

The second is more important, I think. Stephen King talks to us. He speaks for us. He has recorded our world—its successes and its failure, its wonders and its terrors—for over thirty years. He has taken us into a new century by reminding us that we still share the same fears that our parents had. He frightens us, but in a way that allows us to feel a bit of control…if the book ever gets too scary, we can turn on the light and close the book. He gives us experiences that we perhaps all crave but that we cannot safely get in the real world. He sometimes makes our rather tedious lives seem more exciting. He transforms even simple things into images of power and strength…a single red rose, for example. And since he so radically alters who we are when we read his books, we want to *see* those books as well.

Ours is a visually oriented world. Our children learn more about their world through television than through books. They even encounter age-old myths and legends on CD or DVD long before they are old enough even to read books. So naturally, we want to transform the things that effect us deeply into visual images.

Film producers know this. They understand from the sheer number of international editions of King's books that he is touching millions of people across the world. And they know that if even a small percentage of those people—or of the people who have heard King's name but never read his words—buy a ticket, the film will make money regardless of its inherent quality. So films get made. And more films. And more films.

Some of them are powerful in their own right. Some of them just hitch a ride on King's name and don't pretend to do more than that. Most of them fall somewhere in between…enjoyable, fun perhaps, but not particularly memorable.

*Q6. About you. How should I describe you (ex. Professor of English at Pepperdine University?) in my article. Your age if it is ok [Note: It is a Japanese custom to mention interviewees' age in newspapers!].*

I am a professor of English at Pepperdine University (Malibu, California, USA). I have written or contributed to over a hundred books, have published over 400 reviews and articles, and over 1000 poems. I have written extensively on Stephen King, most recently in *Horror Plum'd: An International Stephen King Bibliography and Guide*, published just this month. I have also published books and articles on Orson Scott Card (author of *Ender's Game* and other novels, popular in Japan), Peter Straub (co-author with King of *The Talisman* and *Black House*), and Dean R. Koontz. I am 56, have six children (including in-laws) and almost four grandchildren.

Well—I'm sure you got a whole lot more than you counted on. Thank you very much for inviting me to write this interview. It has helped me think through a number of issues and clarify them, for myself if not for anyone else. I have enjoyed it very much.

If it is possible, could you send me a copy of the article? I would be interested in seeing what you have to say about Stephen King.

Best,

Michael R. Collings

# CONSIDERING *THE STANDS*

[This essay first appeared in *Gauntlet: Exploring the Limits of Free Expression,* edited by Barry Hoffman, No. 2 (1991): 179-185. It has been slightly edited and updated.]

Several years ago I presented an article on the 1978 published version of Stephen King's *The Stand* (which for convenience sake I will refer to hereafter as *The Stand [I]*) to the International Conference on the Fantastic in the Arts. The paper subsequently appeared in Darrell Schweitzer's anthology of essays, *Discovering Stephen King,* under the title "*The Stand*: Science Fiction into Fantasy." As the title suggests, the article argued that in its original format, *The Stand [I]* bifurcates rather neatly. The opening chapters focus on the Superflu and its consequences for humanity. In its emphasis on extrapolation from current technology, this part of the narrative seems essentially science fictional. Key episodes extrapolate from the one question fundamental to all science fiction—"What if?" What if there *were* a Superflu?

What if it did indeed wipe out over 99.6% of humanity?

How would the survivors react? How would they survive? *Could* they survive? If they did, how would their society differ from pre-cataclysmic human societies?

Midway into the story, however, King radically alters his approach. The logical extrapolation from a specific technological event—the Superflu—becomes secondary to episodes that deal less with the re-establishment of society than with issues incapable of clear, rational resolution. With the increasing frequency and importance of dreams, with the introduction of the mystical and evil Dark Man, with the revelation of Mother Abagail as a modern analogue to Biblical prophets and prophecy, the novel shifts from the rational to the irrational, from science fictional extrapolation to quasi-theological fantasy.

The paper was well enough received, both as presented and as published, and for a number of years, through a number of re-readings of *The Stand [I]*, I felt comfortable with what I had suggested.

With the publication of the restored text of *The Stand* (*The Stand [II]*) in 1990, however, it became clear that the neat classification I posited for *The Stand [I]* did not in fact coincide with the realities of King's performance. With the added bulk of the novel, much of it emphasizing the fantastic rather than the science fictional, and with the intrusion of the irrational in dream-visions occurring much earlier than in *The Stand [I]*, it seemed apparent that the novel King had originally envisioned differed substantially from the version actually published as *The Stand [I]*. Fundamentals of structure, characterization, tone, image, even basic theme had been altered by the deletions required for the 1978 publication.

The next question seemed obvious:

Why would King allow such elemental changes in what he must have considered at the time a major opus?

Certainly minor editing, even deletion of selected passages, occurs in the process of bringing many novels from manuscript to final published form. Even *It*, published at a time when King could probably have published almost anything without much editorial intrusion, lost about twenty pages from manuscript to final copy. But in the case of *The Stand*, the changes were so far-ranging that the novel as it finally appeared was in a very real sense *not* the one the author had written.

Part of the explanation, certainly, arises from King's awareness of how unpopular long novels were, if not among all readers then certainly among many critics. In his early reviews, particularly the *Adelina* columns (June-November 1980), he notes the antagonism most contemporary critics express toward 'big books'—and by the most conservative of standards, the full manuscript of *The Stand [I]* could only result in a 'big book,' certainly his longest to that date.

Purely practical considerations might have suggested to King that at this point in his career, it might be politic to edit. King himself says that this was the case. In the foreword to *The Stand [II]*, he writes:

> For the purposes of this book, what's important is that approximately four hundred pages of manuscript were deleted from the final draft. The reason was not an editorial one; if that had been the case, I would be content to let the book live its life and die its eventual death as it was originally published.
>
> The cuts were made at the behest of the account-

ing department. (ix)

King seems to want to make it clear that the deletions were market-driven, pragmatic, required to bring the book out at a cost that would support the $12.95 cover price that Doubleday decided was "about what the market would bear." Over the intervening years, however, some readers and critics have suggested—often on the basis of second-hand, hearsay information—that there were other factors at work in the surgical transformation of King's manuscript into *The Stand [I]*. And here the issue of censorship arises.

It would be foolish, of course, to argue in direct opposition to King's published statements in his preface to *The Stand [II]*. The novel is, after all, his book, and it would seem that King would have little to lose now if he were to reveal the secret machinations of the publishing game in 1978—twelve years (now over thirty years) after the fact and at a time when he had established himself as one of the most potent players in that game.

Reading *The Stand [II]*, however, leads to some interesting possibilities, particularly when one tries to identify the *kinds* of deletions made for the 1978 version. One group are clearly editorial; that is, they streamline the narrative, reducing word- and page-count while retaining the essence of King's vision.

The deletion of what now appears as "The Circle Opens"—the prologue introducing Charlie, Sally, Baby La Von, and the Super-flu—allowed for an incremental intrusion of horror into the narrative, consonant with the science-fictional emphasis of *The Stand [I]*. There is something frantic, irrational, horrifying in Charlie's panicky flight that creates an entirely different opening tone from the stolid, phlegmatic, realistic portrait of Arnette and Hapscomb's Texaco and Stu Redman in Chapter 1. If, as happened in the 1978 version, the opening chapters were to emphasize the rational, the science-fictional, the extrapolative, then the brief introduction of Charlie and family seems too much, too soon.

Other deletions reduced what has become a leading charge against King as writer: redundancy. In the 1978 version, King's examples of the consequences of the Superflu were terse, understated, at times almost reportorially concise. He convinced readers of the reality of the plague but didn't dwell unduly on its accompanying horrors. In *The Stand [II]*, however, the restorations help realize the Superflu by making its universality more obvious, but the multiple episodes threaten to reach or exceed a saturation point; after watching too many people die in agony and loneliness, readers may begin wondering what has happened to the story King wants to tell.

And finally, other deletions streamline the themes of novel as it appeared in 1978. The final chapter of *The Stand [I]* allows for a sense of controlled optimism. Humankind's nuclear playthings still litter the landscape, but Frannie and Stu and the child, Peter, have survived and are together. There is a moment of peace. There is hope. The novel settles into a comfortably SF format, since the disappearance of the Dark Man lets King refocus on his original question: "What if?"

The 'new' last chapter in *The Stand [II]*, however, connects it with other novels and opens fantastical possibilities that King would have understood in 1978 but that most of his readers perhaps would not have. Nine years earlier, King had published a poem called "The Dark Man" that contains a kernel of his vision of Randall Flagg, just as an early short story, "Night Surf," appearing in the same issue of the UMO student magazine, suggests his incipient interest in the Superflu. But the first of the Dark Tower stories, "The Gunslinger," did not appear until October, 1978; *The Dark Tower: The Gunslinger* appeared in book form in 1984, as did *The Eyes of the Dragon*, his third full-length treatment of the character sometimes known as Flagg. In 1978, then, King knew much about who Flagg was and where he might disappear to, but the readers of *The Stand [I]* did not. Ending the story with Stu, Frannie, and Peter gives the truncated 1978 narrative a coherent conclusion.

But there are other deletions that are more problematical than these. In some instances, large sections restored in *The Stand [II]* seem important enough to wonder why they were cut.

Frannie's confrontation with her mother in the formal, nineteenth-century parlor establishes critical themes and motifs for the rest of the novel as it examines the future and the past and the possible sterility of both. Frannie's obsession with protecting her child begins here and makes even more powerful her terrors for her child in later chapters. Perhaps the sheer length of the passage dictated its excision.

In addition, however, there are other deletions that seem suspect primarily because of content. King has never been one to avoid sexuality in his stories. Yet his earlier works do in fact seem at times more restrained than later ones. In *The Stand [I]*, for example, Lloyd Henreid lays awake on the night of June 29:

> Lloyd began to weep. As he cried he rubbed his
> eyes with his fists like a small boy. He wanted a steak
> sandwich, he wanted to talk to his lawyer, he wanted

to get out of there. (181)

The next line indicates that it is now 5 o'clock the next morning. In *The Stand [II]*, however, King adds a paragraph that bridges the missing hours and that simultaneously suggests the general tenor of many minor alterations between the two versions:

> At last he lay down on his cot, put one arm over his eyes, and masturbated. It was as good a way of getting to sleep as any. (280)

An overt, narratively unnecessary reference to what in 1978 might be construed as a conventionally unacceptable sexual activity appears in the restored 1990 text.

Similar, if less obvious, small changes in phrasing alter the tone of dialogue throughout. In the 1978 version, Glen Bateman responds to one of Stu Redman's question with an abrupt "Christ, no!" (233); in *The Stand [II]*, the phrase is expanded to a stronger, but potentially more objectionable, "Christ's testicles, no!" (345). A more extensive but evocative passage occurs with "The Kid"—a section of the narrative that disappeared entirely from *The Stand [I]* and that King refers to explicitly in the preface to *The Stand [II]*:

> ...I have always regretted the fact that no one but me and a few in-house readers at Doubleday ever met that maniac who simply calls himself The Kid...or witnessed what happens to him outside a tunnel which counterpoints another tunnel half a continent away—the Lincoln Tunnel in New York.... (xii)

The Kid's story (587-616) is essential to the new version, fleshing out the sense of insanity that accumulates around the followers of the Dark Man. As King notes, the passage completes a disrupted parallelism between tunnels that amplifies the symbolic value of each. It adds imagistic and mythic strength to Trashcan's Odyssey, making that key character more understandable, his unswerving loyalty to the Dark Man more crucial...and consequently his ultimate defection and destructive fervor more ironically satisfying.

But the passage also recounts The Kid's demand that Trashcan masturbate him, and his subsequent rape of Trashcan with the barrel of a .45 caliber pistol. King refers frequently enough in his stories and novels to "hommasexshuls"; homosexuality is certainly an important motif in *It*, for example. And in the 1990 restoration, twin images of homosexuality and of insane violence—and a foreshad-owing of one of the novel's climactic scene—combine in Trashcan's imagination:

> He was sure that at the instant of The Kid's orgasm he would feel two things simultaneously: the hot jet of the small monster's semen on his belly and the mushrooming agony of a dumdum bullet roaring up through his vitals. The ultimate enema. (*The Stand [II]* 600)

That scene in itself suggests a darkness and a perverseness that might have led to the deletion of the entire passage for an earlier, pre-1980's audience.

Even more disturbing and potentially more devastating is a per-sistent racial undertone in *The Stand [II]*. In a letter to *Castle Rock* (March 1988), Kima R. Hicks expressed concern about King's "con-stant negative reference to blacks":

> In just about everyone of your books, somewhere in the storyline, there is some derogatory comment about a black person. Even in *The Stand*, where one of the central positive forces was an older black woman, there were constant references to 'nigger' and other negative stereotypical remarks. (1)

King's response was reasoned, forthright, and clear: racial epithets occur in the novels because "bigots and idiots" use them, and King in turn uses such characters to "expose rather than promote racism" (1). Dick Hallorann, Mother Abagail, and Mike Hanlon are strong individuals whose very presence in their respective novels stimu-lates abuse and slurs by people "who are possessed of ugly tempers, ugly personalities…or people just too dumb to know any better" (5). Some of King's characters may be prejudiced; King himself is not.

In the expanded Chapter 26 of *The Stand [II]*, which begins with a graphic evocation of the killings at Kent State (the action here transferred to the University of Kentucky at Louisville), King in-cludes a two-page episode in which half-naked blacks systematically execute white army personnel in a deranged parody of baptism: holding a .45 to his victim's head, "'inthenamatofthefathersonand-holyghost,' the big black man intoned, grinning, and pulled the trig-ger" (226).

The text clearly sets black against white. It emphasizes the blacks as half naked, repeating the epithet "the black man in the loincloth." And—symbolically, at least—it exploits white sexual stereotypes and fears as nearly nude (and therefore more 'primitive'?) blacks brutally assault white males with phallic weapons. The Kid's use of a similar weapon as an instrument of sexual conquest and rape later in *The Stand [II]*, and the narrator's deliberate focus on a pair of "pristine white jockey shorts" and a "pink leather loincloth" suggest that the actions described are as much sexual as violent. Even the narrative language of the passage is double edged, denoting insanity while connoting sexuality: "performed," "jerked," "forced," "sweating," "glistening with perspiration," "abortive," "tawdry show."

The passage is, admittedly, relatively short. And given the shifted focus of *The Stand [I]*, reducing the full chapter detailing the insanity resulting from the Superflu to only four pages allows King to concentrate on his major characters—on getting the forces of light clustered about Mother Abagail and those of the dark around Randall Flagg. Yet it is easy to see that this particular episode might have drawn heavy editorial fire for its explicit actions, for its imagery and symbolism, for its suggestion of racial and sexual messages that the book (especially in its 1978 incarnation) does not otherwise carry.

If there were any passages in the manuscript that King was urged to delete, it seems likely that this would have been at the top of the list.

Without King's (or some one else's) evidential support that the manuscript was overtly censored, such charges should neither be leveled nor continued. However, it seems clear that in at least some instances King might have been concerned enough about controversial sexual or racial content that he might have deleted passages he himself felt were otherwise strong and/or structurally important to the novel.

Not all of the changes from *The Stand [I]* to *The Stand [II]* are suggestive in this respect, of course. There is little in the parlor scene that would suggest censorship. But other instances seem problematical. Certainly two lines would not have been critical to total word count; yet King deleted the reference to Henreid's masturbation. The only reason would seem to be its sexual content. Or the single word "testicles" would not have run the book overly long, yet it, too occurs only in the restored text; again, the reason would seem to be its potentially objectionable combination of blasphemy and sexuality.

One point seems clear, however. Regardless of King's rationale for his choice of materials to delete, the restored text is stronger, more coherent, more focused than *The Stand [I]*. Those who saw *The Stand [I]* as among his strongest novels should find that assessment confirmed in the restored text. The re-introduction of long blocks of text deepens and intensifies the mythic nature of the novel, particularly as it re-defines characters' motivations and personalities.

By restoring episodes fraught with racial and/or sexual tension, King creates a narrative compelling in its violence and compelling in its implications for its audiences—whether that of 1978 or that of 1990 (or that of 2009). The addition of the final chapter confirms the position of *The Stand* in King's personal, allegorical investigation of darkness and of evil. The fragile hopes that concluded the 1978 version are undercut and denied; evil may disappear for a season but it is never totally defeated.

Almost without exception, the restoration and changes (including those that update the story to 1990) strengthen the novel. The irrational elements—dreams, portents, omens—arise much sooner, dissolving the sense that the story begins as post-apocalyptic science fiction and then abruptly shifts into fantasy. The ostensible climax—the bomb scene—still occurs with about fifty pages to run, but since so much has been added in previous pages, the final effect is to bring the episode closer to the end of the novel. The result is a fused whole, a more consistent and convincing novel, a cross-generic work that explores the possibilities of extrapolation and revelation, of facts and dreams, of darkness and of light.

**NOTE**: I decided to post this essay on *StarShine and Shadows* (michaelcollings.com), in spite of its being outdated in spots, after a summer spent preparing for a course I was to teach in Myth, Fantasy, and Science Fiction. I selected, in addition to Orson Scott Card's *Ender's Game* and *Seventh Son*, King's *The Eyes of the Dragon* and *The Stand[II]* as required texts, and after re-reading them (and annotating them heavily), went backward and forward in King's canon to examine how they connected with other Dark Tower novels, including *The Talisman, Insomnia, Black House, The Wolves of the Calla,* and *Susannah's Song.*

The experience deepened the understanding that *The Stand [I]* fact represents only a portion of a larger, more coherent vision, one that King has spend over a third of a century expanding and developing; and that the alterations and restorations in *The Stand [II]* not only have literary repercussions but add crucial connective tissue to the epic-in-progress that will (soon, we are promised) lead us to the Dark Tower itself.

# FAITH WITHIN FANTASY:

## STEPHEN KING, RICHARD BACHMAN, AND SEVENTEENTH-CENTURY DEVOTIONAL POETRY

[This essay was presented as a Guest of Honor Address at the Brigham Young University Symposium on Science Fiction and Fantasy: "Life, the Universe, and Everything XXII," Provo UT, February 19, 2004. It subsequently appeared in a slightly altered form as Chapter VII in *Stephen King is Richard Bachman* (Woodstock GA: Overlook Connection Press, March 2008), a revised and expanded edition of *Stephen King as Richard Bachman* (Mercer Island WA: Starmont, 1985.)]

In the mid-1990s, it was announced that Richard Bachman would publish a final, posthumous book in conjunction with a parallel book by Stephen King.

Following closely on the innovative multi-book publication of *The Green Mile* (March-August 1996),* Bachman's *The Regulators* and King's *Desperation* appeared amid a flurry of publicity and expectation. This time, of course, there would be no mystery as to the 'true' authorship when the novels appeared simultaneously, packaged together in a clear plastic case (initially accompanied by a specially printed excerpt of *The Dark Tower IV: An Excerpt from the Upcoming Wizard and Glass*—"A Gift from Stephen King"; then when those copies sold out, by a battery-operated reading lamp). Media hype capitalized on the opportunity to present *both* authors at once. Knowing full well that Bachman was King, and that King was Bachman, readers would have the chance to compare for themselves the authors' respective merits.

More to the point for this study, early information suggested that the novels would use the same characters and story lines, one fil-

---

* For the weeks of 15 September and 22 September, 1996, King shattered normal publication records when *all six* parts of *The Green Mile* appeared on national bestsellers lists *simultaneously. Desperation* and *The Regulators* similarly appeared simultaneously from mid-October 1996 to the middle of January 1997.

tered, as it were, through Bachman's imagination, the other through King's. The publishers—and King—had presented eager readers with a kind of lab practical, with specimens laid out side by side for analysis and critical cross-examination.

As things turned out, some of the anticipated similarities between the books did not materialize, even though on occasion the two quote verbatim from each other. The same supernatural creature inhabits both (or at least, two creatures with identical names and purposes), yet even a cursory reading shows that while characters' names recur in both, the individuals associated with those names differ radically, physically and mentally. A child in one book may bear the same name as an adult in the other. Place-names may be mentioned in both, but actions associated with those locations differ. And while both bear internal trademarks of King's storytelling, he employs those devices and structures to different effects.

Still, the two books inevitably amplified readers' interest in the relationship between author and pseudonym—a relationship King had already overtly explored, for example, in *The Dark Half.* On the one hand, the invitation for comparison was overwhelming, given both the publicity and the circumstances of publication. On the other hand, one could no longer simply refer to a 'King' book or a 'Bachman' book—the purposes that might have impelled King to generate the pen-name in the first place were no longer pressing, and the public knowledge of who 'Richard Bachman' was made impossible any pretense that King intended that readers *not* immediately connect him with both novels. What, then, might readers make of his decision to revive 'Bachman' one more time.

In some senses, the two novels suggest another, earlier set of works, similarly published simultaneously but by a far different author. John Milton published "L'Allegro" and "Il Penseroso," both under his own name, in his 1645 collection of poems. Since then, the poems have almost always appeared as companion pieces; indeed, critics and scholars often use them as touchstones for interpreting Milton's purposes as a poet. Yet after over 350 years of scholarly discourse, the full implications of the poems still seem evasive; we can intimate possibilities but never speak definitively about *why* Milton published them together or why they are at once so similar and so different.

*Desperation* and *The Regulators* might profitably be approached from a parallel critical stance. They are unquestionably similar, yet distinctly different. They represent two sides of the same author, yet they present no clear-cut instructions as to how to read and interpret them. Their publication smacks at least a little of being a publicity stunt (although by August 1996 Stephen King certainly required nothing that blatant to augment his reputation or his sales), yet they also bear the signs of being serious additions to King's remarkable canon. As noted above, their characters' names and landscapes are similar—indeed, in several instances King repeats exact lines and phrases; yet the similarities define no straight-line connections between the stories. Plots and themes resonate between the two, but it remains difficult to say categorically that one or the other represents King's ideas in totality.

As with Milton's companion poems, however, there are a couple of hints that one book might actually carry more weight—more of the author's intentions—than the other. The theme of "Il Penseroso" comports more closely with what we know of Milton's subsequent career, his emphasis on the "sage and serious" uses of poetry as opposed to the more "light fantastic" possibilities. Even a consideration as mechanical as length might give us insight into Milton's preference; while the two contain a number of structural, thematic, imagistic, and verbal parallels that encourage readers to see them as nearly equal in importance, "L'Allegro" tallies 152 lines, while the more philosophical, restrained, balanced, and contemplative "Il Penseroso" extends that count to 176. Greater length suggests greater significance.

A glance shows that *Desperation* is—physically, at least—the weightier book. At 474 pages in the hardcover first edition (498 in paperback), *The Regulators* is a respectable length, longer than the previous 'Bachman' book, *Thinner*, by more than a third. *The Bachman Books,* which collects the first four novels, runs only about 200 pages more than *The Regulators* itself. In fact, measured by sheer page count, *The Regulators* could be considered 'weightier' than such disparate King novels as *Pet Sematary*, *Dolores Claiborne*, or *Gerald's Game* (perhaps the first of King's novels to garner widespread, mainstream critical approval). At 690 pages in hardcover (547 in paperback), however, *Desperation* approaches King and Straub's *The Talisman* and *Black House* in length; equals or surpasses *The Tommyknockers, Needful Things, Insomnia,* and the more recent *Dreamcatcher*; and misses the length of the complex *The Wolves of the Calla* by only twenty-five pages. Neither *Desperation* nor *The Regulators* approaches the length of several of King's acknowledged masterpieces, including *IT* (859 pages in hardcover) or either version of *The Stand* (823 pages in 1978, 1153 pages in 1990), but even so, both fall within the range of some his most powerful stories.

Length by itself does not define significance, of course; one of the criticisms of King's work has always been the length of his storytelling. But greater word count does allow for a greater canvas, opportunities for wider, more expansive vision. In fact, the single criterion of length—coupled with his encyclopedic treatment of his culture and his world—goes far in connecting King with the epic poets of the past…including Milton.

From this single perspective, then, one might venture the opinion that *Desperation* has at least the potential to outmatch *The Regulators* in other criteria as well. Perhaps—in spite of publicity—the two books are not quite as much mirrors of each other as readers initially expected.

A single reading suffices to show that indeed differences between *The Regulators* and *Desperation* far surpass similarities. Reading them, one can easily imagine King exploring two diverging branches of his imagination, creating independent but linked worlds (as he has done more extensively in the Dark Tower books and their multiplex connections with other of his novels), peopling them with equally independent but linked characters, and allowing each to develop toward its own climax and sense of purpose. The books begin to work less as evidence for some kind of King/Bachman dialogue and more as suggestions of two vastly different approaches to storytelling.

King defines these differences, together with their consequences for theme, style, narrative structure, and characterization, before the novels even begin by prefacing each with a tag-quotation, carefully chosen as usual, to establish the tone. The tag for *The Regulators* is appropriately direct, fast-paced, and tough, citing that icon of American popular culture, Steve McQueen, with an archetypal line of dialogue from *The Magnificent Seven*: "Mister, we deal in lead." After an opening chapter devoted to present-tense stage-setting, King provides, as it were, a booster shot for our expectations by reproducing an apparently 'real-world' article, ostensibly from the Columbus *Dispatch*, dated July 31, 1994. The headline fairly screams: "MEMBERS OF TOLEDO FAMILY SLAIN IN SAN JOSE: Four Killed in Suspected Gang Drive-by; Six-Year-Old Survives."

King deftly gives readers 'our' world in a nutshell: its randomness, violence, and death. Nothing in the opening chapters of *The Regulators* will contradict that sense, even as King creates the relatively pastoral imagery of "watermelon and Kool-Aid and foul tips off the end of the bat; it's all the summer you ever wanted and more here in the center of the United States of America, life as good as you ever dreamed it could be..." (Ch. 1). Throughout the book, Steve McQueen rules supreme.

*Desperation* presents a different perspective—radically different and potentially more powerful. The tag-quotation is longer, more complex, more inherently symbolic, and it comes, not from a film character, but from an internationally famous (and infamous) novel, Salman Rushdie's *The Satanic Verses*: "The landscape of his poetry was still the desert...." These words introduce us to an entirely *other* world, a world of poetry almost alien when compared to the mundane Wentworth, Ohio: the forbidding, desiccating, ultimately deadly Nevada desert. No two tags could be more evocative and more different; and the novels that follow remain true to these initial suggestions.

In *The Regulators,* Bachman (referring to the pseudonym will probably be less confusing in this chapter than talking constantly about 'King') begins in a solid world, where things function according to a clear-cut natural order—or at least an order one *feels* is natural—a world where newsboys deliver newspapers without fail, where sprinklers hiss across summer-dry lawns, where neighbors barbecue on backyard grills, where everyone drives an Acura, a Caprice, or a Lumina. It is beyond all else, a *physical* world, populated with common, ordinary *things*: 3 Musketeers bars, Chef-Boyardee Noodle-O's and spaghetti, Hershey's chocolate milk. Initially, Wentworth, Ohio, is as much part of a Bachman world as the landscapes of *Roadwork, The Long Walk,* and *Thinner*...until evil abruptly intrudes.

It is also a prosaic world, figuratively and literally. Bachman (as does King elsewhere) alludes to the larger world of literature in which he functions; here, unlike in *Desperation,* however, that world is stridently prose-oriented. Johnny Marinville, a key character, is a novelist. Initially, he had written "serious prose," garnering a National Book Award for his "novel of sexual obsession"; now, he writes mundane children's books about a detective cat. Imagery throughout *The Regulators* similarly belongs largely to the world of prose, specifically popular-culture prose, with references to Shirley Jackson and Agatha Christie; a hint of something like Bronte's *Jane Eyre* remains vague, avoiding detailed allusion in favor of more generic references to housekeepers in Gothic novels. Cultural icons of suburban Middle America, on the other hand, abound: Newsboys, token Blacks and Bohemians, Action Figures with all of their expensive accoutrements, and—paramount to both plot and characterization—film and television, from *M\*A\*S\*H,* to the films of Sergio

Leone, to B-Westerns of the Fifties, to *Bonanza.*

The text does refer to poetry, but in ways that make it clear that this novel cares little for the niceties and subtleties that poetry admires. Audrey Wyler briefly contemplates the line "Nothing gold can stay," wondering equally briefly if Robert Frost wrote it, then deciding that "It didn't matter" (Ch. 5, part 2). Indeed, *The Regulators* demonstrates a distinctly anti-poetry bias. Where *Desperation* includes a snippet of creditable free verse, *Regulators* offers nasty bits of doggerel, "Little bitty baby Smitty" verses that conjure smirking, grade-school, play-yard humor. Even the characters understand how little a difference poetry makes in this solid, concrete, thing-obsessed version of complacent Middle-America. Peter Jackson "thought of the way Cary [Ripton] had laughed when he, Peter, had told him that next year it would be his turn to howl at shortstop, and felt a sudden pain in his stomach, the organ (not the heart, as the poets had always claimed) most attuned to humankind's tender emotions" (Ch. 3, Part 4).

The essentially prose-oriented, *Thing*-oriented, nature of the world of *The Regulators* surfaces when Seth attempts to communicate with Audrey. Instead of words, he uses images:

> This time many images flickered past. Some came and went too fast for her to identify, but she got a few: an empty Chef Boyardee can lying in the trash, an old broken toilet lying on its side in the dump, a car up on blocks, no wheels, no glass. Things that were broken. Things that were used up. (Ch. 6, Part 1)

The mode of communication here strikingly resembles late Renaissance *Emblems,* visual representations of straightforward *Things* that in turn stand for complex, subtle, often philosophical meanings, readily understood and accepted by the culture at large. There is no need for poetry; the image communicates everything necessary.

In dramatic contrast, *Desperation* is fundamentally poetic—an odd assertion for a novel, perhaps, but in this case demonstrable.

On the level of allusion, if nowhere else, *Desperation* announces its difference from *The Regulators.* As noted above, the opening tag-quotation, while coming from another novel, explicitly introduces, and links, two elements of *Desperation*: the desert and poetry. King frequently incorporates allusion into his novels, perhaps most noticeably in *The Shining* but to lesser degrees elsewhere as well. One might expect, then, to find similar allusions in a book apparently designed to separate poetic wheat from chaff, King from Bachman.

Readers might readily identify echoes of the Bible, of course, including an effective loaves-and-fishes echo (III, 1, iii), an "Angel of Death" allusion (IV, 1, ii), and an evocative glance at the Last Supper: *"This is my body broken for you and for many"*—ironically spoken of a Three Musketeers bar (IV, 5, v). Shakespeare appears equally directly with "'Alas, poor Urine,' [Steve] said. 'I knew him well'" (IV, 5, iii); while a direct reference to H. G. Wells' *The Island of Dr. Moreau* precedes a nicely condensed plot summary of Milton's *Comus*:

> David said, "The sounds I heard from the bottom of the mine—the ones I heard with the Lushan brothers' ears—were like that movie, only in reverse. As if the men were turning into animals. I guess they were. I guess that's sort of what the *can tahs* do. (IV, 1, iii)

John Donne's most famous line (of prose, of course, but even Donne's prose exploits the rhythms and structures of poetry) combines with Biblical poetic imagery when Johnny "held the helmet up, stuck it on his hand like a puppet. 'Ask not for whom the Bell tolls,' he said. 'It tolls for thee, thou storied honeydew'" (IV, 5, iv)

More allusively, and perhaps more crucially, King incorporates a stichomythic dialogue reminiscent of one of the most memorable of the 17th-Century religious lyrics, George Herbert's "The Collar." In an agony of denial and rebellion, Herbert's speaker "…STRUCK the board, and cried, No more;/I will abroad" (1-2), hungering from freedom from responsibility…from God:

> What? shall I ever sigh and pine?
>   My lines and life are free; free as the road,
>     Loose as the wind, as large as store.
>         Shall I be still in suit?

After a series of equally desperate questions and assertions, the speaker decides to take action, to escape:

> I will abroad.
> Call in thy death's head there: tie up thy fears.
>         He that forbears

To suit and serve his need,
Deserves his load.

Then, in a note suggesting all of Herbert's poetry, that declaration is immediately negated by a single line by another speaker, one unseen but deeply felt:

But as I raved and grew more fierce and wild,
At every word,
Methought I heard one calling, "Child!"
And I replied, "My Lord!"

King's lines differ in language and imagery but follow the same progression from rejection to dramatic submission:

"Why are you on earth?" The voice seemed to come from *inside* his head now.
"I don't hear you! I don't hear you!"
"You were put on earth to love God—"
"No!"
"—and serve him."
"No! Fuck God! Fuck his love! Fuck his service!"
"God can't make you do anything you don't want to—"
"Stop it! I won't listen, I won't decide! Do you hear? Do you—"
"Shh—listen!"
Not quite against his will, David listened. (III, 5, iv)

In another dialogue, King explores an answer Milton's contemporary Sir Thomas Browne gave when questioned about the reality of witches. Browne argued quite simply that if witches existed, then God must also: No witches, no God. King's characters approach the same conclusion (one not necessarily implicit in many horror novels, which often revel in a physical manifestation of evil without acknowledging any specific thing to oppose it). Referring initially to the rogue god Tak, David speaks to Johnny:

"He wants what *you* want. For us to leave."
"Then why did he bring us here in the first place?"

"He didn't."

"*What?*"

"He thinks he did, but he didn't."

"I don't have any idea what you're—"

"God brought us," David said. "To stop him."
(IV, 1, I)

Perhaps most startling, King employs a species of imagery unique in English literature to one poet: the seventeenth-century Counter-Reformation Catholic, Richard Crashaw. Nearing the climax of *Desperation,* Johnny Marinville confronts evil at the opening to the *ini,* well of the worlds. In a near-hallucinatory passage, he sees smoke that is muck that is ectoplasm (almost) that approaches the physical. At the ends of the smoke tendrils, he sees

> *Holes.*
> Yes, that was it. Holes like eyes. Three of them. Maybe more, but three he could see clearly. A triangle of holes, two on top and one underneath, holes like whispering eyes, like blast-holes....
> The brownish-black muck twisted toward him, both horrible and enticing, holes that were mouths, mouths that were eyes. Eyes that whispered. Promised. (IV, 5, v)

Holes become eyes become mouths become eyes: a swirl of images that approach the intense and complex physicality Crashaw used to elevate and adore God in "On the Wounds of Our Crucified Lord":

> O these wakeful wounds of thine!
>     Are they mouths? or are they eyes?
> Be they mouths, or be they eyne,
>     Each bleeding part some one supplies.

In *Desperation,* the same imagery functions to demonize and diminish God's opposite.

These allusions act as more than window dressing or exotic exercises in literary one-upmanship. They relate directly to a central concern in *Desperation*, one missing from *The Regulators*: The role of God in the Universe. *Desperation* suggests, albeit in stridently twentieth-century idioms, the same deep seated unease, questioning, and ultimate reconciliation consistently present in much of the religious poetry of the seventeenth-century (not coincidentally an age of similar fragmentation of tradition beliefs, institutions, and social structures). In fact, the novel concludes with close to an affirmation of God; any more explicit, and the book would threaten to shift from fiction to theological pamphlet. In *The Regulators,* Audrey Wyler turns to an 'other' world for physical and spiritual relief, bringing Seth with her to her secret landscapes in Mohonk. While that withdrawal grants them a quasi-immortality, or at least removes them from Tak's power, it remains a solidly earth-bound landscape; as imaginative as it may be, it is formed of the essence of *this* world. David Carver withdraws, not into remembery, but into God. David talks to God...and God answers him.

*The Regulators* is a fascinating exercise in horror, in blending the traditional Western film with Saturday morning commercials for popular Action-figure dolls. But it ultimately asserts the physical. Even the final scenes, as ghostly as they may be, are set in *our* world, *our* landscape. And that landscape is a commercial vacation spot.

*Desperation* removes us *from* ourselves and our world. It thrusts us into a Job-like confrontation between Evil and Good, between Dark and Light...and, unlike his treatment in *Needful Things* and elsewhere, King here gives a name to the Light: God. The characters are present at the scene of the confrontation, not through any desire of their own, but because God wills it.

# STEPHEN KING'S *THE DARK TOWER* IN THE EPIC TRADITION

[This essay was presented to the Brigham Young University Symposium on Science Fiction and Fantasy: "Life, the Universe, and Everything XXII," Provo UT, February 16, 2007]

In the play *1776*, Benjamin Franklin and John Dickinson engage in a bit of satirical repartee that ends with Dickinson saying: "Fortunately, Dr. Franklin, the people of these colonies maintain a higher regard for their mother country." The assertion draws a serious and crucial response from Franklin:

> Higher, certainly, than she feels for them. Never was such a valuable possession so stupidly and recklessly managed than this entire continent by the British Crown. Our industry discouraged, our resources pillages—and, worst of all, our very character stifled. We've spawned a new race here—rougher, simpler, more violent, more enterprising, and less refined. We're a new nationality, Mr. Dickinson—we require a new nation. (Scene 3, p. 41)

Franklin speaks in a political context, in words filtered through a twentieth-century dramatist's understanding of events and characters, but as I began thinking about how to approach *The Dark Tower* and the epic tradition, his words seemed particularly apt.

For a number of years, I have studied Renaissance epic—reading the poems, reading *about* the poems, even reconstructing their general tone, language, and structure in my own epic, *The Nephiad.* During graduate school, I pursued the fortunes of traditional epic from Milton on, through the eighteenth century and well into the nineteenth, when the form appeared largely to fade away. In spite of attempts to write poetic epics, continuing into the present century, few of the results have been critically well received or widely influential, and even fewer—if any—gained anything like popular acclaim.

Worse, given the fundamental definition of epic as a long, narrative poem, the reputation of poetry itself declined to the point that anything more expansive than a lyric poem of twenty-five or so lines seemed almost unapproachable to most readers. The idea of writing a long, coherent narrative in verse became, according to many critics and readers, absurd.

Yet for millennia, epic has been a central means for a society to define itself. And the assumption that such a deep-seated impulse might simply peter out in exhaustion over the span of a few decades seemed, to me at least, equally absurd.

Epic persisted, I felt certain, but where?

The answer surprised me. Armed with a list of conventions that had become intrinsic to literary epic as far back as Virgil's *Aeneid*, with its conscious imitation of structural and stylistic elements defined in Homer's *Iliad* and *Odyssey*, I discovered that there did exist a literary direction that regularly exploited many, if not all, of those conventions.

That direction incorporated the related genres of science fiction, fantasy, and horror.

Again and again, I found novels that seemed to epitomize not only the narrative thrust of traditional epic but did so using far more of the traditional conventions than one might expect of a genre essentially rising from and speaking to, not a classically educated aristocracy (the original audiences for Medieval and Renaissance epic), but rather a less elevated, more middle-class readership. To borrow Franklin's words, this audience seemed "rougher, simpler, more violent, more enterprising, and less refined" than, for example, Milton's "fit audience though few" (*Paradise Lost* VII, 31).

Through several essays written over two decades, I have suggested that the epic impulse informed narratives as disparate in tone, structure, and length as Piers Anthony's Battle Circle trilogy, Frank Herbert's *Dune*, Stephen King's *The Stand*, and Orson Scott Card's *Ender's Game*. Yet each time, I found myself at an obvious sticking-point: as frequently as peripheral epic elements might appear in them, none of the books were long, narrative *poems. Long* they might be, *narrative* they certainly were, and *poetic* they touched upon here and there; but none claimed to be in any contemporary sense of the word a *poem.*

Then it struck me. The problem in tracking the fortunes of epic lay not in the works available but in *me.* I was—I already knew—a bit stubborn. So I kept looking—vainly it turned out—for a work that would fit all of *my requirements*; and if one didn't, rather like Procrustes, I intended to cut and prune until it did.

But I finally realized that my failure to locate a clear-cut example of modern epic stemmed from my insistence that it be a traditional *poem.*

"The world," as Roland of Gilead and other characters reiterate throughout The Dark Tower cycle, "has moved on."

For better or worse, poetry no longer speaks as the highest form of human expression, no longer aspires to Shelley's Romantic definition in *A Defense of Poetry*:

> Poets are the hierophants of an unapprehended inspiration; the mirrors of the gigantic shadows which futurity casts upon the present; the words which express what they understand not; the trumpets which sing to battle, and feel not what they inspire; the influence which is moved not, but moves. Poets are the unacknowledged legislators of the world.

In fact, in large part through the choices of twentieth-century poets as much as through substantive and fundamental changes in social structures, poetry has become very much a minority voice among literary endeavors, palatable only in small, usually lyric, doses.

Instead, the role poetry once enjoyed has been assumed by a more tolerant medium, one more open to the shifts in values and purposes that differentiate the past century from those preceding. Prose—and particularly the prose novel—has now assumed much of the storytelling function once the hallmark of verse, especially in telling stories that help define the essence of a people.

And these conclusions led, finally, to The Dark Tower Cycle.

My first reading of *The Gunslinger: The Dark Tower*, in its original appearance in 1982, half convinced me that I had at last found an analogue to traditional epic, especially in the poetic texture of its prose. And for two decades, I labored under that assumption.

Then I read King's foreword to *The Gunslinger: The Dark Tower I* (2003), in which he implies that one of his purposes in revising the original book was to move away from a poetic texture, to reverse the sense that "language is more important than story, that ambiguity is to be preferred over clarity and simplicity, which are usually signs of a thick and literal mind" (xxvii), and to create "a clearer start and a slightly easier entry into Roland's world" (xxvii). For example, in the first pages of "The Gunslinger and the Dark Man," Roland surveys the bone-strewn amphitheater in which he and the Man in Black meet to palaver:

> *I am in the West, Cuthbert,* he thought wonder-
> ingly.
> And of course in each skull, in each rondure of va-
> cated eye, he saw the boy's face. (276)

Two points are significant: the chapter title, "The Gunslinger and the Dark Man"; and the vocabulary that characterizes the second sentence. In 1969, while a student at the University of Maine, Orono, King published a poem in *Ubris,* the university's student literary magazine. "The Dark Man"—King's second published poem —establishes a *leitmotif* that recurs throughout many of King's later fictions, notably in *The Stand, The Eyes of the Dragon, Insomnia,* and the seven Dark Tower novels: the mysterious and threatening Dark Man. The poem—its title character as well as its poetic texture—seems, in fact, to permeate King's imagination and embody his fundamental preoccupation with the nature of evil—the Dark— as its manifestations contend for human souls with representatives of the White. And in keeping with the genesis of its central image in a poem, "The Gunslinger and the Dark Man" suggests an essentially poetic vocabulary: "rondure," "vacated eye."

In his revisions for the 2003 version, King addresses both of these points. He alters the chapter title, minimally perhaps but crucially. "The Gunslinger and the Dark Man" becomes "The Gunslinger and the Man in Black." The underlying symbolism remains, but the explicit allusion to the earlier poem disappears. "The Dark Man," with its rich suggestions of symbol and ambiguity, becomes the more prosaic (but still, of course, evocative) "Man in Black." And the passage in question reads: *"I am in the West, Cuthbert,* he thought wonderingly. *If this is not Mid-World, it's close by"* (271). The poetry-inspired second sentence disappears entirely; suggestion and allusion are replaced by a prosaic statement of place.

In other instances, King works in an opposite direction to attain the same end, expanding lines that in the original version require the reader to make sense of a compressed, multivalent image. A few pages later in "The Gunslinger and the Dark Man," King writes:

"THEN LET THERE BE LIGHT!"

> And there was light, crashing in on him like a hammer, a great and primordial light. In it, consciousness perished—but before it did, the gunslinger saw something of cosmic importance. He clutched it with agonized effort and sought himself. (286)

The heightened diction of the passage appropriately reflects Roland's vision of worlds and universes dependent upon the Dark Tower; but the final phrase, "and sought himself," again remains open-ended, an invitation to suggestion, allusion, and symbol.

The revised version is longer, less compressed and elliptical, more overt in meaning and diction, more clearly designed to communicate inherent emotion typographically:

> **"THEN LET THERE BE LIGHT!"**
> And there *was* light, crashing in on him like a hammer, a great and primordial light. Consciousness had no chance of survival in that great glare, but before it perished, the gunslinger saw something clearly, something he believed to be of cosmic importance. He clutched it with agonized effort and then went deep, seeking refuge in himself before that light should blind his eyes and blast his sanity. (282)

The changes in wording and sentence structure eliminate multiple possibilities, direct readers to a clearer, simpler awareness of what happens to Roland. Poetic compression has become prosaic exposition.

These changes—and scores of similar revisions—echo an awareness that poetry is no longer the widely acceptable way to tell long stories, to say nothing of its validity as the vehicle for the epic vision.

In the afterword to the original version of *The Gunslinger*, King notes that his projected novel would ultimately approach 3,000 pages or more, adding,

> That probably sounds as if my plans for the story have passed beyond mere ambition and into the land of lunacy...but ask your favorite English teacher sometime to tell you about the plans Chaucer had for

*The Canterbury Tales*—now *Chaucer* might have been crazy." (307)

Those plans included two dozen or more pilgrims—the Tales introduce several not mentioned in "The General Prologue"—all telling two stories coming and two more returning from their pilgrimage to Canterbury, stories that incorporate an extraordinary breadth of characterization and literary forms.

Critics and readers frequently disagree about the precise relation of *The Canterbury Tales* to epic, but one point emerges: when Chaucer began to write the Tales, he had already completed several long narrative poems, including a fragment of *The Romaunt of the Rose* (portions attributed to Chaucer but not with certainty), *Troilus and Criseyde* (1382–1386) and, more significantly, the explicitly epical *Palamoun and Arcite*, later incorporated into *The Canterbury Tales* (c. 1388–1400) as "The Knight's Tale." *The Canterbury Tales* was the work of a mind steeped in the poetic and epic tradition of his day; a mind practiced in writing long narrative poems, some based explicitly on characters from classical epic; and a mind intent upon exploring a remarkably wide range of human experience, suggested by the equally wide range of genres his poem incorporates: epyllion, fabliau, Christian romance, historical narrative, literary confession, exemplum, Breton lay, sermon, hagiography and miracles of the Virgin, minstrel romance, allegory, *de casibus* tragedy, beast fable, satire, prose sermon, palinode or recantation, and others.

He chose to cast his major work—or at least most of it—into the dominant literary for of his day: verse. Prose, and specifically the prose novel, would not emerge for well over a century as a widely viable literary form, not until major changes had taken place in English language, culture, society, and literature. Not the least would be the development of printing; the accessibility of reading and education to wider segments of the populace; and the emergence of a distinctive social class with the skills, wealth, and—perhaps most crucial—leisure to read. Roughly between the middle of the sixteenth century and the end of the eighteenth, poetry as the dominant mode retreated before prose; literary epic deferred increasingly to another vehicle, the novel.

Writers and critics of the time recognized affinities between the two genres. Henry Fielding, one of the first significant English novelists, explicitly connected the genres in the opening paragraphs of his "Author's Preface" to *Joseph Andrews*:

The EPIC, as well as the DRAMA, is divided into tragedy and comedy. HOMER, who was the father of this species of poetry, gave us a pattern of both these, though that of the latter kind is entirely lost....

And farther, as this poetry may be tragic or comic, I will not scruple to say it may be likewise either in verse or prose: for though it wants one particular, which the critic enumerates in the constituent parts of an epic poem, namely metre; yet, when any kind of writing contains all its other parts, such as fable, action, characters, sentiments, and diction, and is deficient in metre only, it seems, I think, reasonable to refer it to the epic; at least, as no critic hath thought proper to range it under any other head, or to assign it a particular name to itself.

Within a century from the publication of what is generally accepted as the greatest verse epic in the English language—John Milton's *Paradise Lost* (1667, 1674)—discussion of the possibility of *prose epic* had begun.

Little more than a century after *Joseph Andrews* appeared, another work unambiguously asserted the continuity of the epic tradition within the prose novel—this time moving away from the rather limited view of the novel as a specifically *comic* epic. Herman Melville's *Moby Dick* (1851) in part treats the prose novel as a vehicle for multiple genres, as noted by Hennig Cohen:

Melville creates spaciousness by a successive layering of literary forms, styles, tones, references, allusions, and particularly the manipulation of language. The "romance of adventure" is formally a combination of personal narrative, drama, and epic including, among other genres, elements of the short story, tall tale, sermons both serious and burlesque, lawyer's briefs, and librarian's catalogue; and its tonalities extend from the grandeur of Elizabethan blank verse soliloquy to the crudities of vaudeville dialect.

My impression on first reading *Moby Dick* nearly forty years ago was that Melville recognized the epic dimensions of his tale but in a sense refused to place his work in competition with the overwhelming literary reputation of *Paradise Lost*. Instead, he chose to secrete his poetry within the context of prose, and in doing so create a complex amalgam of both, drawing upon and exploiting the strengths of each. In addition, as one of his early British reviews noted, he brought to that amalgam a particularly—if not peculiarly—*American* sensibility:

> The book is not a romance, nor a treatise on Cetology. It is something of both: a strange, wild work with the tangled overgrowth and luxuriant vegetation of American forests, not the trim orderliness of an English park. –*London Leader, November 8, 1851*

The second sentence might with good reason just as well apply to King's The Dark Tower as to *Moby Dick*; the back cover of the mass-market paperback edition of the former cites *The Washington Post* reference to volume seven as "A fitting capstone to a uniquely American epic."

In his introduction to the revised edition of *The Gunslinger*, "On Being Nineteen (and a Few Other Things)," King pays overt tribute to the influence of two seminal works: Chaucer's *The Canterbury Tales* (already discussed above) and J. R. R. Tolkien's *The Lord of the Rings*. Tolkien was—and is—a recognized authority on epic, particularly the earliest and greatest English epic, *Beowulf*; his "The Monster and the Critics" remains a fascinating excursion into the poem. Thus it seems instructive that his own foray into modern epic fantasy, *The Lord of the Rings*, present a similar combination of acknowledging prose as the dominant literary form for long heroic narrative and simultaneously affirming the fundamentally *poetic* nature of epic. On the most overt level, *The Lord of the Rings* simply incorporates poetry into its story-telling; more essentially, however, it recreates the texture of epic verse in a number of prose passages. Appropriately, given the influence of the *Beowulf* on Tolkien's portrait of the riders of Rohan (down to re-creating Anglo-Saxon names, place names, and idioms throughout), those passages often attain to a modern analogue of the four-stress accentual heroic verse of *Beowulf,* particularly in battle scenes.

This long, admittedly superficial foray into literary history suggests the directions that several decades of reading and study—ranging from classical and Renaissance epic and epic theory to immersion in recent science fiction, fantasy, and horror—have led me. And it suggests the reasons I waited with eager anticipation for the final volume of *The Dark Tower* saga. From my first reading of *The*

*Gunslinger* in the mid-1980s, it has been a waiting game to see how—and whether—King would bring his tale to a suitably epical climax.

The wait was not in vain.

Now, with the full story told—and the intricate connections established between the seven Dark Tower volumes and many other King novels, especially *The Stand, The Talisman* and *Black House, The Eyes of the Dragon,* and *Insomnia* (named in the Dark Tower as the keystone novel)—the multiple parallels between King's fable and epic become clear. To repeat the kernel of Henry Fielding's discussion:

> . . . for though it wants one particular, which the critic enumerates in the constituent parts of an epic poem, namely metre; yet, *when any kind of writing contains all its other parts, such as fable, action, characters, sentiments, and diction, and is deficient in metre only, it seems, I think, reasonable to refer it to the epic.* (Italics added)

FOR FURTHER EXPLORATION: It is one thing, of course, to assert that a prose novel incorporates most if not all of the traditional characters of the verse epic; it is another to demonstrate that assertion. The most direct way to do so is to isolate a number of epic conventions—structural and narrative devices that have been associated with epic at least since Homer's *Iliad* and *Odyssey,* if not in even earlier surviving epics such as the *Enuma Elish* (the *Babylonian Genesis* ) and the *Epic of Gilgamesh*—and discover how many appear not only in *The Dark Tower,* but in other key works of science fiction, fantasy, and horror.

Here is a proposed listing of some of the more important hallmarks of an epic tale:

1. High style
2. *Propositio* ['proposition']
3. *Invocatio* ['invocation']
4. *In medias res* — ['in the middle of things']
5. Epic similes
6. Arming of the hero
7. Epic catalogues
8. *Deus ex Machina* — Epic machinery
9. The Supernatural; Christian Marvelous

10. Recital of past and future events, often taking place during or after a meal
11. Genealogies of heroes
12. Epic epithets
13. *Nuntius* ['messenger'] and *Mentor* figures
14. Flyting [heroic taunts] and personal combat
15. Epic councils
16. Division into books
17. Descent into the Underworld/Ascent to the Mountain of Revelation
18. Warring nations and rival gods
19. Dual Structure of heroism
20. Heroic/unheroic disguises

# CHRIST-FIGURES IN THE
# FICTION OF ORSON SCOTT CARD

[This essay was presented at the Brigham Young University Symposium on Science Fiction and Fantasy: "Life, the Universe, and Everything, V," Provo UT, 4 February 1987; and published as *Imago Christi*: Christ-Figures in the Fiction of Orson Scott Card," *The Leading Edge: Magazine of Science Fiction and Fantasy* [Brigham Young University] Vol. 14 (Summer 1987): 15-24. The essay was subsequently revised and expanded as a chapter in: Michael R. Collings. *In the Image of God: Theme, Characterization, and Landscape in the Fiction of Orson Scott Card*. Copyright © 1990 by Michael R. Collings. Reproduced with permission of ABC-CLIO, LLC. The original essay is presented here, lightly revised for this volume.]

In "Fantasy and the Believing Reader" (1982), Orson Scott Card argued that the role of the critic is much the same as that of a novelist or short-story writer—to tell a story:

> Literary criticism is the stories we tell ourselves about our stories. When we speak of a literary work's "meaning" we may be telling a story about how the author intended the work to be read, how the proper audience of the work would have understood it, how the work is received by a modern audience, what the work tells us about the author and his community or even how we think the work should have been written and how it compares to that standard of measurement. In all cases, however, we are telling a story—that is, we are giving an ordered account of casually related events. (45)

Several years ago I was speaking to a student about Card's work, specifically about "Kingsmeat," a short story from Card's *Unaccompanied Sonata and Other Stories* (1981). The story had been singled out for harsh criticism—Sandy and Joe Straubhaars' article, "Science Fiction and Mormonism," for example, refers to its "bald sadism," a comment made even more severe by the fact that both author and critic are LDS, yet they apparently could not reach a common ground in interpreting the story.

Even so, the story affected me deeply—on a level I found it hard to articulate. When the student challenged me to make sense of what seemed senseless violence, I went back to the text and read it again, searching for a key to help explain why the story moved me as powerfully as it did.

When I did so, I discovered the value of Card's argument that criticism is the art of making stories about stories and is useful only as long as the critic understands that his or her story is not the totality but only a perspective. "Kingsmeat" had already been subjected to analysis from a perspective that assumed Card to be misogynistic, sadistic, enamored with violence for its own sake. Yet having read *Songmaster* and "The Porcelain Salamander" as well as "Kingsmeat," I was convinced that that "story" misrepresented Card's intentions and his abilities. The Straubhaars' "story" failed to explain "Kingsmeat" or its effect on me satisfactorily.

In a discussion with a book dealer who has become one of Card's most astute and enthusiastic readers, I discovered yet another "story" about "Kingsmeat." He spoke of the tale in terms of his experiences with the Holocaust in Nazi Germany. For him, "Kingsmeat" evoked the ambiguity of collaboration—self-sacrifice to preserve the greater good, even if those one serves never fully understand the nature of that sacrifice. My friend spoke long and persuasively about this "story," one related closely to his own experiences and heritage; for him, it provided a valuable and dynamic approach to Card's fictions.

For me, however, it proved less useful. Not sharing my friend's background—and being substantially closer in age and life experience to Card—I wanted something more direct. This need led me again to the texts—to everything Card has written since "Ender's Game" appeared as a novelette in the August 1977 *Analog*. As a result of that immersion in Card's imagined worlds, I discovered a critical "story" of my own, one that makes the fictions part of a coherent whole, that helps define the nature of Card's heroes, and that explains why I emerge from my encounters with his worlds and his characters a different person.

In *Speaker for the Dead*, the narrator writes that for Valentine Wiggin's children, the facts about Ender's life "became the family legend, and the children grew up hearing marvelous stories of their long-lost Uncle Ender, who was thought in every world to be a monster, but in reality was something of a savior, or a prophet, or at least a martyr" (88). In many ways, this sentence provides an important clue to Card's fictions. From the beginning, many of his central characters have shared this common denominator, struggling through the process of becoming "something of a savior," responding to different situations differently but in each working to bring about a greater good than the individual could legitimately assume for himself—in Card's own terms from "The Finer Points of Characterization," the characters blend pain and jeopardy with a legitimate sense that they are larger than life (II, 38).

"Ender's Game," first a novelette and subsequently a novel, *Ender's Game* (1985), concentrates on Andrew "Ender" Wiggin's recruitment as a child for military training that enables him to defeat the "Buggers," an insectoid alien race ostensibly committed to destroying humanity. In the earlier version, Card makes Ender's Christic parallels explicit. The world needs soldiers, one character argues, and if that requires that one child be denied the freedom to be a child, the sacrifice would be worthwhile; Ender will make it "possible for the others of his age to be playing in the park." The training commander replies:

> "And Jesus died to save all men, of course." Graff sat up and looked at Anderson almost sadly. "But we're the ones," Graff said, "We're the ones who are driving in the nails." (*Analog* 106)

The line controls much of the narrative. Ender is a Christ-surrogate, a child different from other children, whose abilities and talents enable him to encompass the salvation of the human race. To do so requires only that he relinquish his own humanity and, in doing so, almost relinquish his sanity and his life.

Ender is a particularly LDS Christ-figure, however. The choices he must make are real choices; his sufferings, real sufferings. On the opening page of the novel, Card applies the Book of Mormon dictum of opposition in all things: the only way Graff can manipulate Ender into the proper choices is to surround him with enemies. Ender responds by distrusting all accepted notions of how things must be done and penetrating to the heart of each problem, resolving each immediately and for all time. This often requires violence; yet he remains oddly untouched by that violence, an innocent who ultimately does sacrifice himself for the greater good.

This pattern develops fully in *Ender's Game* and *Speaker for the Dead* (and continues to develop throughout the Ender novels, up to and including *Ender in Exile)*, but even a cursory look at characters in some of Card's other early fictions suggests the pervasiveness of this concern.

Card's first book-length forays into science fiction, *Capitol* (1979), *Hot Sleep* (1979), and its revised version, *The Worthing Chronicle* (1983) deal with ostensible immortality through the use of a drug, somec. In each novel, a single character takes responsibility for the burden of directing human life. *The Worthing Chronicle* in particular structures that character on Christic lines, as Jason Worthing brings back to life and educates adult space voyagers whose memories have been lost. He absents himself frequently, going on somec and returning years later to teach their children, while he himself remains essentially unaged and unchanged—a god, in fact and deed.

*A Planet Called Treason* (1979) depicts, as its title implies, the attempt of a planet to expiate the treason of its founding families. Exiled on a planet devoid of metals, the characters must find new ways to develop—some inimical and highly dangerous. Through his experiences among the different families, Lanik Mueller learns to integrate the changes each family has experienced; he suffers a humiliating death, rises transfigured, and finally acquires a control over time that gives him virtual immortality. His life consciously recapitulates the movement of Christ's, in spite of the overt sexuality and graphic violence some early reviewers decried.

In *Songmaster* (1980), Ansset begins as a miraculous child with a miraculous voice, grows to understand the power in his voice, and in doing so distances himself from humanity. Through his struggles, he teaches the Galaxy peace, ultimately reigning as Galactic Emperor and dying voluntarily in the High Tower of the Songhouse. In his life, he becomes the imagistic savior for the individuals whose lives he touches, bringing order and fulfillment out of disorder and hatred: through his death he breathes new life into the static rhythms of the Songhouse, fulfilling his mission as mediator.

In *Hart's Hope* (1983), Card embraces high fantasy but does not abandon his Christic hero. Orem Scanthips recapitulates in human terms Christ's mission as the Son of God. Orem's birth is as mysterious in its way as Christ's—in the context of the novel, it is almost an immaculate conception, certainly a conception shrouded in the religious imagery of the Hart as God. He grows to adolescence distanced from the court and protected from its corruption. He undertakes a journey of maturity, finally arriving at the city of Inwit (the name is Anglo-Saxon and means "Conscience"). He marries the Queen, becoming the Little King, and, through his ability to absorb magic, undoes the evil magic of Queen Beauty and facilitates the return of King Palicrovol—even though doing so costs him the life of his son, Youth, and puts his own life at peril. In the analogical and allegorical world of *Hart's Hope*, Orem is literally the savior, making possible a reconciliation between the true King and Conscience through the shedding of innocent blood. Throughout, Card uses such images as Orem being sold for a bag of silver to solidify the parallels between Orem and Christ.

In 1984, Card moved even closer to his LDS heritage with the non-SF historical novel, *A Woman of Destiny*. Focusing on Dinah Kirkham, an amalgam of several early LDS pioneers but strongly suggesting Eliza R. Snow, Card introduces Joseph Smith into the novel. The presence of a literal prophet in the novel allows Card to make clear and unmistakable allusions to a Christ-figure, allusions that are transformed into allegory in *The Tales of Alvin Maker*, a six-part science-fantasy-in-progress based heavily on LDS history. His central character, Alvin Miller, seventh son of a seventh son and possessor of powerful magic, parallels Joseph Smith in a number of easily recognizable particulars, and thus recapitulates what we might now recognize as Card's primary character: "something of a savior, or a prophet, or at least a martyr."

It would be fascinating to concentrate on each of these novels and explore the complexity with which they develop Christic imagery and Christ-figures—something I intend to do in a full-length study of Card's fiction. But for this symposium, it might be more instructive to look at several short stories, including "Kingsmeat," and see precisely how he generates a sense of the Christic.

*Unaccompanied Sonata and Other Stories* includes several narratives that begin the process. Each fragments the mission of Christ then focuses on a single attribute and explores the ramifications of a juxtaposition of Godhood with humanity.

The clearest example of such a technique occurs in "The Porcelain Salamander," a small masterpiece of fairytale-like fantasy. The story is simple: once upon a time, a merchant's wife dies in childbirth. The man is so distraught that he curses his child—Kiren would be paralyzed until she lost someone that she loved as much as he had loved his wife. He repents of the words almost immediately, but in his world curses have power and the child is unable to move. The father tries to make restitution to her by bringing wondrous gifts from far places—including a small porcelain salamander. Its magic is that it moves; in fact, if it ever stops moving, it will cease to be magical and become simply a porcelain figurine. One day, partially restored through her joy at being with the salamander, Kiren walks with it in the forest; a magical barrier rises, cutting them off from any escape. The wall ends just above Kiren's fingertips; if she could reach it, she could pull herself over and escape. The salamander understands this and offers to stand still so she can climb on it and pull herself to safety. She refuses, but the salamander walks to the wall and stands still—and becomes a porcelain statue. She escapes and the curse dissipates, but her life is changed. She has learned lessons in love and charity, and for the rest of her life, she is a more gracious, generous person.

The salamander suggests Christ. Its incessant movement suggests the various *omnis* associated with Godhood: omniscience, omnipresence, omnipotence. Being "omni-motile," the salamander is distanced from and superior to humanity. It chooses to relinquish that distance, to become part of a world in which things—people and animals—must occasionally stand still. By choosing to do so, it offers its life in exchange for another's. It completes the sacrifice that restores the child to her father and gives her the ability to become fully human; more than that, she shares in small ways the attributes of the salamander: her hands dance, her eyes are "white and lustrous as deep-enameled porcelain," and in their movement, it seems that she can see into another, higher realm.

"Kingsmeat" is far more problematical but perhaps more valuable as an index to Card's techniques. It lacks the fairy-tale qualities of "The Porcelain Salamander," just as it lacks the other's gentleness and wondrous fragility. Instead, "Kingsmeat" confronts us with another facet of the world—its inherent violence and suffering and hatred and death.

A colony world has been invaded by aliens—the king and the queen. At first the aliens stable the colonists as a farmer might stable a herd, regularly selecting a likely specimen and slaughtering it for food. Now, however, the Shepherd (Card capitalizes the name/title) mediates between the aliens and the humans. He selects victims, but instead of killing them, he removes the flesh required for the king and queen. There are few whole people remaining in the colony; almost every one has lost a leg, or an arm, or other body parts. Card does not spare his readers either; one particularly vivid episode shows the Shepherd slicing away a lactating breast On the other hand, the episode also demonstrates the Shepherd's humanity; there is no pain, no blood, and the wound heals almost immediately, and Card recounts the experience with quick, objective language. The Shepherd reconciles his humanity with the demands of an alien morality and consequently finds himself reviled and hated by those he is trying to save.

The story was criticized for its graphic violence, yet the violence is necessary. It is a way to re-create viscerally (i.e., emotionally rather than intellectually) the reality of Christ's Incarnation as mortal and the pain of his sacrifice and confirm us in our testimony of that mission. As both Man and God, Christ sees further, deeper than we: he understands more fully the true significance of events. What might seem cruel may be, in an eternal perspective, the only viable possibility. C. S. Lewis expressed this idea when he spoke of true repentance as being as painful as having a surgeon remove a cancer or a dentist drill to the nerve of a tooth to remove decay.

And it seems inevitable that we read this story on such a level. The title suggests that there is more here than just a science-fiction adventure tale. Capitalizing the word *Shepherd* invests it with great dignity and almost forces us to see in one Shepherd a pale reflection of another, greater Shepherd. In addition, Card's Shepherd assumes the mantle of a saving mission, one not fully understood by those he saves. When the rescue ship arrives, the king and queen are destroyed and the colony is restored; it is clear to all that no blame must be attached to the shepherd or his actions. In fact, the commanding officer orders that the colony honor the Shepherd for his sacrifice.

And here lies the final irony of a difficult and uncomfortable story. The colonists fulfill the letter if not the spirit of the law. In a final analogy with Christ, the Shepherd is stripped of his humanity. Once a year the people enter a certain house to honor him: "There were no large strong hands now.... Only a head and a neck and a spine and ribs and a loose sac of flesh that pulsed with life. The people looked over his naked body and saw the scars." He is, like the Christ in too many lives, kept out of sight, brought out only on ceremonial occasions to be subjected to the attentions of those who have no true conception of who he is or what he has done:

> Then they set down their gifts and left, and at the end of the day the Shepherd was moved back to his hammock, where year after year he looked out the window at the weathers of the sky. They would, perhaps, have cut out his tongue, but since he never spoke they didn't think of it. They would, perhaps, have cut out his eyes, but they wanted him to see them smile. (70-71)

A final story again re-defines the Christic mission and its impact.

"America" is a difficult work that may offend many LDS readers with its overt sexuality.

Sam Monson, the young son of an engineer assigned to Brazil, meets Anamari Boagente, a middle-aged, pure-blooded Indian. Sam represents the European element in America and later becomes the Governor of Deseret, the "last European state in America" (24). Anamari represents the Indian, now beginning a resurgence that will culminate with the conquest of the hemisphere under her son, believed by many to be the incarnation of Quetzalcoatl.

The story is self-consciously mystical as Card blends Mormonism with dream-visions and intuitions of America itself as sentient. The story recounts the two meetings between Sam and Anamari and their unwilling spiral into sexual intercourse as a response to her dream-visions of a resurgent America. Card takes seriously the ideal of America as a promised land—the final words of the story are, "it is the promised, the promising land" (53). And he explores the consequences of absolute fulfillment of prophecy. The Indians had abandoned true worship of the land; Card makes explicit the theological overtones of the story when Anamari warns Sam (and us), "Say *Deus* or *Christo* instead of the land and the story is the same" (44). By succumbing to the love of gold, or the worship of idols, or the corruption of their morality, the Indians subverted their own promises, and the land called to Columbus "and told him lies and seduced him and he never had a chance, did he?"(44).

Now, five centuries later, the Europeans have demonstrated themselves equally unfit to inherit the Promised Land. The time of their punishment having passed, America is calling again to the Indians.

> It sounded so close to what the old prophets in the Book of Mormon said would happen to America; close, but dangerously different. As if there were no hope for the Europeans anymore. As if their chance had already been lost, as if no repentance would be allowed. They would not be able to pass the land on to the next generation. Someone else would inherit. It made him sick at heart, to realize what the white man had lost, had thrown away, had torn up and destroyed. (44)

In a Land that is both God and Christ, Card calls forth a savior, a new Christ to wrest the land from the fallen Europeans and restore it to a purified Indian generation. Through his sacrifice, Sam Monson makes possible the incarnation of a new Christ.

Yet Card never shows us the son. He concentrates instead on Sam and Anamari and their growing awareness that they are players in a drama extending far beyond their own lives. They are saviors, prophets, even martyrs, and through them, the Land will once again be restored and its promises made newly viable.

Within his fictive worlds, Card discovers stories that make us feel the difficulty of Christ's choices, that make new and visceral and integral an understanding of what it entails to become a sacrifice. We see through the facile answers of Sunday School classes and experience vicariously the process of sacrifice, making us more aware of the enormity of Christ's mission. By looking at one facet in each story, then having us read all of the stories, he creates a composite of experience that alters his readers and their conception of the mission of Christ.

# THE RATIONAL AND THE REVELATORY
# IN THE FICTION OF ORSON SCOTT CARD

[This essay was presented *in absentia* at the First West Coast Sunstone Theological Symposium, San Francisco CA, January 31, 1987; and subsequently published in *Sunstone* [Salt Lake City UT] Vol. 11, No. 3, #39 (May 1987): 7-11.]

In an article published in *Dialogue* in 1984, "Refracted Visions and Future Worlds: Mormonism and Science Fiction," I explored some responses to Mormonism in the writings of non-LDS science fiction authors, as well as some attempts by Mormons to write science fiction. Among the latter was Orson Scott Card, certainly the best known—and perhaps the most controversial—LDS writer within the SF community. At that time, I argued that other than generalized references in *Capitol, The Worthing Chronicle*, and stories such as "Quietus," there was little obviously Mormon material in his fiction (112, 113). Card agreed with this assessment, going even further to state the relationship between Mormonism and his fictional worlds:

> I resolved long ago, when I was a playwright trying not to lose more than a few thousand dollars a year writing plays for the Mormon audience, that I would never attempt to use my writing to overtly preach the gospel in my "literary" works…. Faith exists in actions, not in emotions; I speak more about my characters and to my audience in what I make my characters do than in what I have them say or think.
>
> Furthermore, I believe that I present Mormon theology most eloquently when I do not speak about it at all….expressions of faith, unconsciously placed within a story, are the most honest and also most powerful messages an author can give; they are, in essence, the expression of the author's conceived universe, and the reader who believes and cares about

the story will dwell, for a time, in the author's world and receive powerful vicarious memories that become part of the reader's own. ("SF and Religion" 12)

Of course, one of the frustrations (and one of the glories) of writing about living authors is that they cannot be counted on to continue writing stories that fit neatly into preconceived critical theories. While remaining true to the fundamental criteria expressed in his letter, Card has recently published several works that have altered the relationship between his writing and his religion.

Since 1984, Card has reinforced his credentials as a writer with the overtly LDS *A Woman of Destiny* (1984), and the science fiction novel *Ender's Game* (1985) and its sequel, *Speaker for the Dead* (1986). *Ender's Game* garnered both of the top science fiction writing awards for 1986: the Hugo, from the World Science Fiction Convention; and the Nebula, from the Science Fiction Writers of America. Earlier this year, *Speaker* was awarded the 1987 Nebula—making Card one of only two writers ever to receive the award in consecutive years, and the first to receive it for a novel *and* its sequel.

In addition, since 1985, four of Card's stories have appeared in major science fiction magazines, each building upon LDS ideas and set at least in part in a near-future state of Deseret. And finally, the first volume of a six-volume series, *The Tales of Alvin Maker,* is nearing publication. In this series Card explicitly links LDS history and theology to a science-fiction/fantasy framework by using as a central character an analogue of Joseph Smith in an alternate universe in which George Washington was a British commander originally named Lord Potomac, England was divided between a King and a Lord Protector, and folk-magic forms a basis for life.

As Card has gained prominence as a science fiction writer, he has increased the extent to which LDS backgrounds inform his works. *Ender's Game* and *Speaker for the Dead* are extended meditations on and definitions of what being a messiah entails. In the first, Ender Wiggin recapitulates an Old Testament definition of Messiah, protecting Earth against the incursions of ostensibly warlike aliens, the Buggers. This element of his mission is explicit early in the original novella; one character says,

"… At least we know that Ender is making it possible for others of his age to be playing in the park."

"And Jesus died to save all men, of course." Graff sat up and looked at Anderson almost sadly. "But we're the ones," Graff said, "We're the ones who are driving in the nails." ("Ender's Game," *Analog*, 106)

Although deleted from the novel version, the line is important to understanding Ender's role. That he is only eight years old when chosen is as irrelevant to his mission as Christ's youth when he taught the teachers in the temple.

Ender's heritage includes a lapsed Mormon mother who has superficially relinquished her faith but is nonetheless controlled by it on a fundamental, unconscious level. Her actions and reactions help form Ender into the person he must become to save all humanity.

By the end of the novel, however, Ender has discovered that the Buggers were not inimical; in fact, he has caused the genocide of a sentient species. At that point, his mission shifts from temporal salvation to spiritual enlightenment. He becomes the focus for redemption in a literal sense as he emigrates with his sister to a new world, carrying with him a cocoon containing the last remaining Hive-Mother of the Buggers. The concluding lines of *Ender's Game* suggest the essential nature of his quest and his own role in the salvation of an *alien* people:

> So they boarded a starship and went from world to world. Wherever they stopped, he was always Andrew Wiggin, itinerant speaker for the dead, and she was always Valentine, historian errant, writing down the stories of the living while Ender spoke the stories of the dead. And always Ender carried with him a dry white cocoon. looking for the world where the hive-queen could awaken and thrive in peace. He looked a long time. (357)

In *Speaker for the Dead,* Ender completes his quest, discovering an appropriate world and in the process rescuing the Piggies, the third sentient species in the Galaxy. At times, he seems secondary to the vivid characters in Lusitania Colony (a landscape based on Card's experiences as a missionary in Portuguese-speaking Brazil) and to the Piggies themselves. Yet that appearance masks his underlying purpose—to act as mediator, messiah, and savior. In Card's words, Ender was "thought in every world to be a monster, but in reality was something of a savior, or a prophet, or at least a martyr"

(88). His role combines the rational and the revelatory, the scientific and the mystical, a point Card makes clear in passages that consciously juxtapose the two modes of knowing. As two students discuss the recently discovered Piggies, for example, one states that the aliens are "our only hope of redemption." Ender looks at the second student, Plikt, "who he knew would not be able to endure such mysticism. 'They do not exist for any human purpose, not even redemption.' Plikt said with withering contempt" (38).

Only Ender is capable of bridging the gap between reason and revelation, as he functions within the world yet introduces what is, in the context of *Speaker,* revelation; he knows that which no other human could know. Individuals of both other sentient races are equally sensitive to knowledge that cannot be derived rationally; interactions between Ender, the Hive-Queen, and the piggy named Human form the resolution of the novel.

Even more importantly, Ender discovers the obverse of his messianic mission. Having almost sacrificed his life and sanity in *Ender's Game* to save humanity, he must now reverse his role to seal a compact between humans and Piggies. He becomes the crucifier, not the crucified. In a powerful episode, Ender kneels by the body of a slain piggy, a Christ-figure at the foot of an alien cross, crucifying another Savior. Apparent torture becomes a symbol for love and reverence; other traditional mores continuously reverse, as love becomes hate and hatred transmutes into love. Pride of guilt becomes humility. And, without any overt LDS references in structure or narrative, *Speaker* becomes an intensely religious novel that simultaneously avoids platitudes or proselytizing.

*Speaker for the Dead* presents a symbolic treatment of the Plan of Salvation. The Piggies live through three stages that parallel the three estates of human life: "The first life is within the mother-tree, where we never see the light.... The second life is when we live in the shade of the forest, the half-light, running and walking and climbing, seeing and singing and talking. making with our hands. The third life is when we reach and drink from the sun, in the full light at last, never moving except in the wind; only to think, and on those certain days when the brothers drum on your trunk, to speak to them. Yes, that is the third life" (369). The stages of grub, piggie, and tree stand for pre-existence, mortality, and after-life, defining the god-like qualities of the trees and their paternal care for their children. As Ender says to Human about a father-tree, "All the children that he fathered are still part of him. The more children he fathers, the greater he becomes.... And the more you accomplish in your life, the greater you make your father" (365).

Card makes explicit his religious purposes when he writes that in experiencing vicariously the death and transformation of Piggy into father tree, "suddenly we find the flesh of God within us after all, when we thought that we were only made of dust" (385). In fact, one non-Mormon student noticed the three divisions of piggy life and became frustrated because he felt that Card was working toward a symbolic reading, but he could not understand why the stages were important or what Card intended to say through them. They are so integrated into the novel that to extract them as "symbolic" references to Mormonism would destroy the narrative. And yet they only resonate fully to readers aware of the LDS teachings about the Plan of Salvation.

The three stages of existence are fundamental to Ender's story. *Ender's Game* concentrates on Ender's isolation from humanity. He is systematically separated from everyone, beginning with the argument that he must be "surrounded with enemies all the time" (1), a restatement of the Book of Mormon insistence on opposition in all things. Ender cannot become fully human; he is constantly manipulated by others.

In *Speaker for the Dead,* he enters a second stage. He integrates with humanity, exploring for the first time a full range of emotions and experiences. His arrival on Lusitania becomes a symbolic birth as he enters into family relationships and expands the definition of what it is to be "human."

The final, as-yet-unwritten portion of Ender's story, *Ender's Children,* may complete the pattern as an analogical treatment of humanity achieving godhood. It is dangerous, of course, to speculate about unwritten novels, but in this case, Card has told us that the third volume will differ radically from the first two. In answer to the question, "Will there be another *Ender* book?" he responds, "Yes, there will, but it will be even more different from the first two than *Speaker* was from *Ender.* It's cosmic Sci-Fi—discovering what everything is made of, what underlies the laws of the universe, that sort of thing." Card also noted that the novel *cannot* yet be written: "I don't feel I'm mature enough as a writer to handle it yet" (Shirk 12).

Given Card's demonstrated mastery in such novels as *Songmaster, Ender's Game,* and *Speaker for the Dead,* his hesitance over *Ender's Children* suggests that the novel might indeed become an attempt at defining the third estate: what it is to become as a god.

In these novels, Card achieves something rare and difficult. He writes with religious fervor, but without the surface elements of Mormonism. Instead, he infuses the narrative with the "substance" of LDS thinking, the complex of beliefs that acts as the foundation upon which the superstructure of his fiction rests. Although the novels only refer in passing to the lapsed Mormonism of Ender's mother, and many of the characters are stridently and forcefully Catholic, the stories are LDS at heart. Card is confident enough in his own beliefs not to feel any pressure to continually refer to them for artistic justification. As a result, *Ender's Game* and *Speaker for the Dead* do not *sound* LDS *but feel* intensely so. The communication occurs beneath logic and rationality, at an instinctive emotional level.

More recently, however, he has approached directly the question of religious faith in the context of science-fictional extrapolation. Church members who picked up the February 1986 issue of *Isaac Asimov's Science Fiction Magazine* were perhaps startled to see the introductory illustration to Card's "Salvage": a two-page drawing of the Salt Lake Temple half submerged in the "Mormon Sea." Even more startling is the content: the story takes place in a future when most religions have died, when the Temple is apparently important primarily because of stories that it contains hidden treasure. On the surface, the story runs counter to common beliefs within the Church as to what the future holds; Card himself noted after writing it that the story was "threatening to a good many folk doctrines about the future of Salt Lake Valley" (Letter, 20 February 1985).

But beneath the "accident" (to borrow an Aristotelian term) of an imaginary future and a science-fictional extrapolation of "what if" lies Card's "substance": an account of the enduring, often unconsciously enduring, power of faith. Deaver, the non-Mormon character, understands at the end that there *is* treasure inside the half-submerged, empty Temple—an intangible yet infinitely precious treasure that he cannot fully know: "I came to find something here for *me*," he says, "and you knew all the time it was only *your* stuff down there" (74). Structure may decay, the story asserts, but faith abides.

Several months earlier, Card published "The Fringe," a story that was well received by the SF readership in general; so much so, in fact, that it was included in Gardner Dozois' collection *The Year's Best Science Fiction* (1986). This story also takes place in a near-future Salt Lake Valley, an outpost of life against a backdrop of destruction and desolation. Card does not preach in the story, but Mormonism is inherent throughout.

The story was completed in a single weekend, along with "Salvage"—then titled "The Temple Salvage Expedition," while Card was participating in the Sycamore Hill Writers' Workshop in January 1985. Writing the stories was a revelation for Card, who had stopped writing short fiction after publishing forty-one stories between 1978 and 1981. Not only were they stories, but they were stories of a new sort: "'The Fringe' had to be a story," he writes, "It was not an *accidental* story, it was an inevitable one." ("On Sycamore," 11).

Even more importantly, he had discovered something about the relationship between his own heritage and the kind of science fiction he was writing. Speaking of the other writers' reactions to "Salvage," he said:

> The thing that had worried me most—that the intensity of the religious elements in it would put them off—turned out to be not a problem at all. Though few there had particularly strong religious impulses, the sense of holiness that the story depended on seemed to work.
>
> I realized then, that this milieu—of Mormon country underwater, the survivors struggling to keep civilization alive—was viable. ("On Sycamore" 11)

This discovery may have marked a turning point in Card's writing; certainly it reflects positively in "Salvage" and in "The Fringe." Mormonism is critical to both, but on an instinctual level rather than as surface element. Neither story preaches Mormonism per se, yet neither could exists without the underlying assumptions inherent in Mormonism.

This direction is even more apparent in the next story Card published: "Hatrack River" (1986). The editorial introduction to the story states that "the following fantasy is set in eastern Ohio in 1805, and Mr. Card tells us that it uses authentic frontier magic practice." The statement is mildly misleading, although probably not intentionally so. "Hatrack River" comprises the first five chapters of *Seventh Son,* the first novel in Card's series *Tales of Alvin Maker.* As a short story, it is complete and self-sufficient, coming to an acceptable resolution. But reading it in isolation disguises two central points.

First, the Ohio territory represented is not the Ohio we know from history but an alternative-Earth Ohio; the story may be less fantasy than science fiction, extrapolating to an Earth-analogue in which magic is a viable mode of knowing and acting. To understand this point alters the nature of the story.

The second point is even more telling. *Seventh Son* recounts the early years of Alvin Miller, Junior, born a "maker" and holder of unusual powers, even within a society that encourages magic. For most readers, it might seem a fascinating character sketch, bolstered by Card's meticulously re-created folk rhythms in speech, his carefully researched magical practices, and his curiously off-beat references to historical characters that immediately set the story beyond the history we know.

For LDS readers, there is infinitely more to see. "Hatrack River" details the birth of a Joseph Smith-analogue; *Seventh Son* continues his life to age ten. Throughout, Card has intricately interwoven elements of Church history until they are integral parts of the narrative, but in such a way that they are not immediately apparent. In much science fiction, for example, references to gods, angels, or other supernatural beings are frequently intended metaphorically; the authors take great pains to define the intrusions as within the laws of the universe postulated, since to do otherwise would break the conventions of science fiction itself. In *Seventh Son,* Card inverts the process, using incidents, characters, and other elements to symbolize the divine. Point by point, the narrative parallels episodes of Joseph Smith's life, culminating with the well-known incident of his infected leg bone. Card borrows much from the stories that have grown up around that incident, yet he simultaneously makes *his* version seem a logical outgrowth of earlier incidents. Essentially what he has done in "Hatrack River" and *Seventh Son* is to transport Joseph Smith and the Restoration into an alternative frame; the underlying truths remain, but now Card is free to explore and extrapolate *within* the context of LDS theology and history. He has, in fact, written LDS science fiction, a novel "thick with Mormon allegory." And the novel succeeds both as literature and as religious allegory.

One of the most recent Card stories to be published is "America," appearing in *Isaac Asimov's Science Fiction Magazine* for January 1987. In this *tour de force,* Card's Mormon heritage is so important that the editorial head note refers directly to it: "Mr. Card was able to draw upon his first-hand knowledge of Brazil, where he served a mission for the Church of the Latter Day Saints [sic] from 1971 to 1973, to create this powerful story."

The story revolves around two characters: Sam Monson and Anamari Boagente. The first is a "scrawny teenager from Utah," the son of a Yanqui engineer working in the Brazilian jungle; at the end of the story, we meet him again as the governor of Deseret, "the last European state in America." She is a "middle-aged spinster," a pure-blooded Indian proud of her ancestry and contemptuous of most Europeans. Much of the story details their first meetings in the Brazilian jungle, identifying Sam Monson's hatred of his adulterous father, his fear of his dreams, and his increasingly difficult relationship with Anamari. She, on the other hand, develops a deep attachment to the Yanqui youth, even though that attachment often manifests itself in sarcasm. Yet they are inextricably linked, at first through Sam's defiance of his father's orders to stay away from the natives, then later through his dreams. He becomes her revelator, explaining the meaning of her repeated dreams of a huge bird, its unevenly sized wings brittle with corruption. Sam interprets the symbolism: the bird is America, with the wings representing the northern and southern hemispheres. The corruption represents the corruption of European cultures; the healthy places "are where the Indians still live" (40).

Unfortunately, penetrating to the truth of her dreams forces him to penetrate to the truth of his own sexual dreams, in which he couples with Anamari, the "Virgem America." Then, in a dream that merges with reality, the coupling occurs. Before, "she had been a virgin, and so had he. Now she was even purer than before, Virgem America, but his purity was hopelessly, irredeemably gone, wasted, poured out into this old woman who had haunted his dreams" (46).

Almost immediately thereafter he returns to Utah. Forty years later, they meet again, he as the governor of Deseret, she as the mother and emissary of Quetzalcoatl, the incarnation of the Aztec god; she accepts the tribute offered to the true American.

A plot summary such as this is not a particularly effective way to talk about "America," simply because on the deeper levels, the story is *not* about Sam Monson and Anamari Boagente. It is about America, but an America seen from a distinctly LDS perspective.

At first, Anamari says, the Indians knew "the god of the land." They lived with the land in harmony and the land gave them its bounty. Then they forsook the land. The Incas worshipped gold; the Aztecs defiled the land with the blood of human sacrifices; the Pueblos turned forests into desert; the Iroquois took joy in the screams of tortured enemies. They turned from true dreams to the false sleep of drugs: coffee, peyote, coca, and tobacco. And the land rejected them: "The land called to Columbus and told him lies and seduced him and he never had a chance, did he? Never had a choice. The land brought the Europeans to punish us" (44).

When Sam objects that her tale undercuts her professed Catholicism, she responds with a sentence that lies at the heart of the story: "Say *deus* or *Christo* instead of *the land* and the story is the same."

Yet the Europeans did not prosper, either. They poisoned the land with more poisons than the Indians could imagine. And now that the Indians have been punished sufficiently, the land will turn back again to them.

"It sounded so close to what the old prophets in the Book of Mormon said would happen to America," Sam realizes—but with a dangerous twist. Here Card defines the essential "what if" that defines "America" as science fiction. Given the LDS assumption about the destiny of the Americas as fundamental to the fictional world, *what if* the Europeans proved unworthy of the promises? "They would not be able to pass the land on to the next generation. Someone else would inherit. It made him sick at heart, to realize what the white man had lost, had thrown away, had torn up and destroyed" (44).

Thus Card speaks to the central issue of the story, one initiated by the title itself. As fascinating, as mythical and archetypal as Anamari may be (and her name was surely not accidental); as engaging and frightened and narrow and confused as Sam Monson is, they are not the true focus of the story. "America" is about America, the promised land. It is about the machinations the land sets in motion to insure its survival. From the single act their dreams lead Sam and Anamari to perform will come the new God, the new Quetzalcoatl to inherit the promises of the land. The Europeans will dwindle; the Indians again will prosper, recapitulating the cyclical movements so common in the Book of Mormon.

The story ends, in fact, long after the deaths of Sam and Anamari, as the narrator concludes his recollections with the words:

> ...I write this sitting in the shade of a tree on the brow of a hill, looking out across woodlands and orchards, fields and rivers and roads, where once the land was rock and grit and sagebrush. This is what America wanted, what it bent out lives to accomplish. Even if we took twisted roads and got lost or injured on the way, even if we came limping to this place, it is worth the journey, it is the promised, the promising land. (53)

Here we have an explicit statement of the focus of Card's interest: a fictional, extrapolative exploration of the assumptions of Mormonism themselves. He is not, he assures us, attempting to write prophecy of his own; rather, like most SF writers, he uses as speculative future as a milieu for telling the stories" he wants to tell (Letter, 20 February 1985).

And most recently, those stories have centered on essentially LDS themes, settings, and characters, allowing Card to write what may be among the purest examples of *LDS* science fiction as he applies rational extrapolation to a universe of revealed truth.

# LITERARY HEROISM IN THE
# WORKS OF ORSON SCOTT CARD

[This essay was presented at the Brigham Young University Symposium on Science Fiction and Fantasy: Life, the Universe, and Everything VI, Provo UT, February 4, 1988; and published in *The Leading Edge: Magazine of Science Fiction
and Fantasy* [Brigham Young University] Vol. 16 (Winter 1988): 59-69 The essay
was subsequently revised and expanded as a chapter in: Michael R. Collings. *In
the Image of God: Theme, Characterization, and Landscape in the Fiction of
Orson Scott Card.* Copyright © 1990 by Michael R. Collings. Reproduced with
permission of ABC-CLIO, LLC. The original essay is presented here, lightly revised for this volume.]

In differentiating between "science fiction" and "sci-fi," Norman
Spinrad recently argued that the essence of "sci-fi," and of all com-
mercial fiction, lies in strict adherence to a predetermined "Plot
Skeleton" that precludes character development,

> which is ultimately what almost all fiction that at-
> tempts to touch the heart and higher philosophical
> brain centers of the reader must be about. Which is
> perilously close to saying that "sci-fi" and "literature"
> are by definition antithetical. (181)

According to Spinrad's thesis, Orson Scott Card's *Ender's Game*
remains at the level of "sc-fi" largely because Card has pursued Plot
Skeleton to the detriment of character.

Elaine Radford's idiosyncratic "Ender and Hitler: Sympathy for
the Superman" similarly contends that characters in *Ender's Game*
"are constructed of the highest grade cardboard, but since Norman
Spinrad has already detailed Card's amazing lack of originality in
plot and character construction, I won't indulge in a literary hatchet
job here" (11). In spite of her denial (since she proceeds with a "literary hatchet job" nonetheless), she asserts that Card's fictions desperately lack adequate character development and thus fail as literature.

The surprising thing is not that such assessments have reached the public forum, but rather that the attacks focus, wholly or partially, on what other readers consider one of the greatest *strengths* of Card's fiction: characterization. Card himself has assessed the importance of characterization in articles such as "The Finer Points of Characterization," defining what constitutes strong characters and suggesting that his aesthetic and critical empathy lies less with modern, experimental fiction than with more traditional forms— specifically, the "romance" tradition. More to the point, perhaps, Card argues in "Fantasy and the Believing Reader" that fantasy (including science fiction as he writes it) does not lend itself to critical reading. Instead, it demands "epick" and "mythick" readings—that is, it defines the reader as a member of a community or as a member of humanity at large. Card's use of the term "epick" is important, particularly in light of his approach to character. Science fiction often incorporates remnants of earlier traditions, transformed superficially to accommodate narratives hinging on technological developments and future worlds. In a study of epic heroism, John M. Steadman discusses the attempts of Renaissance poets to imbue their heroes "not only with the martial arms of classical and romantic worthies but also with the moral and theological virtues of the Christian knight" (*Paradoxes*, 3). To a degree, Steadman's concerns parallel Card's, who speaks as an LDS science fiction writer to a community that includes, at the opposite extreme, the anti-heroic impulses of the cyberpunks.

Spinrad and Radford argue that Card's characterization is flawed, yet my experience in reading Card's novels suggests the opposite. Of the conventional elements of fiction, characterization seems in fact the most fully developed. In spite of Card's longstanding love affair with maps and map-making, for example, setting often seems merely plausible rather than a reflection of the intricate world-creation one finds in J. R. R. Tolkien or Frank Herbert. Novels such as *Capitol* or *A Planet Called Treason* rely in part upon setting, but this concern lessens in later novels. *Ender's Game* shows little overt concern for the physics of the Battle School; in *Speaker for the Dead,* the town, the forest, and indeed the world seem as much metaphorical as actual. Yet this is not a failing in the narratives. In most instances, a few well-placed brush strokes of detail sufficiently create the setting Card's narratives require.

Much the same might be said of plot. In *Ender's Game,* for example, the essential conflict is implicit in the Stilson episode of the opening pages; the remainder of the story clarifies the relationships between Ender and his world. *Speaker for the Dead, Wyrms,* and the Alvin Maker tales incorporate carefully woven plot lines, but again,

the final sense is less of plot manipulating character than of characters making inevitable, often irrevocable, decisions on the basis of
who and what they are.

This does not argue a flaw in either conception or execution in
Card's fiction. Instead, it asserts that he is aware of an area in which
he excels, perhaps because of his extensive background in theatre,
certainly because of his concern for the primacy of character. This in
turn leads to an approach in Card's novels that not only disputes the
conclusions of critics such as Spinrad and Radford, but also argues
that they have in fact inverted an important direction in Card's fiction. In a genre that emphasizes an ever-changing, futuristic orientation, the best-novel Hugo and Nebula awards for 1986 and 1987
went to books that were, in one essential element at least, conservative and traditional. In *Ender's Game* and *Speaker for the Dead,*
Card presents a traditional hero. He looks back over the centuries to
restate, in a science-fictional format, the "Hero Monomyth," a paradigm for heroism that recurs in the literature of virtually every human culture. The pattern incorporates eight specific stages:

1. *Miraculous conception and birth,* including the
   hiding of the new-born child—a motif familiar
   through the Incarnation of Christ but also having
   parallels in classical, Norse, and Egyptian mythology, as well as in the tales of Quetzalcoatl among
   the Aztecs;
2. *Initiation of the hero-child,* often resulting in (or
   from) his displaying unusual knowledge, as when
   Christ instructed the teachers in the Temple;
3. *Withdrawal from family or community for meditation and preparation,* often accompanied by the
   hero's refusal to submit to temptation;
4. *Trial and Quest,* the "agony and rewards of adult
   life," with the quest either for an object—such as
   Gilgamesh's search for the secret to immortality,
   Jason's for the Golden Fleece, or Percival's for the
   Holy Grail—or to complete an action, as in the stories of Hercules, Faust, and Christ;
5. *Death,* often as miraculous or unusual as his birth.
   As David A. Leeming argues, "In death, the hero
   acts, psychologically, for all of us: he becomes a
   scapegoat for our fear and our guilt";
6. *Descent into the underworld,* during which the hero

confronts the reality of death and attempts to over-
turn it;

7. *Resurrection and rebirth,* a logical culmination of
   confronting death as well as the completion of the
   quest. The hero "overcomes death physically and is
   united with the natural cycle of birth, death, and
   rebirth";

8. *Ascension, apotheosis, and atonement,* through
   which the hero is "taken out of the cycle and
   placed in a permanent state in relation to the cosmos and to the creator-father god." (Leeming, *Mythology,* 6-8)

Within the Christian tradition, Christ fulfills all eight stages of the
paradigm, a logical discovery in light of his role as mediator between humanity and God. In actual practice, however, heroic figures
may not necessarily complete the full paradigm; in order to share the
mythic, archetypal strengths of the hero, the character need experience only some of the stages. According to Donald M. Burleson, "It
is generally significant to find even half of these things in any one
account" (174). As defined by scholars of mythology and literary
symbolism, the paradigm enables us to penetrate to the depths of the
human soul. Leeming introduces his collection of epic and heroic
tales by arguing that "Myth is as real as human concerns are real. It
is when we lose our ability to feel the mythic that we lose contact
with that which is most basically and universally human. In a real
sense a society loses its soul when it can no longer experience myth"
(*Mythology,* 5).

In his novels, Card restores the "soul" of humanity by recasting
traditional elements of archetypal heroism into new forms while retaining the essential outlines of the paradigm. Beginning with *Capitol* and its intriguing figure of Jason Worthing and continuing
through the Alvin Miller tales (in "Hatrack River," for example,
with the miraculous birth of the hero, and in *Red Prophet* with Alvin's withdrawal into the wilderness and preparation for future action), Card consistently draws central characters who meet at least
half of the eight characteristics required. Several—including Lanik
Mueller in *A Planet Called Treason* and Orem Scanthips in *Hart's
Hope*—meet six or seven. The most complete example of heroic development, however, occurs in *Ender's Game.* Ender Wiggin fulfills
all eight stages of the monomyth; then, as if to emphasize Ender as
an archetypal hero, Card repeats the cycle almost in its entirety in
*Speaker for the Dead.* Adding a further level of complexity, *Ender's*

*Game* and *Speaker for the Dead* move the hero partially through a third cycle which will presumably culminate with the as-yet-unwritten *Ender's Children.*

In *Ender's Game,* we meet Andrew Wiggin and immediately understand the unusual nature of his birth—he is a "Third," a third child in a society that allows only two. Even more unusual, his birth was mandated by the government, setting in motion ripples of guilt from his lapsed-Catholic father and lapsed-Mormon mother. They see in Ender not only a breaking of their vows not to have more than two children but also an image of their own deeply hidden need to multiply and replenish the earth. He becomes a constant accusation of their failure of faith *(Ender's Game,* 23). From the beginning, he is different, set apart.

The novel's action begins with Ender's initiation. Deprived of his monitor, a device which allows protective surveillance, he is thrust into a situation in which he must demonstrate his ability to function without external support. Again and again, this motif repeats as Ender learns about his powers and is consequently (and constantly) introduced to higher levels of awareness. This sense of repetition is important in the novel, since Card treats the Hero Monomyth with greater complexity and sophistication than merely following a straight-line pattern. Instead, he allows the elements to interweave, to double back, to create layers of cycles within cycles, all leading to the ultimate resolution in the final chapter. This process is particularly evident in the intermediate stages of the Monomyth: withdrawal leading to trial and quest. Again, what we see is not single-minded adherence to a predetermined pattern but rather a series of increasingly wider circles composed of multiple manifestations of Trial and Quest. Every cycle, more serious and wider-reaching than the last, begins with Ender's search for acceptance as an individual and as part of a clearly defined community—something that, as a Third, he was denied.

In effect, Ender is isolated from the beginning, a situation defined overtly in the opening dialogue, as disembodied voices dictate that the child must be "surrounded" by enemies at all times (1). He is removed from a mother and father who love him, but distantly; from an older brother who threatens to destroy him physically or (worse) psychologically and emotionally; and from a sister whose love runs to the opposite extreme. She threatens to subvert his strength through gentleness. Ender's emotional ties must be severed, because to save humanity—and himself—Ender must first act as an individual. He must make an adult-level decision without the traditional ties and background that would allow him to do so. As a result of his first interview with Graff, Ender assumes the most generalized quest-level in the novel: saving humanity from the Bugger invasion.

To do so requires that he relinquish what fragmentary personal identity he has attained. He leaves his parents' house, and leaves behind everything demonstrably *his,* including his name; for the rest of the novel, he is "Ender" instead of "Andrew," the saint's name his parents chose. He has effectively been removed from the normal circuits of human society. But he does not yet understand what that means, just as he does not yet comprehend the extent of his own powers. Thus Card initiates a series of increasingly expansive quest-cycles, each repeating in miniature the essential movement of the Monomyth. The Launchies provide a partial substitute for Ender's severed relationships. Through his handling of crises—Bernard's antagonism in particular—Ender defines new communities that include himself. The chapter detailing Ender's first fully successful interaction with the Launchies ends with an image of community: Ender and Shen "laughed together, and two other Launchies joined them. Ender's isolation was over. The war was just beginning" (57). The last statement is true, just as the one preceding it is, in light of the rest of the narrative, false—Ender's true isolation has just begun. By forging relationships with the Launchies, he has merely impelled himself to the next stages of isolation, into an almost tribal structure, with Ender as an authority figure. He experiences empathy for those just like him and understands more fully the cruel necessities behind certain adult behavior. His first actions as commander of Dragon Army recapitulate his own experiences as Launchie, but in reverse. He subjects Bean to the same stress he endured, realizing that precisely that sort of opposition will bring Bean to his full potential and thus enlarge Ender's potentials as a leader.

As Card traces Ender's experiences, he also allows Ender opportunities for withdrawal, meditation, and preparation, primarily through the device of the Giant's Game. The game functions as a metaphor for Ender's psychological development, for those times when he retreats into himself in order to understand internally what is happening externally. His entering the game often signals a transition between stages, as he learns to rely on his internal responses for strength and understanding.

As the tension intensifies, Ender is forced to struggle toward yet a larger community identity for himself and for his soldiers as Dragons. But as before, the adults refuse to let him remain on the plane of static acceptance within the community; they change the rules, so that each victory merely establishes new parameters for a subsequent challenge.

Ultimately, Ender is forced into denial. With the decimation of Dragon Army, beginning with Bean's transfer to the command of Rabbit, Ender refuses to fight "I don't care about their game anymore," he says, consciously distancing himself from "them" and from the "game" that has thus far given the novel its title (242). He threatens to move too far from the community, to divorce himself too completely from responsibility for others.

The immediate consequence of this threat is that Ender is returned briefly to Earth. Graff's purpose in taking Ender to Earth is explicit: in order to want to save humanity, Ender must feel *part* of humanity, a feeling that has largely disappeared during his training. Graff must ensure that Ender reconnects to the world from which the adults have systematically isolated him. Graff returns Ender to his earliest ties in his meeting with Valentine and in his immersion in the bowl of sky, the lake, the landing.

All of this—roughly three-quarters of the text of *Ender's Game*—prepares for the Final Quest on behalf of humanity. Ender becomes anew a member of the human community but shares almost no personal ties with others. On Eros, those surrounding him become disembodied voices speaking to him, listening to him, urging him onward. The one exception is the Mentor-figure of Mazer Rackham, who alone has preceded Ender on the quest and who alone can give him knowledge and understanding. Mazer attained partial victory in Ender's quest but fell short of completely understanding himself, the enemy, and the requirements of battle. Mazer can only point Ender along the way; ultimately, Ender must move beyond everyone else and act on his own.

Eros provides the setting for the final permutation in the series of cycles that constitutes Ender's development as a heroic figure. With the destruction of the Bugger home world, Ender both refuses to participate further in the adult-imposed "games" *and* culminates his quest: the defeat of the Buggers and the salvation of humanity. In a deeper sense, Ender has completed his bonding with Earth and humanity: "He saw Graff and remembered the woods outside Greensboro, and wanted to go home. Take me home, he said silently to Graff. In my dream you said you loved me. Take me home" (319).

With Ender's final "game," the quest stage of his development—and the level of plot resolution demanded of generic, formulaic "sci-fi"—reaches completion. The Earth has been saved; the alien invaders, destroyed. If Ender were simply a Heinleinian juvenile hero, the action of the novel would close at this point.

But Card's purposes run deeper than the superficiality of "sci-fi." At the moment of triumph, Ender collapses. In archetypal terms, his collapse constitutes the Death of the Hero. He sleeps in darkness for five days, enduring a complex of dreams that recapitulates his life and makes sense of the specter of death that has haunted him. Although short—barely over one page—the episode suggests a state distinguishable from life. Here Ender passes what "might have been a single day; it might have been a week, from his dreams it could have been months. He seemed to pass through lifetimes in his dreams" (331).

During this state Ender figuratively descends into the Underworld to discover the key to life. On a subconscious level, he works through his guilt as images of love and hate, victory and defeat, and life and death blend to sharpen his awareness. This episode effects his transformation from "sci-fi" hero to archetypal Hero:

> And always the dream ended with a mirror or a pool
> of water or the metal surface of a ship, something that
> would reflect his face back to him. At first it was al-
> ways Peter's face, with blood and a snake's tail com-
> ing from the mouth. After a while, though, it began to
> be his own face, old and sad, with eyes that grieved
> for a billion, billion murders—but they were his own
> eyes, and he was content to wear them. (331)

At least one reviewer has disparaged. the treatment of the League War, in which Card focuses on this dream-state and allows the war itself to be reported later by messenger (a motif echoing Greek tragedy). However, the emphasis parallels Card's overall approach to characterization. Ender's internal struggle is more critical than the external, 'political maneuverings of unstable Terran states. His return to life and light signals his rebirth; in the terminology of the Monomyth, Ender is resurrected from his death-like dream-state into full awareness of his new relationship with, and responsibilities for, humanity and the Buggers.

The final chapter, appropriately titled "Speaker for the Dead," opens without the isolated adult-human dialogue that characterizes the preceding fourteen; for the first time, Ender's awareness of external events is placed on a par with that of Graff, Anderson, and the others who have been manipulating his life. Although there are still elements of manipulation, Ender is now fully aware of them. He accepts Valentine's challenge and literally ascends into space; he parallels that act with a figurative ascension as governor of a new human community. At twelve years of age, he stands at the apex of a community such as he has struggled throughout to achieve acceptance in. But little is said about his governorship, since it is the least important element of his transformation. To the extent that he functions as governor, he is still within the circle of humanity, and so *Ender's Game* must conclude with his excision from that circle and apotheosis into the "Speaker for the Dead." The new title itself suggests something beyond the human—a "Voice from the Dust," with theological, LDS overtones implicit in title as well as in the image of a book revealing the truths of a lost people. In this final chapter, the discovery of the Hive-Queen allows Ender to make restitution for the error imposed "on him by a fearful and ignorant adult world. He becomes the Savior-figure, not simply politically for his *own* species, but literally for the aliens he destroyed.

In terms of Ender's development through a [proposed] trilogy of novels, it is significant that by the beginning of *Speaker for the Dead* the name "Ender" has become associated with the military "victory," while Ender's efforts in attaining the second, greater "victory" (i.e., writing his two books of "scripture," *The Hive-Queen* and *The Hegemon*) establish him as "Something of a savior, or prophet, or at least a martyr" (88). With the final line of *Ender's Game*, Ender is effectively "taken out of the cycle" of humanity, a process which culminates his transition into an archetypal hero. However, the process continues in *Speaker for the Dead*, becoming analogous to the withdrawal stage of an even larger mythic pattern and ending, perhaps, with Ender's decision to remain on Lusitania, subjecting himself for the first time to the inevitability of a normal life span and literal death.

The centrality of the Hero Monomyth in *Ender's Game* is evident. What is equally important is that the same paradigm recurs in almost every Card novel. Jason Worthing in *Capitol, Hot Sleep,* and preeminently in *The Worthing Chronicle* mirrors the archetype, from the oddities of his birth as the son of a Swipe to his centuries-long sleep/death and resurrection as a god-figure restoring his children to the truth of their heritage. In *A Planet Called Treason,* Lanik Mueller may not have had a miraculous birth, but he clearly fulfills the remaining stages; the final chapters are among Card's clearest portrayals of human deification. *Songmaster*'s Ansset moves from foundling and apprentice songbird to Galactic Emperor, to a figurative death as he returns to Songhouse, and finally to apotheosis through literal death in the High Room of the Songhouse. In *Hart's Hope,* Orem Scanthips similarly moves from miraculous birth through trial and quest, although Card truncates the pattern, closing the novel just prior to the possible death of the hero. Even here, however, the paradigm re-emerges in the final paragraph:

> Did you think this was the tale of Orem Scanthips? His tale was finished when Youth died. In Orem's short life, he has already earned his name: Hart's Hope. (261)

*Wyrms* similarly includes elements of archetypal heroism as it explores the prophesy that the seventh seventh seventh Heptarch will be the Kristos, the savior of the world. Written in the semi-allegorical mode Card had mastered in *Hart's Hope, Wyrms* recounts the transition of the heroine, through the mediation of Will and Ruin, from Patience to King. The novel concludes with an image of eternity as Agranthemen Heptek and others make annual pilgrimages to the Mother Wyrm, where they "listened to her wisdom and received her love and joy. So also did their children, and their children's children, through all the ages of the world" (263).

Even in their unfinished state, the *Tales of Alvin Maker* represent even more clearly the development of the archetype, with the first two volumes defining the miraculous birth and childhood, initiation, and withdrawal and preparation of the hero for his ultimate confrontation with the Unmaker and the fulfillment of his vision of the Crystal City in *Red Prophet.*

Throughout his works, Card consistently focuses on character in conflict: his characters suffer great pain, they are placed in true jeopardy, and they are larger than life ("Finer Points" II, 37-38). But even more importantly, they transcend the narrow limits of romantic heroism to approach the level of mythic archetypal heroism that allows them to transcend the equally narrow limits of their individual narratives and speak not only for themselves but. ultimately, for all humanity.

# THE STORY THAT
# BINDS THEM TOGETHER:

## ORSON SCOTT CARD'S *THE FOLK OF THE FRINGE* AND THE STRUCTURE OF THE MEDIEVAL MYSTERY CYCLES

[This essay was presented the Brigham Young University Symposium on Science Fiction and Fantasy, "Life, the Universe, and Everything IX," Provo UT, February 8, 1991; and subsequently presented in a much revised form to the Philological Association of the Pacific Coast, 89th Annual Conference, Las Vegas NV, November 16, 1991. It appears in print here for the first time.]

In the "Author's Note" to *The Folk of the Fringe,* Orson Scott Card acknowledges his debt to the art of dramatic pageantry in creating what he calls the "original story" of the collection, "the one at the root of all the others and…the hardest to write" (295):

> Ironically, after I signed the contract for the book that would contain "Pageant Wagon," I was asked to write the new script for the Mormon Church's Hill Cumorah Pageant, the oldest and best and most resonant of the Church's pageants. It was a mark of great trust in me, and I spent the winter of 1987 working on nothing else. The result was a script that I was proud of, given the institutional needs and pressures that must shape such a work. I also came to understand far more clearly just what such a pageant is for, how it feeds the hunger of a community; if I had not written *America's Witness for Christ*, the real Hill Cumorah Pageant, I could not have written *Glory of America*, the mini-pageant that is performed in "Pageant Wagon." (297)

Far from remaining a "satirical yet powerful fifteen minute pageant that would be a commentary on the self-congratulatory pageants that Mormons are wont to put on" (296), the pageant-within-a-story grew in scope and complexity until it formed a nucleus for five independent but interlinked stories. As the idea was transformed from sketches toward a musical comedy to narrative, it also seems to have undergone a metamorphosis of intention. The story becomes not only a story about such pageants but also a representation *of* such a pageant. Thus even though events in "Pageant Wagon" are occasionally peripheral to the stories of earlier characters, they are central to an underlying theme in *The Folk of the Fringe*—a collection of stories that, taken together, creates a verbal pageant of faith, survival, and regeneration.

Card implies that the Aals' rickety flatbed truck fulfills more important functions than just transporting an itinerant acting company through an inhospitable land. The truck is a vehicle for salvation: first when the company physically rescues Carpenter in "The Fringe"; again when it rescues Teague physically and spiritually in "Pageant Wagon"; and finally when it becomes a nexus for community and cultural salvation.

Bearing its advertisement for "Sweetwater's Miracle Pageant" the truck links Card's stories to a central dramatic forms of the Middle Ages, the Mystery Cycles—extended sequences of interrelated plays performed during the fourteenth and fifteenth Centuries in England. When Card's characters describe *their* presentation, they blend medieval and contemporary terminology: "We who travel in, on, and around this truck are minstrels of the open road. Madrigals and jesters, thespians and dramaturges, the second-rate sophoclean substitute for NBC, CBS, ABC, and, may the Lord forgive us, PBS" (148). When Deaver Teague comments that they are "Show gypsies," the actors' reactions indicate that he has misunderstood their definition of the company: "Ollie's father winced and Ollie snapped off the inside light and the truck sped up, rattling more than ever. Maybe they were mad because they knew all the stories that got told about show gypsies, and they figured Deaver was being snide when he said "*pageant* wagon" like that" (149).

It seems more likely, however, that the Aals are reacting to their perception that they were more than just Show gypsies, that Sweetwater's Miracle Show is more than an itinerant pageant. Even though the company is troubled by marginally corrupt, frequently antagonistic suspicious city officials, by an unsavory reputation (at least partially undeserved), and by having to travel from town to town, their show is a powerful force for community. Their pageant,

*Glory of America,* helps bond the fragmented society around the Mormon Sea (Great Salt Lake). They travel under the commission of the Prophet; and, as Deaver Teague discovers, their calling exceeds mere entertainment. The company is to define and re-unify a ravaged community: "For a while tonight [the audience] saw and heard and felt the same things. And now they'd carry away the same memories, which meant that to some degree they were the same person. One" (215).

The medieval Mystery Cycles (also referred to as 'miracle' plays) fulfilled a similar role in their societies. W. A. Davenport discusses the plays as celebrations of shared religious ceremonial occasions, employing extensive dramatic performances of plays that "told the Christian story, from the Creation of the World to the Last Judgment, in a series of short tableaux with dialogue" (1-2). Such plays were commonly presented by guildsmen on traveling stage-wagons—originally called simply *pageants*—that wound through the streets of Coventry or York or other centers. The plays had theological as well as entertainment value in recreating human history from beginning to end, but "the coverage of the ages of history and the ages of mankind is selective and spare enough for one to see the patterns forming" (Davenport 127). Through these patterns, the plays instruct and edify by defining the parameters of Christian life, by blending literal history with the "interpretation of History through Christian faith. So myth and prophecy join the chronicle of ancient times, as they do in the Bible, to form a complete account of life from the Creation of the World to the Last Judgment of men" (Davenport 4).

Nearly all of the academic discussions of the Mystery/Miracle Cycles emphasize that the cycles display a unity that transcends the meanings of individual plays. According to Martin Stevens, for example, the Corpus Christi cycles were "not so many interchangeable structures built to carry out the same function, but carefully constructed frameworks that, like cathedrals, have about them a unique beauty and understanding not only of the subject that they all have more or less in common but also of the way in which they make that subject come alive in each of their dramatic settings" (11).

Human existence is portrayed as part of an overriding pattern; human history becomes a revelation of divine intention. Variations on the Creation, Fall, Redemption, and Judgment provide the surface content of the plays, but beneath that lie more critical functions. The Mystery Cycles established "the patterns of correspondence, the forecasts of the future and the echoes of the past, the symbolic prefigurings of the role of Christ, the fulfillment of the pre-known destiny" (Davenport 127) essential to medieval Christianity.

A similar purpose underlies Card's "Pageant Wagon." Called by the Prophet (157, 179), Aal's troupe entertains the people of a dark, hostile land. Their arrival is a parade; their performance, a public highlight. They may (and perhaps other pageants do) leave behind them a "string of pregnant virgins and empty chicken coops" (149)[*], but that does not invalidate their primary function: to Name, and by Naming to consolidate. As Deaver says to Katie after the performance of *Glory of America,* "I saw you take an audience and turn them into one person, with one soul" (218). That soul is the surviving American soul, the Mormon soul that has endured in spite of nuclear bombs that create the Mormon Sea, in spite of pogroms and hatred and bigotry, in spite of a lifestyle that is brutal and demanding and unforgiving.

In spite of everything, *Glory of America* asserts that the essential spirit of the people endures. When, near the end of the pageant, 'Betsy Ross' stands alone in the spotlight and asks of the American flag, "Does it still wave?" (214), the audience responds as one. For that moment (and subsequent moments, until the experience fades into memory) the people *are* one. Katie disparages the company's dramatic achievements; the actors are, she contends, merely repeating memorized lines. But Deaver is uniquely both part of the pageant and part of the audience. He can see the play's effect on the audience and can understand it more completely than Katie because for the first time he feels the emergent sense of community. He sees the joy that transforms a bitter, petty functionary into a smiling father and husband (215).

Perhaps because "Pageant Wagon" was conceived as a musical comedy, the pageant's effect on Deaver and its fictional audience may spill over into the reader as well. The play is, as Katie is aware, only marginally *drama.* The history it reproduces is questionable; its characters, wooden and stereotypical. But those are precisely the strategies that made the Mystery Cycles effective, if not as drama then as statements of a culture. Davenport's description of the cycles

---

[*] Note the recurrence of the "pregnant virgin" as a primary motif in "America," although without the obvious satirical content. Deaver Teague cannot believe in such things; the term is an oxymoron that justifies his ironic, distanced approach to religion, belief, and humanity. In "America," the term is used consciously (by Card, and through him, by Anamari Boagente) with all of its Christic, mythic resonances. As with the Mystery Cycles, one story foreshadows, another echoes.

can stand almost unaltered as a description of Card's *Glory of America* as well:

> Many of the named historical figures in the cycles are represented simply as 'tableau' figures and given the speeches necessary for them to fulfill their function in unfolding the story. But some figures were far more developed and the main method of development was to use historical instances as exemplification of moral ideas. This is one main way in which the bare material of Scripture was expanded, so that in the individual example one saw the types of mankind. Hence Herod becomes the type of the ranting tyrant, boasting of worldly power, and brought down as punishment for pride; Pilate becomes a more complex version of the holder of power, because he holds in trust worldly justice as well as worldly command." (7)

Hence we see America's "bumbling fool of a President" and "the evil Soviet tyrant" in the Aals' pageant, both threatening to "out-Herod Herod" or "out-Pilate Pilate." In their nearly slapstick interchange, Card defines the critical human types that lead to holocausts. In the abrupt transition from comedy to tragedy that prefigures the end of old America and the beginning of the new, a third character enters. The most heroic range rider in the ravaged lands around the Mormon Sea, Royal Aal (Marshall Aal's estranged brother) defies history and strides onto the stage: "Then he reached down to the President's body—to lift him up? No. To draw out of his costume the gold and green beehive flag of Deseret" (213). Type reveals truth; pageant becomes reality: "This time the flag rose slowly; the anthem of Deseret began to play. Anyone who wasn't standing stood now, and the crowd sang along with the music, more and more voices, spontaneously becoming part of the show" (213).

The essence of America has been re-defined, and with it the essence of Mormonism: "George Washington, Betsy Ross, Joseph Smith, Abraham Lincoln, Brigham Young, all part of the same unfolding tale. Their own past" (211). In spite of the weaknesses and failings Card details throughout "West," "Salvage," and "The Fringe," the essence remains, like the prayers inscribed on crumpled bits of metal and carried into the submerged depths of the Salt Lake Temple. The surface structures may have been damaged, even in part destroyed; but the essence remains.

"Pageant Wagon," then, is what it describes. It is the story of a near-future analogue to the Miracle plays, of a stage wagon that travels from point to point bringing entertainment and spectacle into difficult lives, and that at the same time binds actors and audience into a unity of belief and story and community. And, like the great Mystery Cycles, that story is only one episode in a larger pageant, Card's verbal pageant of the essence of faith and endurance.

There are good reasons to consider Card's approach in *The Folk of the Fringe* as at least as closely analogous to the medieval cycles as to contemporary, more narrowly focused pageants such as *America's Witness for Christ,* a commemoration of the Book of Mormon and its place in Mormon belief, celebrated annually near Palmyra, New York. Considered as an independent story, "Pageant Wagon" evaluates such pageants while simultaneously presenting one. In a sense, the story *is* such a pageant. Readers are invited not only to share Deaver Teague's responses to it, but to assess their own responses as well. "Pageant Wagon" is only one story of five, however; and even within the confines of the story, *Glory of America* is at best only one element in a complex drama of relationships.

"Pageant Wagon" is, according to Card's account, the "root" story of the collection. Beyond the meaning and value of its own narrative, however, "Pageant Wagon" also defines a mode by which to read *The Folk of the Fringe.* It ties the other stories together by defining the framework upon which they are assembled; it instructs readers in how to approach the sequence of stories…as a pageant, a series of tableaux that at times seems more tapestry than recitation of human actions. In speaking of the Mystery Cycles, Davenport writes that their form is essentially

> episodic and panoramic. The short pageants are complete in themselves, but they depend for their logic on what precedes and follows; on the other hand, the contents of the cycle could vary, from year to year, without the essential idea of the "play" being harmed. The pieces of the mosaic are organized by an all-over simple structural design, consisting of beginning (Creation and Fall), middle (Incarnation), and end (Redemption and Judgment). (5)

Similarly, *The Folk of the Fringe* could easily have been told with alternate tales. Card admits as much when he talks about episodes for "West" that were conceived before he had fully developed his central character (294-295), or when he says that he could have published "Pageant Wagon" in an earlier version. But more importantly, *The Folk of the Fringe* is structurally "cyclical and panoramic." The culminating tale, "America," surrounds and encompasses the other episodes; it is at once the first (chronologically) and the last (sequentially) of the stories Card chooses to tell. Other stories depend on it and on each other for interwoven threads that clarify and define. And ultimately they fit into Cards own mosaic of Beginning, Middle, and End.

"West" is a paradoxical story of Creation and Expulsion from Eden. In this case, *creation* is ironic, since the new (in the form of Card's small group of Mormon survivors) rises from the ashes of the old America. "West" is a story about order and stability in conflict with disorder and instability that reaches from the individual to encompass and disintegrate first the family (as in Jamie Teague's life history) and finally society as a whole. In a world where everything has changed, only one constant remains: the Promise of Zion in the Salt Lake Basin. The group's goal is never in doubt, not even when they reach the seductive haven of Jamie Teague's Blue Ridge cabin. As an image of a new paradise, the mountains invite; but the focus of "West" is implicit in its title. In spite of the temptations to remain, the group moves west, toward Zion, with their "hired" guide. He guides them physically through the eastern mountains, but more critically they guide him spiritually through the accumulated guilt of a ravaged childhood. By accepting their openness he accepts their love; that love brings him into unity with himself and with others.

By the end of "West," the new world is clearly in focus. The small party is met by outriders from the flooded Salt Lake Valley and brought to the new capitol city, Zarahemla. Incorporated into Mormon Sea society, each of the characters finds a place, while retaining a sense of group unity: "Being the sole company ever to come in from the Greensboro massacre, that gave them a story that bound them together" (83). In this way, "West" becomes a story of creation—creation of trust, of faith, of life, of health and understanding, and of love in the ruins of a world destroyed by their opposites.

"Salvage" parallels the Mystery plays based on Noah and the flood. Like those plays, it represents a world drowned as a consequence of its own sin and error. Like the antediluvian world, that world is also dead, a point that Deaver Teague recognizes more instinctively than those still obsessed with resurrecting the material remains of the past (88). In spite of his cynicism, however, Teague (the only character from "West" who did not fit into Mormon Sea society) is desperately searching for something; and he believes he has found it in rumors of gold hidden in the flooded Salt Lake Temple. The temple becomes the focus of his faith, just as it has always been and continues to be the focus of the "epick" of Mormonism.[*] In it he will find the life he desires:

> It was down there, waiting for him; the future, a chance to get something better for himself and his two friends. Maybe a plot of ground in the south where it was warmer and the snow didn't pile up five feet deep every winter, where it wasn't rain in the sky and lake everywhere else you looked. A place where he could live for a very long time and look back and remember good times with his friends, *that was all waiting down under the water.* (99-100; italics added)

In this flooded world, Teague undergoes painful lessons on the nature of faith and belief. Finding the true treasure that the flooded temple preserves—the prayers of the faithful, inscribed on bits of metal—he realizes how completely outcast he is from society around the Mormon Sea. He is the only one who does not know that the temple is still the center of the Faith, that its story is part of the epic of the people it serves. For him, the flood waters of the Mormon Sea are merely the physical symbol of a barrier he can never pass. He feels pain for his two Mormon friends: "They still lived in the drowned city, they belonged down there, and the fact they couldn't go there broke their hearts. But not Deaver. His city wasn't even built yet. His city was tomorrow" (108). After the flood come dreams of new beginnings.

"The Fringe" is Incarnational. Its central character is the crippled Carpenter, condemned by palsy to a computerized wheelchair. He is one of Card's many Christic characters. Thematically and imagistically, he is the Carpenter who brings justice and mercy to a desert land. He is the teacher, the interpreter of the law who speaks harsh truths in simple parables. He voluntarily leaves the haven of the University to save the children of the Fringe. He communicates only through his computer terminal, but, as even his tormenters recog-

---

[*] For a definition of Card's use of "epick" as a distinctive critical term, see his "Fantasy and the Believing Reader" *Science Fiction Review* (August 1982): 45-50.

nize, his power is the power of the Word (123).

Card's description and authorial comment force us to see Carpenter as Christic. Carpenter's rigid, palsy-twisted body stretches "across his wheelchair like a mocking crucifix" (118). Like Card's Christic Shepherd in "Kingsmeat," he makes difficult decisions for the highest good of the community and accepts the consequences for himself: "I will bear what I must bear, as well—the grief, the resentment, and the rage of the few families I have harmed for the sake of the rest" (121). Attacked by the sons of the men he accused of selling black market wheat, he refuses to defend himself. He refuses even to speak. As they lower his chair into a wash, knowing that it will soon channel a flash flood that will kill the crippled teacher, he still does not speak. He struggles to retain key truths: "Children are innocent in the eyes of God, Carpenter reminded himself. He tried to believe that these boys didn't know what they were doing to him" (126)—in other words, "Forgive them, for they know not what they do."

Left to die, Carpenter faces his private Golgotha. He re-lives decisions and re-defines values that will probably lead to his death. When he is rescued by the Aals and brought back to town in their pageant wagon, he refuses to identify his assailants, understanding that they will pay sufficiently through their own guilt. His justice is tempered with ironic mercy, and the story ends oppressively as Carpenter watches one of the boys walking away, the wind catching at his jacket as if he were a kite:

> But it wasn't true. The boy didn't rise and fly. And now Carpenter saw the wind like a current down the village street, sweeping Pope away. All the bodies in the world, caught in that same current, that same wind, blown down the same rivers, the same streets, and finally coming to rest on some snag, through some door, in some grave, God knows where or why. (137)

Carpenter has shown them the path; they must choose for themselves to follow it.

"Pageant Wagon" suggests a middle ground. It deals explicitly with the issue of living in a fallen world. It defines family, community, and belonging, not so much theologically as culturally and socially. The Deaver Teague rescued as a child by the pioneer party in "West," and who later tries to fill an inner emptiness by diving for gold in the flooded temple, here finally discovers the thing he has been searching for. The story is complex, as are all the family relationships among the Aals. Card touches on all levels of emotional involvement: love, hate, fear, hope, greed, ambition, lust, forgiveness. The story functions most clearly, however, in suggesting the *possibility* of community and unity. If Carpenter's cruel but necessary actions divide a town and destroy families, Teague works in the opposite direction. He unifies. Through him a diseased family is brought to the possibility of health; an angry young man is shown an outlet for a rage he can neither define nor control. And most important, Deaver Teague receives a final sense of identity. In a dream, he sees his mother and hears her speak his real name, a name he has not remembered since the mobbers killed his family and he was found by Jamie Teague. As he wakes, the dream-image of his mother's face merges with the reality of Katie Aal's, and "when he shaped his true name with silent lips, he knew that it wasn't true anymore. It was the name of a little boy who got lost somewhere and was never found again. Instead he murmured the name he had spent his life earning" (239). In healing others, he has been healed. As Lillian Marks Heldreth comments "Because Card does not deal in cynical endings, life begins to work itself out for Deaver, but because Card is not a Pollyanna, everyone is not made blissfully happy, either— just enabled to go on living relatively productive lives" (52).

"America" is admittedly a 'fantasy' in the sense that Card does not try to provide scientific, extrapolative explanations for what can only be interpreted as dreams, omens, and prophecies. Yet it is critical to the collection and to its sense that "there was a purpose behind all the loss and suffering" (239). It deals with Last Things: Redemption and Judgment. It narrates the culmination of America's Promise and the reversion of that promise to the Indians, now that the Europeans (including most of the remaining Mormons) have proven incapable of living up to the Land's expectations and demands. On the surface, "America" seems to be about sexuality and repression, guilt and punishment. Beneath that surface, however, lies an extraordinary vision of a Promised Land capable of sending dreams that lead to its own fulfillment, of moving human actors across the stage as it needs and desires. The story consciously layers itself (and thereby the preceding stories) with the stuff of myth and legend, as both the narrator (Carpenter) and the characters are themselves fully aware. And, no matter how else it might be read, it culminates the dramatic sequence of *The Folk of the Fringe* with the narrative of God's judgments on the land—and the culture—that Card has defined and explored throughout.

Each of the stories in *The Folk of the Fringe* is complex, sophisticated, and engaging; as Heldreth concludes, "These are good stories. Enjoy, whether you are Catholic, Baptist, Quaker, Mormon, or Zen Buddhist" (52). Each manifests the power of Card's storytelling. Beyond that, however, the collection presents an intriguing parallel to and analogue of the purposes, structures, and emotional and spiritual effects of the great Mystery Cycles. Card's tales create, people, develop, unify, and finally judge a fictional world; but in doing so, they fulfill similar functions for two distinctive communities that do exist. *The Folk of the Fringe* creates a verbal pageant that gives imaginative life to the essential ideals of America and of Mormonism.

# ORSON SCOTT CARD
# AND MYTHOPOEIC FICTION

[This essay was presented as "Orson Scott Card: An Approach to Mythopoeic Fiction," the Guest of Honor Speech to Mythcon XXVI, Berkeley CA, August 5, 1995; it was published as "Orson Scott Card: An Approach to Mythopoeic Fiction. Guest of Honor Speech: Mythopoeic Conference XXVI." *Mythlore*, Issue 81 (Summer 1996): 36-43, 50-51; and subsequently expanded as an Appendix to *Storyteller: The Official Orson Scott Card Bibliography and Guide* (Woodstock GA: Overlook Connection Press, 2001), 441-461.].

Occasionally my own not-yet-forgotten undergraduate training in semantics surfaces to remind me of the importance of definition, particularly of words we all assume we understand. A word such as *Mythopoeic* is open to a variety of definitions, to say nothing of the even more elusive word *fantasy,* a word that may be, as the bibliographer E. F. Bleiler writes, "almost all things to all men" (Manlove, 1). Even narrowing the field to "mythopoeic fantasy" invites an enormous range of possibilities, including the consensus definition for this conference:

> the fiction of the Inklings (J. R. R. Tolkien, C. S. Lewis, and Charles Williams); the winners and finalists of the Mythopoeic Fantasy Award, which is given for works in the spirit of the Inklings; and other books that are to a significant degree like them. (Bratman)

While this may be relatively vague, it is as useful or more useful than the standard dictionary definition of *mythopoeic* as "productive of myths; myth-making." This bare-bones definition is largely unhelpful, as a matter of fact, because many such fantasists do not claim to be actively *making* myth; rather, they systematically incorporate pre-existing mythic patterns into their works. It would be difficult, for example to appreciate the intricate texturing of a *Perelandra* without understanding how cultural myth can be interwoven with story; even in a novel as "earthbound" as *That Hideous Strength,* myths—both ancient and modern, magical and scientific—blend to augment the power of Lewis's storytelling.

More recently, Orson Scott Card is among those contemporary writers who have explored the possibilities of mythopoeic fiction from the perspectives of Tolkien and Lewis. Card argues that the essence of the fantastic is "belief," in that the fantastic is effective to the degree that readers become "participatory" and embrace for the moment the universe of the story—including the myths it asserts—and allow the story to *change* them ("Fantasy" 48). There are, he argues, three ways of "believing" a story: *epick, mythick,* and *critick,* respelling each to differentiate it from its conventional homonym:

- "Epick is all story that is received by a group as its own story—as true *of that group.* It is all story that tells who *we* are as opposed to who *they* are."
- "Mythick is all story that is received by readers as true of all human beings, and therefore lets each reader define himself as like or unlike the characters in the book. It is believed on a personal, not group level."
- "Critick is all story that is received by readers as being detached from them. It defines the reader neither as a human being nor as a member of a group. Rather, critickal readers evaluate the meaning or truth of the story consciously, usually detaching the meaning from the story itself" ("Fantasy" 45, 46).

*Epick* and *Mythick* do not require conscious decisions to believe; the reader simply accepts or rejects the fundamental assumptions of the story: "The self is named by the story, and so to doubt the story is to rename the self" ("Fantasy" 45-46).

This differentiation is central to Card's writing, because the approach the reader takes *does* ultimately affect the way the reader perceives the text:

Because critical readers read, not believing, but instead identifying and detaching meanings from the story, they are incapable of properly receiving a story that was written mythickly or epickly: They cannot receive a story that was written from belief. Likewise, mythick and epick readers, because they believe as they read, do not usually discern and detach meanings. The two methods are not compatible. ("Fantasy" 46)

In addition, many stories do not respond well to critickal readings; the story breaks down to mere convention, particularly in fantasy:

> Critics examine it and find strong-thewed heroes saving damsels in distress, magic rings and prophecies, dark forces opposing the bright light of goodness, and the critics say, "Cardboard characters. Endless repetition of meaningless conventions. Hack writing. Childish oversimplification of good and evil. Obviously written for the adolescent mind. Wish-fulfillment. Bourgeois and fascist and sexist and racist. Pure trash." And ah! the most damning epithet of all: "Escapist." ("Fantasy" 47)

But fantasy often exerts power over us precisely because it *cannot* be reduced to distanced, critical statements of meanings: symbolic, metaphorical, allegorical, or otherwise. Even the "damning epithet" is itself incorporated into the way Card looks at such literature. Negative "escapism" occurs, not in reading mythopoeic fictions, but rather in creating the distanced, dispassionate, analytical and critical readings that sever story from reader:

> The detached reader is escaping, not from that set of fictions called reality, but from that most dangerous and fearful of all things, the true story. The closest thing to true communication between two human beings is story-telling, for despite his best efforts at concealment, a writer will inevitabl[y] reveal in his story the world he believes he lives in, and the participatory reader will forever after carry around in himself and as himself a memory that was partly controlled by that other human being. Such memories are not neatly sorted into fiction and real life in our minds. I know, of course, that I never stood at the Cracks of Doom and watched Gollum die. But that faith in the distinction between my own actions and the actions of fictional characters is merely another story I tell myself. In fact, my memory of that event is much clearer and more powerful than my memory

of my fifth birthday. ("Fantasy" 49)

Thus Card, like Lewis and Tolkien, ultimately depends on Myth (with the capital "M," to suggest those patterns of believing that order our perceptions of the universe) not so much to assert a meaning or moral as to *communicate* stories that become memories that in turn touch upon what he sees as the true underpinnings of those stories.

Of course, this statement requires that I now attempt the impossible—at least given Card's assertions about the nature of reading and understanding: I must attempt to give a *Critickal* reading of a writer who approaches Story as *Epick* and *Mythick*.

Paradoxically, this attempt is made easier by the fact that, while the word *mythopoeic* might still remain vague, abstract, even ambiguous, two of Card's three ways of believing are fundamentally mythopoeic. Both "Mythick" and "Epick" require a commitment from the participatory reader to coherent patterns of belief that not only inform the story but that also define readers as belonging to *specific* groups and sharing *specific* identities. Two interconnecting "epicks" help define Card and his works: the "Epick of Mormonism" and the "Epick of America"; but encompassing both is the most fundamental and far-reaching of all, the "Myth of the Sacrifice."

Card has commented that he sees himself as an outsider. Critics such as John Clute and Joe Christopher have noted the sense of "self containment" (Christopher 2) in Lewis's works—the fact that, as an Ulster Protestant born in Catholic Belfast, Lewis belonged to a "surrounded but proselytizing faith" (Clute 244). A similar sense of religious isolation highlights Card's works. In "On Sycamore Hill," Card talks about how he came to write two short stories in *The Folk of the Fringe.* One evening, as the rest of a workshop group left for dinner, Card remained behind. He thought at first that he wanted to work on his stories, but the real reason had little to do with an unfinished story; it was in fact his awareness that as a Mormon, he was not truly part of the group:

> This wasn't my community. These guys were Americans, not Mormons; those of us who grew up in Mormon society and remain intensely involved are only nominally members of the American community. We can fake it, but we're always speaking a foreign language. (9)

In a very real sense, then, portions of Card's fictions are "epick"—Story that "is received by a group as its own story—as true *of that group.*" While Card is certainly interested in writing to as large an audience as possible, there is a core of meaning in his work that defines the primary group to which he perceives himself as belonging; these stories tell his "Epicks of Mormonism."

Readers are often aware of generally religious implications in Card's fictions. Gareth Rees points out in an online review of *The Worthing Chronicle* that the novel clearly defines Card's "moral imperative" that pain and grief are necessary for growth:

> Even if, like me, you find this attitude disturbing and reeking of hypocrisy, we must take it seriously as it is a respectable belief within the Christian community. Indeed, it is perhaps a necessary belief for people otherwise unable to reconcile their belief in a loving and omnipotent God with the state of the world. Viewed in this way, *The Worthing Chronicle* is an attempt to justify God to His creation, a task that would tax a Milton, and it is not surprising that Card fails.

Rees does not accept the story Card is telling and thus, for him as a reader, books such as *The Worthing Chronicle* fail; yet Rees nevertheless recognizes that Card, like Milton (and not coincidentally, Lewis), constructs stories on religious bases that simultaneously lend them power and make them liable to attack from nonbelievers.

Initially, religious elements appeared sporadically in Card's science fiction and fantasy stories, while *Capitol, A Planet Called Treason,* and *The Worthing Chronicle* suggested generalized Mormon references to some readers. By the early 1980s, however, Card's use of the "Epick of Mormonism" became more overt. Between July 1982 and March 1983, he combined Mormon themes with the form of Lewis's *The Screwtape Letters.* Published in an underground newspaper to a limited audience, "Notes of a Guardian Angel" (chapters 1-6), narrated the trials and growth of a young Mormon boy, and used Lewis's story both as a model and as a literary warrant to incorporate—to borrow Lewis's phrasing—"angels" instead of "space ships" into his fiction (cf. Lewis, *Of Other Worlds,* 69)

But with *Seventh Son* (1987), the Mythopoeic Fantasy Award winner in 1988, Card openly invited a much wider readership to share elements of his religious heritage. This first volume of the saga of Alvin Miller in an alternate-universe America where magic, science, and religion all work re-creates as fiction the "Epick" of portions of the Mormon past. Card so seamlessly incorporates episodes based on the early life of Joseph Smith, the first president of The Church of Jesus Christ of Latter-day Saints, that historical motifs become as integral to his story as if he had imagined them.

Perhaps the best example of this occurs late in *Seventh Son*. Young Alvin fractures his leg while trying to save a millstone from breaking (not coincidentally, this stone is literally "carved out of a mountain with no hands" and helps establish Alvin as a "Maker"). Alvin heals his leg but cannot heal a spot of darkness in the bone itself, the signature of the Unmaker—a figure closely allied to Lewis's Un-man in *Perelandra*. Alvin realizes that the diseased spot must be surgically excised. As his older brother Measure prepares to operate, Alvin refuses wine to dull the pain. "I can stand the pain and hold right still, iffen you whistle," he assures his brother, who successfully removes the bit of bone that otherwise would spread and kill the young Maker (219).

The original of this episode is one of the best known stories in the Mormon community about the early life of Joseph Smith, ideally suited to Card's purposes in *Seventh Son*—to illustrate Alvin's courage, moral intensity, and spiritual power. Significant details are altered but the power of the pattern remains, allowing Card to speak to Mormons and non-Mormons alike in a story informed with specific spiritual and moral values and at the same time equally engaging as an alternate-universe fantasy.

The five-part, seventeen-hundred-page Homecoming series further develops the "Epick of Mormonism." On the planet Harmony, a computer-entity, the Oversoul, manipulates the family of Nafai to leave the city of Basilica and wander for years in the wilderness until they finally arrive at the place where the original colonists arrived forty million years before and where their ships have remained in stasis, awaiting this moment. Activating the ships, Nafai's group returns to Earth to reestablish humanity on their home planet. Throughout, Card displays his hallmark creativity, peopling both Harmony and Earth with fully developed cultures, both human and alien; generating internal and external discords to complicate Nafai's mission; even exploiting the complexities of time and space as he had done in *Capitol, A Planet Called Treason, Speaker for the Dead,* and *Xenocide.*

But underlying what seems a relatively conventional SF plot is something extraordinary. Early in *The Memory of Earth* (Homecoming Vol. 1), Nafai and his brother glance back down the road from the city gates: "If Nafai and Issib had delayed even ten minutes more they would have had to make this trip in the noise and stink of horses, donkeys, mules, and kurelomi" (16). *Kurelomi* is an unusual word, but most SF and fantasy readers would willingly accept such a nonce word used, apparently, to assert an alien environment. Mormon readers, however, would note that the word echoes a Book of Mormon passage describing an "exceedingly rich" society, where individuals owned horses, asses, and elephants, and "cureloms and cumoms" (Ether 9:19). .

Some dozen pages later, when Nafai's father describes a vision sent by the Oversoul concerning the imminent destruction of Basilica and ultimately of the entire planet, there is a moment of recognition potentially as startling as the lamb and the lion passage at the end of Lewis' remarkable *The Voyage of the "Dawn Treader."* What Wetchik describes is Lehi's vision of the destruction of Jerusalem, taken from the Book of Mormon. Wetchik and his four sons become analogues to Lehi and his four sons. The Palwashantu Index that Nafai must kill to obtain parallels the Brass Plates. And from that moment it becomes clear that the plot movement throughout the Homecoming Series is based explicitly on narratives from the Book of Mormon.

If incorporating Mormonism were all that Card had attempted in the Homecoming novels or the Alvin Maker series, he would, I think, remain an excellent writer working on a narrow, parochial level. His just presenting Mormon history and theology in fictionalized form would have disturbed many readers, Mormon and non-Mormon alike. On-line reviews and discussions of these novels have frequently hinted at the basic assumptions that Alvin Maker, for example, is no more than Joseph Smith dressed in the trappings of alternate-history fantasy, and that the Homecoming novels contain little more than warmed-over Book of Mormon narrative—occasionally, in fact, the word *plagiarism* has surfaced, implying for some that readers were never intended to notice similarities between Card's fictions and his religious heritage.

Such comments miss Card's point entirely. Alvin Miller is not *just* Joseph Smith; nothing in Joseph Smith's life records suggests that he spent a year wandering the wilderness with Tecumseh or that he was present at a cataclysmic battle at Detroit. Nor is there anything in the Book of Mormon to foreshadow the pivotal role of women in the Homecoming series, or the central point that once humans nearly destroy themselves on Earth, the planet will be inherited by evolved rats and bats. To suggest that *all* Card is doing is recreating Mormon theology is to argue that all Lewis does in *Pere-*

*landra* is to crib from Genesis, or that *Till We Have Faces* is *only* the Cupid and Psyche myth retold. Such assertions as much ignore the power of Lewis's fiction as they miss the power of Card's.

But Card only *begins* here; a close reading examining the text for Mormon elements suggests, in fact, that Card uses direct references sparingly, primarily to move the plot forward. For much of the time in the Alvin Maker series, *The Folk of the Fringe, Lost Boys,* and the Homecoming series, in fact, he concentrates on filling in the rough outlines of cultures, beliefs, and social practices that make his science-fictional and fantasy worlds function. In more essential areas, he moves on to broader implications and to more expansive "epicks" that incorporate wider and wider audiences and tap into the power of more pervasive cultural Myth.

The process is best illustrated in the Alvin Maker stories. *Seventh Son* echoes much that is narrowly Mormon, but Card also suggests broader interests. Taleswapper mentions Ben Franklin's reputation as a wizard, possibly even a Maker; but Franklin himself claims that "The only thing I ever truly made was Americans" (135; see also "Pageant Wagon"). By "Americans" Franklin means more than just people born in a certain geographic location; by rewriting American history, Card illuminates the inner vision of what accepting that name means, justifying Taleswapper's rhetorical question: "Now tell me, Alvin Junior, was old Ben wrong to say that the greatest thing he ever made was a single word?" (139).

The second volume, *Red Prophet,* departs almost entirely from the "Mormon Epick" of *Seventh Son* to concentrate on the "Epick of America"—here, the conflict between "Reds" and "Whites." Again, Card's treatment is consciously mythic. His "Reds" have a direct relationship with the Land that no White can ever know, except Alvin; not coincidentally, the same motif appears in "America," a story that defines the essence of Card's view of "the promised, the promising land" (*Folk,* 273). This relationship intensifies the already mythic relationship suggested in tales about "noble savages" living harmoniously with Nature. Card's "Reds" feel the greensong, and through its power, can call animals for food, run for days without wearying, and enhance their true stewardship over the land. Card is no doubt aware that this version of the story is in part historically untrue; yet he is equally aware of the power of the myth and capitalizes on it, just as Lewis knew as he was writing *Out of the Silent Planet* that there were actually no "canals" as such on Mars. (*Of Other Worlds* 50). Card's "Reds" may not reflect historical reality in every detail, but they do reflect one popular version of the myth of

America's beginnings.

In addition, *Seventh Son* is essentially private; *Red Prophet* is public. In the first volume, young Alvin never moves more than a few miles from home; the story emphasizes private belief and family struggles. In *Red Prophet,* the eleven-year-old Alvin ranges across the face of America, in company with the great Ta-Kumsaw (Card's Tecumseh-analogue), and participates in visions, councils, and battles that ultimately define the face of the new America and help to determine the relation of both Red and White to the waiting land. In doing so, Card is consciously expanding the scope of the myths he incorporates. (In a conversation several years ago, he noted that while *Prentice Alvin* is highly localized, in parallel with *Seventh Son,* the next volume, the then unpublished *Alvin Journeyman,* would again expand outward to incorporate not only American but European history, as Alvin discovers the implications of public, political uses of power).

Late in *Red Prophet,* the prophet, Tenskwa-Tawa, speaks to Alvin's brother, Measure: "The bigger a man is, the more people he serves.... A small man serves himself. Bigger is to serve your family. Bigger is to serve your tribe. Then your people. Biggest of all, to serve all men, and all lands" (185). In the Alvin Maker series, Card begins by serving his own tribe, restructuring the story of Joseph Smith in a magical universe. As the series has progressed, however, that focus enlarges until in *Red Prophet,* Card emphasizes the larger context of the American nation, with its promises of freedom and liberty; and the third volume, *Prentice Alvin,* deals explicitly with another "Epick of America," the struggle against slavery. While Mormon elements occur, this volume is more directly about what America can and should be; it is about freedom and justice on all levels, from the personal to the public. The Alvin Maker series builds on the "Epick of America" to suggest not only lost opportunities in the past but potentials for the present; it is designed to elicit those remaining elements of greatness in the American Myth of dream and belief

The "Epick of America" and the "Epick of Mormonism" similarly combine in *The Folk of the Fringe,* originally called "Tales of the Mormon Sea." Card's concern for America-as-Myth permeates the apocalyptic dream-visions of "America" and the carefully crafted theatricality of *Glory of America,* performed in "Pageant Wagon," as he forges these two mythic strands into one Story:

> It seemed a little strange that a show called Glory of
> America should have an equal mix of Mormon and

American history. Bur to these people…it was all the same story. George Washington, Betsy Ross, Joseph Smith, Abraham Lincoln, Brigham Young, all part of the same unfolding tale. Their own past. (210-11)

The pageant defines the Myths that hold one community together. Card is not proselytizing for either, neither the truthfulness of Mormonism nor the sanctity of the America Dream. Instead, he creates a story about community that combines these Myths into a single entity. As *Glory of America* ends,

> The shouting faded, the clapping became more scattered. The faint audience lights came on. A few voices, talking, began among the crowd. The applause was over. The unity was broken. The audience was once again the thousand citizens of Hatchville….
>
> Suddenly Deaver realized something…. For a while tonight they saw and heard and felt the same things. And now they'd carry away the same memories, which meant that to some degree they were the same person. One. (214-15)

This is the power of Myth—the power to weld participants into a single community of structured memory and vicarious experience. In some cases, Card writes specifically for Mormon readers who will understand the full power of Card's images; in others, he writes specifically for Americans, who will recognize the power of the Myth of America, regardless of how far it might diverge from present reality; and, in stories such as "America," *Red Prophet,* and the Homecoming series, Card even warns readers of dangers to the integrity of those Myths. In *Red Prophet,* Tenskwa-Tawa sees an America divided, with Reds in the west and Whites in the East. In all other visions,

> the Red men dwindled, confined to tiny preserves of desolate land, until the whole land was White, and therefore brutalized into submission, stripped and cut and ravished, giving vast amounts of food that was only an imitation of the true harvest, poisoned into life by alchemical trickery. Even the White man suffered in those visions of the future, but it would be many generations before he realized what he had

done. Yet here—Prophetstown—there was a day—
tomorrow—when the future could be turned onto an
unlikely path, but a better one. One that would lead to
a living land after all, even if it was truncated; one
that would lead someday to a crystal city catching
sunlight and turning it into visions of truth for all
who. lived within it. (234)

In the vision of Tenskwa-Tawa, there is hope; in the America of the
1990s, we already live in the hopeless, desolate, dying land the Red
Prophet struggled to avoid.

Card's exploration of mythic power extends beyond these
"Epicks" of Mormonism and of America, however. Even earlier
than his overt embracing of Mormonism and America as themes, he
had asserted more encompassing mythic patterns. As the Red
Prophet said, the greatest service is to "serve all men, and all lands."
Among Card's earliest stories are a number that attempt to touch on
some of the most important Stories. In "Ender's Game" (1977),
"Kingsmeat" (1978), "Hart's Hope" (1980), "The Porcelain Salamander" (1981), and others, Card investigates the "Myth of the Sacrifice," the mediator, the advocate, the Christ-figure. These stories
are sometimes harsh and brutal, since he is concerned not simply
with easy answers but with difficult realities, particularly when the
sacrificial figure is only partially, or perhaps not at all understood by
the ones who need salvation.

The epitome of the sacrificial Christic figure in Card's fiction is
Ender Wiggin, whose very existence meets the needs of the larger
community, and whose career as military genius, as itinerant inter-
planetary mediator and advocate, as apostle to aliens, and as human
link with the generative powers of God (emphasized in the title of
the fourth volume, *Children of the Mind)* is based on serving larger
and larger communities. As such, these stories anatomize the role of
mediators—most often Ender Wiggin but occasionally others as
well—in an attempt at understanding the psychological and spiritual
dimensions of sacrifice within the context of Christic imagery and
meaning. These novels occasionally discuss God overtly but they
are essentially *about* atonement, sacrifice, mediation, and their effects on community.

Episode after episode in *Ender's Game* resonates with Christic,
biblical meaning, as when Ender as savior of humanity is aided by
the chosen twelve closest to him and most capable of carrying out
his mission (217); when, following the destruction of the buggers'
home planet, Ender descends into the darkness of quasi-death for

five days, during which he sees, understands, and accepts the consequences of his actions (330-32); and finally when, with the defeat of humanity's perceived enemies, he becomes "the child-god, the miracle worker, with life and death in his hands" (338). By the end of the novel, Ender has come as close as is humanly possible to being a Christ-figure, sacrificing all to save all, accepting the responsibility of a billion, billion deaths (331).

In *Speaker for the Dead,* Ender is now quasi-immortal; through time-space dilation, he has aged only a few years while three thousand years have passed for the rest of humanity, a motif Card initially explored in *Capitol* and *The Worthing Saga,* concluding there as here that such is a false immortality, an illusion gained by isolation from human community. Again, Ender is explicitly linked with messianic, mediational functions. To his sister's children, he is "their long-lost Uncle Ender, who was thought in every world to be a monster, but in reality was something of a savior, or a prophet, or at least a martyr" (88). He is the apostle to the piggies, who recognize his Christic function. Most significantly, he must witness the compact between humans and piggies by reversing his role from *Ender's Game.* Instead of being the sacrifice, he must sacrifice the alien named Human. To Ender's bitter comment that he is "cold and ruthless" enough to solidify the covenant in the only way the piggies will accept, Novinha responds that he is also "compassionate enough...to put the hot iron into the wound when that's the only way to heal it." And, as Ender understands, "as one who had felt his burning iron cauterize her deepest wounds, she had the right to speak; and he believed her, and it eased his heart for the bloody work ahead" (374). He performs a passage into Life-after-Death that Human and others describe in terms of miracles and covenants, sacrament and resurrection, brotherhood and ascent into the light (380-81, 384). In the words of Bishop Peregrino, the Speaker's interference with the established structure of things on Lusitania has turned into revelation: "It was the miracle of the wafer, turned into the flesh of God in his hands. How suddenly we find the flesh of God within us after all, when we thought that we were only made of dust" (385).

Even before *Xenocide* was published, Card acknowledged that the sequel to *Speaker For the Dead* would be difficult to write: "It will be even more different from the first two than *Speaker* was from *Ender.* It's cosmic Sci-Fi—discovering what everything is made of, what underlies the laws of the universe, that sort of thing" (Shirk 12). "Cosmic Sci-Fi"—the same kind of Story that Lewis weaves in the Ransom novels, as we gradually understand the connections among all things within the Fields of Arbol, through Maleldil as Creator. Card's discussions of philotes and philotic webs seem intended less as scientific, extrapolative suggestions about the actual functioning of universe and meta-universe than as metaphorical ways of defining the underlying Myth of creation and generation that shape his stories, especially the Story of Ender Wiggin, "sometimes monster, always something of a savior, or a prophet, or at least a martyr."

To varying degrees, Card's readership has responded to the power of Myth as it percolates through the Stories that embody it. Yet the same acknowledgement of mythic power also makes these novels vulnerable to attack. As happens occasionally in Lewis studies, critics who do not accept Card's Myths as true may have difficulty accepting the Stories Card uses to define them, as when the Ender novels are rejected as neo-Hitlerian, male-oriented power-fantasies perpetrated by a misogynistic, myopic, militaristic anti-feminist (Radford); or when *A Woman of Destiny* is written off as a predictably formulaic romance (Quaglia). But for readers open to the Myths these writers explore, the Stories become things of enormous potential. And, in their own way, the Myths become means by which more difficult books can be approached and understood.

Much like Lewis's *That Hideous Strength,* Card's most recent single-volume novel has elicited strong criticism for doing what it should not and for not doing what it apparently should. Yet, when one looks at it closely, *Lost Boys* (1992) is a logical conclusion thus far to Card's interlocking approach to three essential Mythic patterns.

*Lost Boys* seems on the surface a far cry from mythopoeic fantasy. In fact, most of it seems barely fantastic at all; only in the final pages does Card leave the world as we know it and enter another world, where Myth becomes Reality; but even there, he makes it clear that terms such as *fantasy* and *reality* are only relative in this novel. As Step Fletcher says about his son's apparent problems facing reality, "It's the real world that he's living in, only just as we thought, he sees it more deeply and truly than the rest of us" (376). In addition, long portions of the novel discuss the mundane concerns of making a living, of defining relationships, both family and social, of home and school and job. One reader writes that the novel is simply about a "struggling computer programmer with a strong religious...background and a son who is having weird experiences with video games. I really was caught up in the trials and tribulations of the programmer's life, but the subplot of the boy is always kinda *[sic]* creepy in the background" (Ingram). Another reviewer summarizes the novel as being about "a family who lose a difficult child to a murderer, but when he comes back as a ghost they are able to give him the perfect Christmas he never had when he was alive" (Rees, "Maps").

Both responses are fundamentally inaccurate. Stevie's story is not a quirky subplot; it is the rationale for the entire novel, with Step Fletcher's difficulties at work defining one of several reasons why Step is unable to rescue his son until too late. The novel discusses Mormons and Mormonism, but not in the sense that its purpose is to convince readers that Mormonism is true; instead, religion illuminates Stevie's decisions, particularly his need to stop a vicious, spreading evil. And the Fletchers do not merely give Stevie "the perfect Christmas he never had when he was alive" (which is simply false to the novel); but rather their child finds the strength to bring one final, nearly "perfect" Christmas to the families of a killer's innocent victims. By rejecting Card's underlying Myths, these readers miss the power of the novel. It becomes merely, as one reader said recently, a very sad book.

The case is complicated by the fact the short story "Lost Boys" differs radically from the novel. This becomes immediately apparent in the tone of the original opening paragraphs:

> Kristine and the kids and I moved to Greensboro on the first of March, 1983. I was happy enough about my job—I just wasn't sure I wanted a job at all. But the recession had the publishers all panicky, and nobody was coming up with advances large enough for me to take a decent amount of time writing a novel. I suppose I could whip out 75,000 words of junk fiction every month and publish them under a half dozen pseudonyms or something, but it seemed to Kristine and me that we'd do better in the long run if I got a job to ride out the recession. Besides, my Ph.D. was down the toilet. I'd been doing good work at Notre Dame, but when I had to take out a few weeks in the middle of a semester to finish *Hart's Hope,* the English department was about as understanding as you'd expect from people who prefer their authors dead or domesticated. Can't feed your family? So sorry. You're a writer? Ah, but not one that anyone's written a scholarly essay about. So long, boy-oh! (73-74)

This does not sound like the opening to a fiction; this is Orson Scott Card talking about his own life, his own family, his own frustrations. The story continues in this way for several more paragraphs, providing at the least insights into Card's biography. Only with the introduction of an oldest child, "Scotty," does the story assert itself as fiction; Scotty is the vehicle by which Card tells a Story that is, in essence, his own "Epick," his own Myth.

When he took the story to the Sycamore Hill Writers Workshop, it was sharply criticized. Card quotes Karen Fowler as saying, "By telling this story in first person with so much detail from your own life, you've appropriated something that doesn't belong to you. You've pretended to feel the grief of a parent who has lost a child, and you don't have a right to feel that grief" ("Lost Boys" 89). Card's response is that "Lost Boys" contains a private Myth. Responding to Fowler's comments, Card discovered that

> this story wasn't about a fictional eldest child named "Scotty." It was about my real-life youngest child, Charlie Ben.
>
> Charlie, who in the five and a half years of his life has never been able to speak a word to us. Charlie, who could not smile at us until he was a year old, who could not hug us until he was four, who still spends his days and nights in stillness, staying wherever we put him, able to wriggle but not to run, able to call out but not to speak, able to understand that he cannot do what his brother and sister do, but not to ask us why. In short, a child who is not dead and yet can barely taste life despite all our love and all our yearning.
>
> Yet in all the years of Charlie's life, until that day at Sycamore Hill, I had never shed a single tear for him, never allowed myself to grieve. I had worn a mask of calm and acceptance so convincing that I had believed it myself. A story that I had fancied was a mere lark, a dalliance in the quaint old ghost-story tradition, was the most personal, painful story of my career—and, unconsciously, I had confessed as much by making it by far the most autobiographical of all my works. (90)

The story added a new dimension to Card's use of Myth by allowing him to include himself directly in confronting a truth that defines his life as a father.

When Card expanded the story into a novel, that private myth retreated. Step and DeAnne Fletcher replaced Scott and Kristine; Stevie, Robbie, and Betsy replaced "Scotty," Geoffrey, and Emily; the new child was Jeremy Zapata Fletcher instead of Charlie Ben. But *Lost Boys* retained touches of Card's private Story. The Cards moved to Greensboro, North Carolina, while the Fletchers moved to Steuben, North Carolina; but significantly the Fletchers set out from Vigor, Illinois—echoing Vigor Church near the Hatrack River area that Card used as a landscape for the Alvin Maker novels. Even as Card removed Orson Scott Card as character from the story, he replaced him with allusions to Orson Scott Card, author of other books that begin the process of exploration and discovery continued in *Lost Boys.*

Beyond this personal level, *Lost Boys* also illustrates Card's three consistent themes. The "Epick of Mormonism" is specifically represented. Throughout, Card provides his insights into the practical, everyday workings of a religion that, for him, is the focus of his life and his family's lives. He is so persistent in providing these details that it is easy to see why readers might feel that he is proselytizing; but the Mormon references are so functional, so integrated to the narrative that rereading the short-story version, where religion is rarely mentioned, reveals a thinness that mere word count cannot explain. For Step and DeAnne Fletcher, religion is real. Blessings work. Prophecy is possible. Prayers can be answered, although not always in the ways one might either wish or expect.

Thus, the Fletchers of all people should be prepared when Scotty's life is touched by transcendence. Yet initially they fail their own beliefs. In *That Hideous Strength,* Lewis's Mother Dimble can kneel in evening prayer, in front of a near stranger, without any embarrassment; Card's Step finds it more difficult to do so. And in spite of their frequent contact with the spiritual, both Step and DeAnne persist on defining Stevie's "problem" in secular terms, including sending him to a psychiatrist, only to find that Dr. Weeks wants to *cure* Stevie of his religion, since she sees it as fostering an unhealthy mental state. Yet she encourages her own son to associate with the Mormons, since among them his obsession with obtaining invisible powers and becoming a god will pass (she hopes) relatively unnoticed.

Still, the Mormonism remains secondary to other concerns. The novel is set in contemporary America. If in *Red Prophet* Tenskwa-Tawa has a horrific vision of a land poisoned and dying, devastated by the Whites, Step Fletcher *lives* in that vision. He brings his pregnant wife to a town enveloped by fumes from nearby tobacco factories; DeAnne constantly battles nausea because of the stench. His home is invaded several times by hordes of insects—June bugs, spiders, roaches. Each time, the insects are seeking to escape a violation of the land as the killer buries yet another young victim in the dirt beneath the Fletcher's home. Even the steps taken to rid the house of the insects are themselves poisonous, the residue of the insecticide forcing the Fletchers out of their house and ironically inviting the killer inside.

And, most tragic of all, their world is a world of deception, greed, anger, and evil. A fellow Mormon, who should have provided strength and support for the new family in the area, perverts religion to her own end, frightening young Stevie with self-serving "prophecies" and false "blessings." The teacher who should have helped Stevie develop ties with his new community ridicules him to bolster her own self-importance. A young man who offers to baby-sit the Fletchers' children turns out to be a sex offender so near to being a mere "creature" that Step hesitates even to speak his children's names when the man can hear. And, of course, at the center of the plot is the serial killer, the murderer of young boys, whose actions impel Stevie's need to redeem the killer's victims.

This is the America of reality, a place where Myth dissipates, a place already well on the way to the devastation and defeat that opens *The Folk of the Fringe*. Yet even here there are remnants of hope: new-found friends provide comfort and community; and by believing the unbelievable, a police investigator confirms the meaning of Stevie's sacrifice. In the end, the place that saw the difficult birth of one son and the death of another becomes the community the Fletchers had been seeking:

> Step and DeAnne buried their oldest boy in a cemetery on the western edge of Steuben, surrounded by thick woods full of birds and animals, a living place. They both knew as they stood beside the grave that their days of wandering were through. They had been anchored now in Steuben, both by the living and by the dead. Little Jeremy would enter Open Doors [Clinic] when the time came; flowers would be tended on this grave. (447)

If *Lost Boys* remained merely an extended version of one man's private story, a story about the workings of a specific religion, or even a story about what America has become, then the novel would indeed be just "a very sad story." But there is more. Card's works, no matter how terrible, frightening, sad, or even apparently inconclusive, struggle to move beyond the family, the tribe, even the people, to "serve all men, and all lands," and *Lost Boys* is no exception. This novel works because each level is an inherent part of something larger. And structuring the story is the Myth of Sacrifice.

Stevie is not just a "problem child" who sees imaginary friends, plays phantom video games, and ignores his parents. He is a vehicle by which Card can mourn his own "lost boy"—yes: but on a much larger scale, he is an icon for innocence and purity. As Detective Douglas says:

> There's some people who do things so bad it tears at the fabric of the world, and then there's some people so sweet and good that they can feel it when the world gets torn. They see things, they know things, only they're so good and pure that they don't understand what it is that they're seeing. I think that's what's been happening to your boy. What's going on here in Steuben is so evil and he is so good and pure that he can't help but feel it. The minute he got to Steuben he must have felt it, and it made him sad…. The rest of us, we've got good and evil mixed up in us, and our own badness makes so much noise we can't hear the evil of the monster out there. But your Stevie, he can hear it. He can hear the names of the boys [and]…your Stevie takes those names, and he makes friends out of them. (374)

Douglas is close to the truth, but even he does not fully understand that Stevie achieves more than just naming the lost boys. In a climactic exchange, Step threatens to ban Stevie from the computer, Stevie's main connection with the lost boys. "You can't," Stevie cried, "That's the only thing they're staying for! If I can't play they'll go away!" (410). Step answers that maybe the boy is spending entirely too much time playing Atari.

> "Not as much as you spend on the IBM in there," said Stevie.
> "That happens to be my work," said Step. "That happens to be what pays for our house and our food

and Zap's doctor bills."

"Are you the only one in the family who has work to do?" Stevie demanded. (410-11)

Several pages later, DeAnne makes the correct connection, even though neither she nor Step understands it completely:

"The funniest thing," said DeAnne. "You know when he said, 'You're not the only one with work to do?' or whatever it was he said?"

"Yeah, I didn't know whether to be delighted to see him showing so much emotion or appalled that for the first time in his life he was yelling at his father."

"Do you know what went through my mind when he said that?" said DeAnne. "I thought, 'Wist ye not that 1 must be about my father's business?'" (412-13)

At this point *Lost Boys* ceases to be merely a sad book and becomes a powerful one, because Stevie is pure and good and perceives the tear in the world…and he has the courage to act to stop it. Through his courage, he can hold onto the lost boys long enough to teach them one thing that brings hope out of tragedy: how to be seen.

It is not an accident that the story closes on Christmas, nor is it as one reader suggests a "schmaltzy" manipulative ploy on Card's part (Rees, "Maps"), any more than it is a schmaltzy manipulative ploy on Lewis's part to signal the collapse of the White Witch's power by the appearance of Father Christmas. Instead, at the season of Birth and Hope, the lost boys both give and receive a final gift: as the killer

was led away, as the bodies were brought out of their hidden graves and under the police lights of that bitter cold Christmas Eve, one by one the boys inside the house no longer had the strength or the need to keep trying anymore, and they said goodbye, and they were gone. One moment there, the next moment not there. Then their parents left, weeping, clinging to each other, with just a whispered word or two from Douglas. "Tell no one," he said. "You don't want your boy's name in the press. Just go home and thank God you had a chance to say good-bye. One small mercy in this whole cruel business." And the parents nodded and agreed and went home to the loneliest Christmas of their lives, the Christmas in which questions were answered at last, and love was remembered and wept for, and God was thanked and blamed for not having done more. (442)

This is a tremendous weight for one boy, one Story, to bear; and Card's control comes perilously close to breaking. Yet I think that control does hold; the story does ultimately imitate the deeper, brighter Story that Card wants to tell. There may in fact be "monsters in the mall"—evil close to us, unseen and unidentifiable except for its consequences; but there are also those willing to sacrifice in order to bring that evil into the light and defeat it. Card gives us the externals—an apparently disturbed child, whose parents struggle to find clues as to how to cure him—with the resolution only becoming fully understandable at the end of the story. With Stevie's parents, readers are invited to watch him make difficult decisions; yet the readers do not understand his preliminary decisions any more than Step and DeAnne do. The intensity and power of Stevie's sacrifice require that it be revealed at precisely the correct moment, transforming what had seemed to be a "realistic" novel into a deeply "mythopoeic" one.

In speaking about the *eucatastrophe* of fairy stories, Tolkien provides a paradigm for the final effect of a story such as *Lost Boys:*

> The consolation of fairy-stories, the joy of the happy ending: or more correctly of the good catastrophe, the sudden joyous "turn" (for there is no true end to any fairy-tale): this joy, which is one of the things which fairy-stories can produce supremely well, is not essentially "escapist," nor "fugitive." In its fairy-tale—or otherworld—setting, it is a sudden and miraculous grace: never to be counted on to recur. It does not deny the existence of *dyscatastrophe,* of sorrow and failure: the possibility of these is necessary to the joy of deliverance; it denies (in the face of much evidence, if you will) universal final defeat and in so far is *evangelium,* giving a fleeting glimpse of Joy, Joy beyond the walls of the world, poignant as grief. (85-86)

In its final pages, Card's text emphasizes the effects of this pattern:

the sudden "turn" that, far from providing emotional closure, reveals that on more fundamentally mythic levels, the story opens outward, inviting readers "further in and further up" (Lewis, *Last Battle* 173); the "sudden and miraculous grace" that brings consolation by intruding the supernatural into the frighteningly real world Card has re-created, a world of serial killers and missing children. And the final paragraphs of *Lost Boys* provides precisely the emotional response that Tolkien defines in "On Fairy Stories":

> It is the mark of a good fairy-story, of the higher or more complete kind, that however wild its events, however fantastic or terrible the adventures, it can give to child or man that hears it, when the "turn" comes, a catch of the breath, a beat and lifting of the heart, near to (or indeed accompanied by) tears, as keen as that given by any form of literary art. (86)

# THE EPIC OF ENDER

[This essay was presented as the Guest-Scholar Address at EnderCon, Utah Valley State College, Provo UT, July 6, 2002. The convention celebrated the twenty-fifth anniversary of the publication of Orson Scott Card's *Ender's Game*. The essay has been expanded for this volume.]

## DEFINITIONS AND PERMUTATIONS OF EPIC

More than thirty years ago, one of the leading contemporary scholars of Renaissance epic theory posited a key differentia between that period and ours:

> For a heroic poet no idea was more crucial than the concept of heroic virtue. This was the *raison d'être* of the epic; and if this form rivaled tragedy as the highest and foremost of literary genres, one reason was the superlative *Ethos* of its protagonist. The epic poet did not merely imitate an action; he also imitated Character. He did not simply portray "highest deeds"; he also portrayed the "godlike virtues" from which they sprang. Action itself proved and demonstrated character; and character, in turn, exhibited a moral idea. Whatever "profit" or "delight" the poet imparted through imitation derived its value primarily from the concepts behind the poetic image. The concrete example hinged on the abstract idea, the particular on the universal. In his "epic person." he laid the "pattern" of an ideal hero; in his heroic image he embodied the Platonic archetype.
>
> Unfortunately, *virtus heroica* is another of the ideals that separate us from the Renaissance intellectual milieu. In the age of Prufrock and the "anti-hero," it has lost its philosophical significance along with its relevance for poetry. Where it still survives, it haunts the remote frontiers of polite letters, the

near-wildernesses of popular fiction. Banished from the more sophisticated Parnassus with its archaic vehicle—the heroic poem—it lingers in the Limbos of outer space, the deserts of the American West, and the shadows of the metropolitan underworld. Stripped of his Mycenaean armor, the *theios anēr*—the "God-like man"—dons the badge of a deputy sheriff or the space helmet of an astral voyager. The blurbs of the comic strip have replaced the classical hexameter; the heroes of Troy have shrunk to the dimensions of a Dick Tracy, a Red Ryder, or a Superman. (Steadman, *Characters*, 13-14)[*]

John M. Steadman's comments suggest an essential trivializing of epic/heroic virtue as we enter the initial years of the twenty-first century; yet in a larger sense, his assessment seems more valid than—and certainly more positive than—perhaps even he realized. In a very real way, the epic impulse, persistently present in human society from the *Epic of Gilgamesh* through such twentieth-century works as David Jones' *Anathemata*, Charles Williams' *Taliessin through Logres,* and Frederick Turner's *The New World* has in fact survived its apparent demise in the more than two centuries following the publication of Milton's *Paradise Lost*—centuries characterized by the abdication of poetry as the primary literary form, the development and rise of prose fiction, the eventual abdication of heroic virtue as a central interest in such fictions (epitomized by the naturalistic and realistic schools of the late nineteenth and early twentieth centuries), and the subsequent rise of a genre of prose fiction that fuses epic impulse with prose narrative, heroic virtue with moral explorations, and epic characters with epic actions—actions that ultimately effect the destinies of cities, nations, continents, worlds, and galactic systems.

This genre is, of course, Science Fiction and Fantasy.[†]

---

[*] Darko Suvin arrives at a similar conclusion on the relation of SF to epic; in "The SF Novel as Epic Narration: For a Fusion of 'Formal' and 'Sociological' Analysis," he states "I would…say that modern SF is then—in proportion to its meaningfulness—under the hegemony of the epic" (*Positions,* 77).

[†]Along with Card himself, I do not see the barriers between the two sets of fictions—fantasy and science fiction—as particularly relevant to discussions of the moral centricity of either. Cf. Card's Guest of Honor Speech, Brigham Young University Symposium on the Impact of Science Fiction and Fantasy, "Life, the Universe, and Everything XV, Provo UT, March 1, 1997; the speech was a read-

An epic is more than the sum of its conventions; yet for the past 3,000 years or so[*], the *form* of epic has been generally defined by the relative presence or absence of specific conventional devices. Certainly mere presence is not sufficient to elevate a conglomeration of conventions to the level of cultural epic, or even to the level of a poem that survives its own time. G. G. Trissino's *L'Italia Liberata* is, by consensus of most readers, a theoretically (and conventionally) perfect poem with only one serious drawback:

> Trissino's epic of the emperor Justinian's conquest of the Goths, a blend of patriotism, religion, and heroism that seemed to be perfect according to all the canonical rules of art except one—no one derived any pleasure from reading it. A competent, if conventional, critic, Trissino was a dull poet. A great and noble action was uselessly sung if it was unread. (Hainsworth, 142)[†]

As a matter of fact, for a goodly portion of the epic's long history, its very nature has been ostensibly determined by the poet's facility with the conventions seen as imperative to any epic. Much of Milton's greatness, for example, stems from his ability to simultaneously use and negate classical and Christian conventions for Renaissance epic, themselves studiously copied from Homer as transmitted by Virgil and earlier Renaissance poets.

It should not, then, come as a surprise to discover that in a genre that strongly suggests the essence of epic—the survival of heroic virtue—one might also discern vestiges of the conventions of the form, especially in a writer such as Card, whose knowledge of Spenser and Milton attest to his general awareness of epic theory as well.[‡] With that in mind, it should prove fruitful to look at a few of

---

ing of the introduction to the forthcoming *Worlds of Ice.*

[*] Accepting as a generalized date the 850 B.C. Richmond Lattimore proposes for the composition of the Homeric epics(20); while earlier epics certainly exist, they conform less universally to the specific devices discussed in this paper.

[†] See also E. M. W. Tillyard, p. 223-225 ("Trissino is not a great critic any more than a great poet" [225]); Judith A. Kates, pp. 44-447.

[‡] Card has discussed both authors as influences (cf. Collings, *In the Image of God,* pp. 23-24); in addition, his graduate work at Notre Dame concentrated on Spenser, to the extent that his poem, "Prentice Alvin and the No-Good Plow" represented a

the traditional conventions of epic, specifically as they relate to Orson Scott Card's *Ender's Game.*

## Narrative poem

An epic is, by consensus, a long narrative poem.

And that is about all that critics finally agree upon when attempting to define a form that has produced disparate works for some 5,000 years of human history. Yet even that skeletal definition requires careful attention when the reader tries to link contemporary science fiction to classical/Renaissance epic.

Science fiction is, in general, narrative—that much is also agreed upon. While anomalies such as Brian W. Aldiss's spectacular exercises in non-narrative prose in *Report on Probability A,* and parallel exercises in non-linear narrative such as Aldiss's equally impressive *Barefoot in the Head,* or Samuel R. Delany's massive *Dhalgren* occur, SF by and large retains a solid commitment to narrative—to storytelling as the highest art.

Science Fiction is also (often notoriously) long. The Delany title mentioned above comes immediately to mind (for a number of years, Delany could honestly claim to have written the *longest* SF novel yet), as do the even longer narrative sequences implicit in such novels-and-sequels series as Frank Herbert's almost interminable Dune saga or Piers Anthony's ever-burgeoning Xanth tales. And, while works such as Stephen King's SF-oriented, apocalyptic novel *The Stand* and two remarkably similar works—Dean R. Koontz's *Strangers,* and Robert McCammon's *Swan's Song*—triggered criticism based solely upon their length, by and large most readers of SF willingly embrace length.

Often they clamor for it.

But poetry?

Here is the first sticking point in any attempt to trace the development of epic in contemporary society.

Speaking of Richard Francis Burton's poetic translation of Luis vaz de Camões' great Portuguese national epic, *Os Lus'adas* (1870), William C. Atkinson discusses at length the difficulties of rendering a sixteenth-century Portuguese poem into nineteenth-century English idiom. Burton's object, Atkinson argues,

---

conscious attempt at mastering Spenserian archaism in diction and form. The poem in turn led to the Alvin Maker series. For a listing of possible epic conventions, see "Stephen King's *The Dark Tower* in the Epic Tradition" [above].

was to provide such a poem as Camoens might have written had he been born instead an Englishman, although the attempt to write Elizabethan English in the nineteenth century already overlooked the detail that no readers of that age had survived. Nor was this all, for in a vain effort to convey further the impression of sixteenth-century Portuguese he clogged his style with hyperbaton, syncope, apocope, aphaeresis, diaeresis, paragoge. The interests of the modern English reader were nowhere consulted, and the upshot was as could have been foreseen: his version, the most ambitious of all and the most firmly rooted in scholarship, fell from the press stillborn, unreadable.(31-32)

Atkinson's comment addresses a key issue in discussing twentieth-century manifestations of epic: simply put, that poetry no longer establishes the consensus medium for heroic discourse—or, perhaps, for discourse in general. In an age such as the that of Homer or of Virgil, when much prose itself was often written in highly poeticized forms, verse could assume a wide audience. In the twentieth century, when much of the dominant poetics has caused a separation (if not an outright rift) between poet and audience, when poetic attempts at the epic such as T. S. Eliot's *The Wasteland,* Charles Williams' *Taliessin through Logres* * or David Jones' *The Anathemata* present even diligent readers with almost insuperable obstacles, the mere act of presenting an epic fable in verse form seems tantamount to an invitation to failure.

Conversely, in an age when prose has become, tacitly if not overtly, the dominant verbal form, it seems appropriate to agree with Atkinson that prose may in fact be an acceptable form for epic; his purpose in translating Camões' poetry, he writes, "aims at rendering a service to the living, not pious tribute to the dead, and is concerned therefore with the substance, not the form, of the original" (32).

Card is himself a poet of no mean skill or ambition. Adept at recreating the idiom and tone of past times, as evidenced by "Prentice Alvin and the No-Good Plow" and by the full-length prose version of that poem in the Alvin Maker series. In addition to several

---

*One of the ironies of reading Williams' poem is that C. S. Lewis's discussion of the poetry in *The Arthurian Torso* is in some important senses more revealing, and ultimately more satisfying, than the poetry itself.

poems published in periodicals including *Anthology of Speculative Poetry #4, Amazing, BYU Studies, The Ensign,* and *Sunstone,* he has completed several book-length manuscripts of poetry.

One implication of Card's dual interest in poetry and prose—and of his extensive background in both—is that when he approaches an epic fable such as that lying at the heart of the Ender novels, he allows the strengths of poetry to augment his prose. In a sense, his prose moves toward the texture and density of poetry. More specifically, at moments of crisis, of climax, of resolution in *Ender's Game,* for example, Card consciously allows himself to shift from carefully crafted prose rhythms to the overt rhythms of poetry. The lesson comes from Shakespeare, whose rhymed couplets frequently punctuate critical scene- and act-divisions. And if Card does not indulge himself in self-consciously poetic couplets, he does emphasize specific moments with modulated rhythms that suggest poetry.

At the end of the novel's first scene, as the doctor remove's Ender's monitor, Card emphasizes the terror—and guilt—the doctor feels. In a scene reminiscent of a key moment in *Songmaster,* Card's hero is thrust into a living agony unanticipated by those around him. The physical and psychological consequences of an unthinking moment seem staggering: Ender might have died. The passage concludes with the doctor's instructions to his nurse—and his condemnation of himself: "Keep him here for at least an hour. Watch him. If he doesn't start talking in fifteen minutes, call me." Then, as summary to the action, and a devastating critique aimed at himself, two final lines: "Could have unplugged him forever. I don't have the brains of a bugger" (9).

The lines are prose; yet the natural rhythms of key phrases—"unplugged him," for example—suggest that the lines might be read metrically. And if we do that, the internal sight-rhyme and slant rhyme of *forever* and *bugger* force themselves on our attention. In essence, Card has written line that strongly suggests dactylic hexameter (with one missing syllable in the final foot):

> **Could** have un/-**plugged** him for/-**ev**-er. I / **don't**
> have the / **brains** of a / **bug**-ger.

The emphasis on *could* in the first sentence (achieved through the simple device of deleting its obvious subject, *I*) seems to require a similar emphasis on its parallel, *don't,* in the second, throwing the entire passage into a rocking but regular rhythm. In effect the line not only closes out the first intensely emotional scene in the novel, but does so using an acceptable English approximation of the traditional heroic or epic measure of classical Greek and Latin.

Such examples are perhaps not frequent; but they are both intentional and functional.

## Heroic virtue

Norman Spinrad argues that the only science-fiction story worth telling (as opposed to "sci-fi" story) in *Ender's Game* and *Speaker for the Dead* occurs *between* the two novels, in the final pages of *Ender's Game* and in the—for Spinrad—awkward and unbelievable opening pages of *Speaker for the Dead.* In a rather formal, generic way, the comment is apt, insofar as *Ender's Game* defines essentially an Achillean hero—a military hero whose actions effect the fate of his people, as do Achilles' in the *Iliad*; and *Speaker for the Dead* suggests a Virgilian hero—one who subsumes his own needs and desires to a greater good, specifically establishing a stable community, epitomized by Aeneas in Virgil's *Aeneid.*

Traditionally, what falls between these two sorts of heroes is the Odyssean hero, the hero of wandering, whose voyage outward and return inward recapitulates similar movements in the poet's and the readers' imaginations. What has emerged in epic studies as a critical commonplace is the argument that the hero developed in the *Odyssey* differs significantly from the hero in either the *Iliad* or the *Aeneid.* The Odyssean hero is substantially more ambivalent—a trait based on Odysseus's recurring epithet, "polytropos," or "many-turning"—cunning, clever, deceitful. Critics often suggest that, while the *Iliad* seems to be the earlier poem, based primarily on linguistic forms, the *Odyssey* is in its own way more 'primitive,' demanding more of the reader in order to establish empathy with the isolated, wandering, often deceitful hero.

To turn to more contemporary literature, George Slusser has discussed the Odyssean motif in science fiction at length, specifically as it occurs in Arthur C. Clarke's *2001: A Space Odyssey.* Similarly, I have analyzed the tripartite divisions of Piers Anthony's *Battle Circle* as recreating Achillean, Odyssean, and Virgilian heroic models ("Argument"). To the extent that this evaluation is true, Card's decision to bridge the 3,000-year-gap between the close of *Ender's Game* and the opening of *Speaker for the Dead* supports his overriding theme of community in both novels. The first ends as Ender completes his first task: helping to establish a community of humanity linked by more than external fear of the buggers. The second begins with the first clear step toward establishing a second level of community: a private community into which Ender might fit, and a public community consisting of the three ramen species: human, piggy, and bugger.

For Card to interrupt his quest for community with an Odyssean wandering would disrupt his progress toward theme, as well as presenting perhaps insuperable difficulties in balancing the narrow focus of *Ender's Game*, the relatively narrow focus of *Speaker for the Dead* (two parallel sets of episodes separated by twenty subjective years) and the enormous possibilities of Ender Wiggin as Speaker for the Dead, spending six months on any one world before traveling to the next, searching for the appropriate place to seed the bugger colony. The point of the intervening millennia is precisely that *nothing* significant occurred, at least nothing at once significant and directly related to Ender's self-imposed quest to restore the buggers. Action there might be, and adventure aplenty, with opportunities for disquisitions philosophical, theological, social, political, and personal.

But *nothing* that relates to Ender's quest.

Thus, whether consciously or not, Card establishes a transition between the two novels that allows for continuity in Ender's search for community, and that disallows digression into Ender's experiences as Speaker for the Dead. To much the same effect, incidentally, Card has indicated that he has no plans to write the story of Peter the Hegemon, even though he has been urged to do so. That story is complete in the first two volumes; all that would be left for Card as Storyteller would be to recount the episodes leading to a conclusion his readers have already reached.* And in a critical sense, Peter's 'true' story emerges in *Xenocide* and *Children of the Mind,* in which he is reconstructed and, again, released onto an unsuspecting universe.

**NOTE**: The recent publication of *Ender in Exile, First Meetings,* and the multiple volumes of the Shadow series does not seriously impact these observations. *Ender in Exile* does in fact take place between *Ender's Game* and *Speaker for the Dead,* but takes the action only a few (subjective) years beyond the first novel and incorporates only two voyages, rather than the multitudes that would compose the remainder of the 3,000 year history. Even so, the outlines of an Od-

---

*Orson Scott Card, "Question and Answer," XVth Annual Brigham Young University Symposium on the Influence of Science Fiction and Fantasy." March 27, 1997.

yssean hero might still be discerned in its details. There is wandering, as Ender resigns his governorship and takes to space with the implicit goal of reaching, not his home, but the yet-to-be-discovered home for the Hive Queen. There is a heroic disguise of a sorts, as Ender begins the process that will subsume his identity under the 'mask' of Speaker for the Dead. There is isolation as Ender embarks on his journeys accompanied only by Valentine, his sister. But the novel functions best, perhaps, in initiating Ender's transformation into Virgilian hero, sacrificing his own wishes and desires for the good of his colony, then resuming his voyage with the intent of founding a new nation—not the Rome of Aeneas, but the new world of the Buggers.

In terms of this discussion, the Shadow novels stand outside the purview of Ender's epic quest. He is present, but primarily as a memory, and the stories told are not his. Peter and Bean move to the fore as central characters—heroic persons, if you like—and might profitably be discussed as heroes of their own epics. But they do not alter our perception of Ender in any significant way.

### In Medias Res

As far back as Horace's *Ars Poetics*, it has been accepted that epics must begin *in medias res*—literally 'in the middle of things.' The tradition was already considered ancient in Horace's day (65-8 BC) since it was based primarily on Homer's example. Both the *Iliad* and the *Odyssey* begin in the middle of the action. The *Iliad* ultimately recounts the whole of the Trojan War but begins in its final week. The past and future events recounted throughout the poem, frequently during Epic Councils, complete with set-piece dialogue and elevated, formal diction. Similarly, the *Odyssey* begins just after Odysseus has lost all of his shipmates; in an early banquet scene, he recounts the preceding years of his wandering and the rest of the poem completes the ten years it takes for him to reach Ithaca. The majority of epics in the centuries to come assumed the same narrative stance: Virgil's *Aeneid* and Milton's *Paradise Lost* are among the most important of them. In fact, in the opening line of his poem, Milton promises to speak "Of Man's first Disobedience," but he doesn't actually get around to doing so until the ninth book of twelve. Ultimately, however, he recounts events from the Creation itself to the expulsion of Adam and Eve from the Garden and the beginning of human history.

*Ender's Game* models this same tradition. It begins appropriately enough in the middle of things—the day Ender loses the monitor that has set him apart from other children. What has gone on before, we learn gradually, over the course of the book, often through the dialogues that open chapters, echoing Epic Councils, as well as through Ender's discussions with his Mentor-figure, Mazer Rackham. And the novel concludes by simultaneously ending the Bugger War and opening a new era in human history.

## Epic simile

Similes are relatively simple literary forms: comparisons using "like" or "as." They are generally used to illustrate an unfamiliar idea or thing by likening it to something familiar. The "epic simile," on the other hand, can be enormously complex, extending over multiple lines and incorporating an encyclopedic knowledge of the poet's world, cultural heritage, and religion, among other areas. It becomes a vehicle by which the poet can introduce added meaning into the poem. As with the other conventions, this one originated with Homer and was applied to great effect by succeeding epic poets. The first of several bee-similes in Homer, for example, occurs in Book II of the *Iliad*, comparing the armies arriving by ship to "tribes" of bees. Virgil subsequently compares the great city of Carthage to a hive of bees. Milton's fallen angels are compared to bees in Book I of *Paradise Lost*. Each succeeding poet knew how his predecessors had used and amplified the image and could count on readers not only to understand the immediate comparison but also to recall it in its previous manifestations in other poems. Frequently epic similes are so long and complex as to seem digressive, but a close reading reveals that they are a mechanism by which the poet can introduce new ideas and images, allude to the great myths and stories of the past and import their power into his own poem, and provide readers with a new, frequently unexpected perspective of the subject at hand.

J. B. Hainsworth approaches the topic of epic simile from a structural point of view—how does including an overt comparison impel the epic narrative forward? "Short similes," he notes, "are universal"; but the longer similes particularly associated with Homeric epic are more genre-specific and function-specific:

> Since their content is not at all confined to echoes
> of the heroic world, the similes [in the *Iliad* and the
> *Odyssey*] make an important contribution to the epic
> breadth of view. And they are useful for another rea-

son. Much of what Homer described was outside his audience's direct experience. It could be stirring stuff for all that, but how much more effective if it could be brought within the imaginative experience of an audience. The simile invites, almost compels, its hearer to visualize the two scenes, the action and its likeness. (28-29)

In a long and complex narrative such as an epic poem, such a technique may prove invaluable.

In terms of contemporary science fiction and fantasy, however, some critics argue that the presence of simile itself militates against the genres. By definition (some definitions, at least), science fiction and fantasy (and horror, for that matter) *are* literatures of images, of metaphors and similes, in which the worlds and the peoples invented to inhabit those speculative landscapes in some senses represent vehicles of comparisons, with humanity itself as the persistent tenor. Rosemary Jackson, indeed, argues that by virtue of its subversive relationship to comparison, the Fantastic denies metaphor, and by extension, simile:

When it is 'naturalized' as allegory or symbolism, fantasy loses its proper non-signifying nature. Part of its subversive power lies in this resistance to allegory and metaphor. For it takes metaphorical constructions literally. Donne's famous metaphor 'I am every dead things', for example, is literally realized in Mary Shelley's *Frankenstein*, and in Romero's film *Night of the Living Dead.* It could be suggested that the movement of fantastic narrative is one of *metonymical* rather than *metaphorical* process: one object does not *stand for* another, but literally becomes that other, slides into it, metamorphosing from one shape to another in a permanent flux and instability. (267)

It might thus seem appropriate in a novel such as *Ender's Game* that there are few extended comparisons; after all the *game* that figures so prominently in the title and in the narrative becomes, we discover in the final chapter, a metaphor for larger, more critical issues, including the nature of humanity, the nature of sacrifice, and the nature of community.

Yet even so, there are moments in *Ender's Game* when the

structure of comparison becomes critical, opening the text in unexpected ways. In the opening lines of Chapter 2, the disembodied voices that introduce each chapter assess Ender's responses to losing his monitor:

> "All right, it's off. How's he doing."
> "You live inside somebody's body for a few years, you get used to it. I look at his face now, I can't tell what's going on. I'm not used to seeing his facial expressions. I'm used to feeling them."
> "Come on, we're not talking about psychoanalysis here. We're soldiers, not witch doctors. You just saw him beat the guts out of the leader of a gang."
> "He was thorough. He didn't just beat him, he beat him deep. Like Mazer Rackham at the—"
> "Spare me...." (14)

The abrupt intrusion interrupts an attempt to define Ender Wiggin—an attempt that remains central to the novel. At the same time, the simile potentially opens the novel to incorporate portions of an heroic narrative not strictly part of Ender's story or of Ender's Game. Just as Homeric similes functioned in part to allow the poet infinite opportunities to expand his base story—through catalogues of warriors and weapons, through genealogies, through recitations of previous battles and heroic encounters, through supernatural intrusions into human affairs, and so on—so the reference to Mazer Rackham could allow infinite opportunities to bolster the military backgrounds to the story. Card refuses to indulge in those opportunities, however, suggesting but not developing a central simile that will ultimately prove more crucial than the speaker knows.

Toward the end of the third chapter, on the other hand, Card incorporates two seemingly off-handed similes that will echo throughout the novel and that Card *will* develop. As Graff describes the Battle School to Ender, he says: "We've scraped together everything mankind could produce, a fleet that makes the one they sent against us last time seem like a bunch of kids playing in a swimming pool" (27). Ender, however, is concentrating on his mental image of Mazer Rackham's fleet in the videos of the bugger invasions:

> And then he thought of the films of the buggers that everyone had to see at least once a year. The Scathing of China. The Battle of the Belt. Death and suffering and terror. And Mazer Rackham and his

brilliant maneuvers, destroying an enemy fleet twice his size and twice his firepower, using the little human ships that seemed so frail and weak. Like children fighting with grown-ups. (28)

Two key references remain largely undefined: The Scathing of China and The Battle of the Belt. But the similes of children in a swimming pool and of children fighting adults become, again, central to the story. Several chapters later, at the beginning of "The Giant's Drink," Card describes the children at the Battle School as they "filed clumsily into the battleroom, like children in a swimming pool for the first time." Ender pushes his body into null-gravity: "He wasn't flying, he was falling. This was a dive." And later, when the students have acclimated to nullo conditions, they "drifted lazily in many directions, waving their arms, trying to swim" (54-55). What was initially a simile—and perhaps a trite one at that—becomes realized in an extended passage that covers most of two pages and that becomes a recurring motif in the novel. Dink Meeker's free-style floating in the battleroom, a self-defined signal that he understands more than the other children about what is really going on at the Battle School, similarly parallels Ender's free-style floating in the lake on Earth, an action that is the prelude to *his* understanding his relationship with Valentine, with humanity in general, and with the Buggers.

Swimming, then, functions initially as a visual, perhaps tactile comparison between a known action and an unknown action. Readers familiar with swimming can identify more easily with the battleroom, can in part imagine the sense of freedom it extends, and thus can empathize more completely with Ender, Dink, and the others as the battleroom becomes the single focus of their lives.

Similarly, the reference to the students being "like children fighting with grown-ups" will resonate again during the climactic final battle in the Battle School, with Ender's exhausted army pitted against two fresh armies. Against all decorum, Ender sends five soldiers to perform the victory ritual at the enemy's gate, thus effectively asserting victory even though they were out-numbered, out-maneuvered, and out-classed. When Ender is unfrozen, he confronts, not the child-commanders of the 'enemy' armies, but his instructor:

Ender was smiling. "I beat you again, sir," he said.
"Nonsense, Ender," Anderson said softly. "Your

battle was with Griffin and Tiger."

"How stupid do you think I am?" said Ender. (190)

Ender understands that in the Battle School, the true conflict lies between the child—himself—and the adults who surround him, isolate him, and refuse to help him. What he does *not* understand—yet—is that the same holds true for the larger Game he plays, the game of Human versus Bugger. There, too, children are pitted against adults. Ender fights Mazer Rackham physically and psychologically; Ender and his toon leaders fight the teachers at Command School as the students grow closer together and bond in the face of a perceived enemy; and Ender and his toon literally fight the bugger fleet, destroying humanity's enemies at their Home Planet. Only in the final chapter does Ender discover the great irony that the final battle was unnecessary; the buggers were not returning to destroy Earth. And at that point, in what Spinrad slightingly refers to as a bridge between the novel and its sequel, Ender finally understands the adult 'game' sufficiently to dedicate his life to winning it on his terms—to give life to the Hive Queen and her eggs.* The simile encompasses the novel; and, more importantly, it opens outward to direct Ender and the reader into *Speaker*.

The initial similes, which functioned as little more than sketches of images, expand until they take on an epic intensity, coloring the entire narrative. Great things—the salvation of all humanity—have been compared to small things—children swimming in a pool. It is one characteristic, in fact, of the epic simile, that great things are compared to small things

> without any loss of grandeur, the danger of such
> similes being that the smallness of the thing to which
> the subject is being compared will lower the subject
> rather than elevate it by understatement. The three
> major epic poets succeed, however: Homer compares
> a warrior's courage to that of a house-fly that auda-
> ciously bites a man who is shooing him away (*Il.*

---

*Thus providing an indication as early as Chapter 3 that Card intends all along that Ender bear the enormous burden of guilt he willingly assumes in Chapter 15— and, I think, negating Spinrad's claim that the novel is about "Ender's repressed incestuous sexuality, buggery as the villain of the piece, the capture of adolescent libido for militaristic purposes, and Ender's feeling of guilt in what should have been his climactic hour of triumph" Spinrad (*Science Fiction*, 69).

XVII, 570-2); Virgil compares the builders of Carthage to bees busily pursuing their labors (I, 430-6);
and Milton compares Satan and his legions to the
pygmies, 'that small infantry/Warr'd on by Cranes'.
(Blessington, I, 575-6)

And subsequently, by the way, to ants. Card carefully describes the
buggers—to the extent that he provides any concrete descriptions—
as being ant-like. Gradually, however, that comparison loses in importance to the continual and increasing suggestion of something
bee-like about them—their Hive and, most critically, their Hive
Queen.

In the penultimate chapter—in truth the final chapter of this portion of Ender's story—Admiral Chamrajnagar attempts to describe
to Graff the "mysteries of the fleet," the almost ecstatic visions that
will open up to Ender Wiggin. Graff responds that the admiral has
made it "sound like a priesthood." "And a god," the admiral answers,

And a religion. Even those of us who command
by ansible know the majesty of flight among the
stars. I can see you find my mysticism distasteful. I
assure you that your distaste only reveals your ignorance. Soon enough Ender Wiggin will also know
what I know; he will dance the graceful ghost dance
through the stars, and whatever greatness is within
him will be unlocked, revealed, set forth before the
universe for all to see. You have the soul of a stone,
Colonel Graff, but I sing to a stone as easily as to another singer. (Ch. 14, p. 222)

While not a simile, the comparison of dancing, of unlocking, revealing, setting forth greatness is surely critical at this point in the text.
True, Ender is about to defeat the buggers—defeat them thoroughly
and utterly, almost beyond any hope of restoration—but that is not
really how Card intends to demonstrate his hero's greatness. Instead,
everything that has gone on before Chapter 14, everything in Chapter 14 itself, becomes prologue to the larger epic Card intends to tell,
beginning in Chapter 15, "Speaker for the Dead," and continuing
through *Speaker for the Dead, Xenocide,* and *Children of the Mind.*[*]

---

[*]In this connection, it is significant that Norman Spinrad's eccentric interpretation

This single lyrical passage—one of the few such passages in the novel—establishes an expectation, a focus, for the remainder of the story yet to come, while at the same time explicitly introducing the epic-creating image of the singer and his song.

Even in these few points, tracing connections between *Ender's Game* and the epic tradition seems useful in understanding and appreciating Card's achievement in the novel. It would be equally possible to discuss at length other of the conventions associated with epic, particularly:

- **High style**—a genre-specific vocabulary, including neologisms and alternate meanings, that triggers what Samuel R. Delany calls the "reading protocols" unique to science fiction and/or fantasy and immediately categorize the work as such;
- **Arming of the hero**—both in terms of Ender's battle suit and of the machinery he becomes almost identifiable with as he plays his games;
- *Deus ex Machina,* **Epic machinery, or Christian marvelous**—the revelation of instant galaxy-wide communication through the use of the *ansible* functions as an intrusion of the apparently

---

of *Ender's Game* requires that the last chapter be virtually jettisoned:

> Throw out the final chapter, which seems to exist mostly as a bridge to the sequel, *Speaker for the Dead,* and the novel reaches its proper sci-fi climax when Ender destroys the home world of the Buggers.
>
> The hero destroys the villains and gets the girl.
>
> But the girl he gets is his sister, and in his hour of victory what he feels is not triumphant vindication, but *guilt.* (*Science Fiction,* 27)

What Spinrad misses entirely are the epic ramifications of that final chapter, Card's version of a Miltonic 'critique of heroism' that undercuts the epic pretensions of a militaristic hero and initiates discussion of a more complex mode, a hero of wisdom and sacrifice. Card has noted in private discussions that *Ender's Game* was intended as a prolegomenon to *Speaker for the Dead*; to speak of its final chapter as merely a bridge—a "perfunctory anti-war statement" (Spinrad, *Science Fiction,* 27)—invalidates Card's extended vision. In a final commentary on *Ender's Game,* Spinrad faults it for not being a tragedy; he fails to note that it attempts to epic.

'supernatural' into Ender's story; the aliens and the otherwise inexplicable advances based on their science might also be considered;

- *Nuntius* **('messenger') and** *Mentor* **figures**— this would include Mazer Rackham and his contribution to Ender's battles;
- **Descent into the Underworld/Ascent to the Mountain of Revelation**—particularly as it functions during Ender's five days of unconsciousness at the close of the novel and his subsequent ascension into the mysteries of space;
- **Warring nations and rival gods**—this forms the core of events in *Ender's Game*: the battle between humans and buggers and, to a lesser extent, the ongoing war between adult and child.

# CLIVE BARKER'S
## *THE GREAT AND SECRET SHOW*:

## REALISM IN HORROR FICTION

[This essay was presented to the Brigham Young University Symposium on Science Fiction and Fantasy: "Life, the Universe, and Everything XX," Provo UT, February, 2002.]

One fundamental consideration of horror fiction is the relation between the reader and the fictive landscape. Gothic horror (exemplified by Poe, Lovecraft and the writers of the Cthulhu mythos, and others) often attempts to divorce the reader from an objective reality as soon as possible. Within the first paragraph of "The Fall of the House of Usher," for example, the reader is asked to exchange familiar physical landscapes for a frightening landscape of the mind:

> During the whole of a dull, dark, and soundless day in the autumn of the year, when the clouds hung oppressively low in the heavens, I had been passing alone, on horseback, through a singularly dreary tract of country, and at length found myself, as the shades of the evening drew on, within the view of the melancholy House of Usher. I know not how it was—but, with the first glimpse of the building, a sense of insufferable gloom pervaded my spirit.... There was an iciness, a sinking, a sickening of the heart—an unredeemed dreariness of thought which no goading of the imagination could torture into aught of the sublime. (231)

The technique appears with even greater clarity in the opening lines of "The Pit and the Pendulum": "I was sick—sick unto death with that long agony; and when they at length unbound me, and I was permitted to sit, I felt that my senses were leaving me" (246).

The reader is thrust at once into the speaker's subjectivity (including the never-to-be-defined reference to 'they'); and the story never allows that subjectivity to merge with an identifiable external reality. The story's settings, actions, and characters remain steadfastly segregated from verifiable fact. The same technique appears in other Poe stories, including the elliptical "The Masque of the Red Death" and "The Oval Portrait."

Readers of many Lovecraft stories are similarly impelled into worlds that exists only in Lovecraft's imagination. In "The Outsider," for example, Lovecraft's second sentence is simultaneously Poesque and (to use Lovecraft's own word) grotesque: "Wretched is he who looks back upon lone hours in vast and dismal chambers with brown hangings and maddening rows of antique books, or upon awed watches in twilight groves of grotesque, gigantic, and vine-encumbered trees that silently wave twisted branches far aloft" (46); eventually the references to "chambers," "brown hangings," and similar words assume new meanings that are integral to the horror itself. Perhaps the most idealized example, however, occurs in the first sentences of "The Picture in the House," which exemplify as they define:

> Searchers after horror haunt strange, far places. For them are the catacombs of Ptolemais, and the carven mausolea of the nightmare countries. They climb to the moonlit towers of ruined Rhine castles and falter down black cobwebbed steps beneath the scattered stones of forgotten cities in Asia. The haunted wood and the desolate mountain are their shrines, and they linger around the sinister monoliths on uninhabited islands. But the true epicure in the terrible, to whom a new thrill of unutterable ghastliness is the chief end and justification of existence, esteems most of all the ancient, lonely farmhouses of backwoods New England; for there the dark elements of strength, solitude, grotesqueness and ignorance combine to form the perfection of the hideous. (30)

In such stories, neither Poe nor Lovecraft takes particular pains to convince readers that the world portrayed is the 'real' world, or that the disruptions suffered by that world impinge on the reader.

An alternate approach, persistent in much contemporary horror, works in the opposite direction by requiring that the story relate explicitly to the reader's objective world. The disparity between what the reader sees beyond the confines of the book and what happens within that book creates the disjunction that in part gives horror its *frisson.* Stoker's web-hung castles and heart-stopping, midnight rides through haunted ranges draw their strength not only from the intensity of his imagery but from their juxtaposition to the tone of Jonathan Harker's prosaic journals. Stephen King's landscapes encompass not only vampires, werewolves, haunted hotels, haunted automobiles, and revenant pseudonyms, but also New England city parks where people picnic and eat Ding-Dongs, and macadamized rural roads where oil trucks barrel along at high speed, sometimes striking cats...and sometimes children. Dean R. Koontz moves even closer to the real world in his fictions, many set in the Southern California landscape Koontz knows well. *The Bad Place,* for example, almost invites readers to take out city maps and follow characters' routes; and it is possible, it seems, to read *Shadowfires* and then drive from Los Angeles to Las Vegas and almost identify the exact gully where Eric Leben encountered nests of rattlesnakes. Again and again, Koontz's fictions rely on a sense that the landscape is *here,* that the world represented is *ours,* that the characters are people just like us; then into that familiar, comfortable-seeming world intrudes something irrational and horrific.

The technique is, as these examples suggest, both commonplace and potent. The closer the reader identifies with the objective reality we agree to share, the greater the horror when that reality is disrupted.

Either approach seems appropriate. Both work for different effects. Both require different techniques. Both can lead readers to the unique pleasures of terror and horror.

Occasionally, however, a writer confuses approaches. The result is frequently a frustrating novel, perhaps appealing within its own confines but ultimately ambiguous.

Clive Barker often finds himself in these mid-grounds. His strength as a story teller is evident in a number of tales in *The Books of Blood.* His novels, however, have not received the praise that his short fiction has. *The Damnation Game* was, for some readers, unreadable; it began with a promising premise, then spun off into indecisiveness. *Cabal* is even more frustrating with its blending of realistic landscape, surrealistic character, and poetic diction, with lines often more elliptical than direct, events more suggested than defined.

In *The Great and Secret Show,* however, Barker illustrates the difficulty horror writers may lock themselves into by creating an imbalance between reality and horror. The novel begins with a promise of verisimilitude. Initially, characters, settings, and actions are extreme but marginally realistic in presentation, at least until the revelation of what is contained in the mounds of letters in the Omaha Central Post Office

When the novel shifts toward present time, however, beginning in Part Two, "The League of Virgins," two serious problems develop. The first, and perhaps least important, relates to the setting—a small town called Palomo Grove. There is no problem with the assertion of a fictitious town in Ventura County, California, nor even in placing that town in geographical relationships with actual landscapes—witness H. P. Lovecraft's Innsmouth and Dunwich, Stephen King's 'Castle Rock,' and other similar locales. And, according to an interview with Barker, he intended the setting to reflect reality: "...the little town of Palomo Grove is a real town, and based upon research that I did in that town, and pursued the details of getting that right as much as I possibly could" ("Telephone Interview" 78).

For the first few chapters dealing with Palomo Grove, the setting seems acceptable. Abruptly, however, Barker defines his geography too narrowly; he specifically identifies Palomo Grove as one town of several in Simi Valley, California (III, 1, 110), or, as he calls it in the interview, "the Simi Valley."

At that point, the setting lost the sense of verisimilitude it had attempted to establish, because Simi Valley *is* a town; it is in fact the only town in a small, narrow valley, and the physical landscape Barker describes bears little resemblance to the real place. Simi Valley has no Hill, with its semicircular stratification of socioeconomic status, nor is there a multi-story Mall even resembling the one he describes. More critically, when Barker has characters leave Palomo Grove, their movements seem inaccurate. The family of one girl moves from Palomo Grove to Thousand Oaks, "only to find that their reputations had followed them" (III,1, 111)—not at all surprising since Thousand Oaks lies less than ten miles from Simi Valley. The school in both towns are rivals, people from one area shop in the other, and both towns straddle a major route from the Coast Highway to the San Fernando Valley. Certainly Thousand Oaks would lie close enough to Simi Valley for Jo-Beth to be among the first to returned to the ruined town "when it was deemed safe to" (VII, 8, 677-678); but given the trauma she has endured in Palomo Grove, it seems too close to be a haven of healing.

At the point where Barker pinpoints the location of Palomo

Grove, then, *The Great and Secret Show* became problematical. The sense of disjuncture is intensified, however, by the rapid development of a second level of inaccuracy, this time more critical because more closely tied with necessary developments in Barker's plot.

Several years ago, I wrote a paper that argued that references to Mormonism appear more frequently in Science Fiction and Fantasy than to most other religions. While many of the conclusions in that paper have been modified over the years, my contention remains that when Mormons or Mormonism appear in fantasy (of either the light, the high, or the dark varieties), the references usually deny any strict theology and work instead on the level of cultural assumption. Mormonism in general becomes a structure to be manipulated as part of the plot, rather than a structure of belief.

In *The Great and Secret Show,* Barker makes a point of noting that several key characters are Mormons. The first references are, admittedly, elliptical, almost off-handed. One of four girls about to become, unwillingly and unknowingly, a member of the League of Virgins is cast as a Mormon. We discover this apparently incidental bit of information obliquely. She wants to meet a boy; she approaches him and, suddenly inarticulate and shy, she "recited all her personal details shamelessly; even asked him in a sudden rush of optimism, if he was a Mormon. That, she'd later decided, had been a tactical error" (II.1, 66).

The assertion of her Mormonism allows Barker to develop an intriguing tension in the narrative. A girl belonging to a religious group noted for its conservative attitudes toward drinking, smoking and pre-marital sex suddenly reverses the direction of her life. Like the other three girls, Joyce becomes obsessed with sex—or more accurately, with bearing a child. Her resultant inner turmoil surfaces early in the story; in the same paragraph that reveals her disastrous approach to Randy Krentzman, Barker also notes that "If Arleen had been seriously interested in Randy's affections then Joyce might have gone right around to the Reverend Meuse and asked him if he could hurry the Apocalypse up a little" (II.1, 66).

And there the novel threatened to disintegrate.

A Mormon girl, asking that the Apocalypse be advanced just because of her jealousy? Not likely perhaps, although at least possible. But the reference to 'Reverend Meuse' (and later to 'Pastor John') were unsettling, not because of their appearance in a horror novel but simply because Mormons *never* refer to their ministers (who are after all lay men and women) as either "Reverend" or "Pastor."

The bobble in terminology might seem trivial, particularly at this stage in the novel. After all, the reference is superficial, with no relevance to church structure or theology. But even though Barker correctly identifies the name of the Mormon Church (a rarity among many non-Mormon writers), he seems to have intruded the references without researching sufficiently to re-create the particular jargon of Mormonism.

The resulting crack in the façade of realism and verisimilitude—like the puncture the Gaffe tears in the fabric of our universe—never quite closes. For a while, it seems as if Joyce's Mormonism is merely way of providing a thumbnail character sketch. Mormons don't drink. Mormons don't smoke. Mormons are conservative about sexuality. Therefore Joyce's pregnancy becomes ironic and atypical.

However, Barker does not let the reference slide. Ultimately it becomes Joyce's responsibility to "tell the whole truth, without excision or addition, and to lay the story of the League of Virgins to rest" (II, 3, 104). One girl is dead; one is insane; one has left town. That leaves only one in Palomo Grove…the Mormon.

Initially, Barker focuses on her Mormonism as a means of defining how difficult it is for her to keep the secret, especially since she is pregnant and she alone of the four had a specific religious heritage that militates against premarital sex. In addition, her father's religion becomes important: "Dick McGuire was not a strong man, either in spirit or body, and his Church was wholly unsupportive in the matter, siding with the non-Mormons against the girl. The truth had to be told" (II, 3, 104). Barker does not explain how a group as tightly focused as most Mormon congregations would break with history and tradition to confront the girl (by the end of the novel, in fact, he contradicts his own image with the comment, "The Church of Jesus Christ of Latter-day Saints looked after its own" [VII, 8, 680]).

Nor does he explain why, in the next paragraph, he evokes a scene with the girl, six parents, and Pastor John, "the spiritual leader of the Mormon community in the Grove and its surroundings" (II, 3, 104). Mormon "spiritual leaders" are usually called bishops; if the area is small enough, one might be a "Branch President." And if the area is larger, he might be the "Stake President." But never "Pastor." Seventeen years later, however, Joyce still refers to him as "Pastor John" or as "the Pastor" (III, 2, 116; III, 5, 162; IV, 10, 263; and others). A reference to calling "the church" only to find that the Pastor is "not available," having gone to comfort a new widow, implies that this Pastor works full-time for the congregation and presumably lives at the church (IV, 2, 185), another point of departure between Barker's Mormons and actual ones.

When Joyce says that the names of the biological fathers were unimportant because they were "just men," Pastor John responds, "Are you saying the Devil is in you, child?" (II, 3, 105). While Mormons believe in the Devil, Pastor John's question seems foreign to their usual vocabulary and structure. This difficulty recurs when Barker describes conversations between the adult Joyce and an older Pastor John: "Talk of the world as a Valley of Death, haunted by faces capable of unspeakable malice. That was the chief comfort Pastor John gave Momma [Joyce]. They agreed on the presence of the Devil in the world; in Palomo Grove" (III, 2, 118). For Mormons, this world is uniquely positive; it is a time of trial and temptation, to be sure, but potentially far more than that. Mormon phraseology and theology work against a simplistic "Valley of Death" image. Similarly, Pastor John's frequent references to "the McGuire woman" (IV, 10, 272; and others) rings hollowly; any Mormon leader who had known a woman in his congregation for seventeen years would refer to her as "Sister McGuire." Nor is Pastor John exempt from scrutiny; at a crucial scene, Barker reveals his authorial biases when he refers to the Pastor as "the God-fearer" (IV, 10, 275), sarcastically highlighting the Pastor's personal hypocrisy and Barker's underlying critique of twentieth-century religion, most frequently exemplified by his hybrid version of Mormonism. In the face of the horrors Barker imagines as impinging on the world, "God's agency—in the form of the Pastor—[is] valueless" (V, 2, 315).

Other references to Mormonism become even more confusing. At one point, Joyce's daughter Jo-Beth reflects on the intensity of her emotional attraction to a stranger. Barker couches her reflections in religious terms, and (unusual in popular fiction) he uses correct terminology:

> If all the Sunday teachings she'd dutifully attended had instructed her in anything, it was that revelation came when and where least expected. To Joseph Smith, on a farm in Palmyra, New York; news of the Book of Mormon, revealed to him by an angel. Why not to her then, in circumstances no more promising? Stepping into Butrick's Steak House; standing in a parking lot with a man she knew from everywhere and nowhere? (III, 3, 136)

Barker accurately notes that Joseph Smith received *news* of the Book of Mormon on a farm in Palmyra, not the book itself—that event came later, some distance from Palmyra. And even the word choice—Joseph Smith, instead of 'Joe Smith,' and Book of Mormon instead of 'Golden Bible,' 'Mormon Bible,' or any of several alternatives—resonates as authentic.

But then, only a few paragraphs further down, Jo-Beth's twin brother, Tommy-Ray, brews coffee; its scent fills the kitchen. His drinking coffee may not be unusual, since it is early established that he has deeper connections with his evil father than Jo-Beth. But her reaction to coffee in the house is startling. When Tommy-Ray challenges her about the events of the previous night, she says, "Want to pour me some of that coffee?" (III, 3, 137). There is no explanation why someone thinking in terms of Joseph Smith and the Angel Moroni moments before would drink coffee and thereby blithely break one of the best known external prohibitions of the Church that Joseph Smith founded. More curious is the lack of any reaction from their mother, Joyce, who could at least smell coffee brewing even if she rarely comes downstairs.

Elsewhere, the façade of Mormonism dissipates just as quickly. Jo-Beth realizes that evil exists: "the terrorist, the anarchist, the lunatic." All may be abetted by forces beyond the human; but she also realizes that "it was never more important that she sought the company of those whose definition of good was unshakable" (V, 7, 354). For Jo-Beth, this means Lois Knapp, owner of the Mormon Book Store. Yet when she arrives at the Knapp home, there is no mention of religion, theology, or goodness in conflict with evil. Instead, Barker presents the illusion of characters of contemporary (and inane) television situations comedies and soaps. In the midst of sanitized lust and the quasi-nudity of men's-underwear advertisements, Barker allows only a brief reference to religion when Jo-Beth states that she doesn't drink liquor. Her host's immediate comment undercuts that assertion, however. His wife, he notes, "denied herself," but he believes that what God doesn't see won't hurt him (either Mal Knapp or God).

The Mormon Book Store in Palomo Grove is a central location, one of half a dozen specifically described and pivotal in the plot. Again, however, there is an odd sense of unevenness in Barker's treatment of it.

The first reference to it is simply as "a book store" where Jo-Beth works days (II, 3, 135). Mrs. Knapp, the owner whose "dress and features" were "plain to the point of severity," first suggests its religious nature when she counter's Jo-Beth's tardiness with the terse comment that "The Lord's work is not to be taken lightly" (II,

3, 142).

The store's explicit connection to Mormonism is spelled out on several pages, unusual for their accuracy in representing LDS history and belief. When Howie Katz returns to the store to find Jo-Beth, he encounters the redoubtable Mrs. Knapp. Under her scrutiny he investigates the shelves. He sees the name of the church for the first time: The Church of Jesus Christ of Latter-day Saints, spelled correctly and accurately reproduced. He notes, again accurately, the connections many Mormons make between Jesus Christ and the "Great White God of ancient America...Quetzalcoatl in Mexico, Tongo-Loa god of the ocean sun in Polynesia, Illa-Tici, Kukulean or half a dozen other guises." His subsequent reference to all of these manifestations as "the perfect whitebread hero" is definitely not Mormon, but in this context is not intended to be so (IV, 4, 210).

Even more surprising, on his next pass through the shelves, Katz finds a picture-book history of Joseph Smith and reproduces verbatim a passage that is seminal in LDS theology and belief: "I saw two Personages, whose brightness and glory defy all description, standing above me in the air. One of them spake unto me, calling me by name..." (IV, 4, 211). The remainder of this critical passage is reproduced accurately and completely, including the phrase "sacred grove" that appears in virtually all LDS references to Joseph Smith's experience.

Almost immediately, however, Mrs. Knapp breaks in, and Barker's treatment of the rest of the scene relies more on stereotypical representations of older "Christians" confronted with young, long-haired types—compounded with Mrs. Knapp's persistent lying about Jo-Beth's whereabouts. But Mrs. Knapp, "good Christian that she was, seemed determined to have him out of the shop," making full use of her "versing in hypocrisy" (211-212). She abruptly ceases to be concrete, recognizable Mormon and becomes abstracted Christian hypocrite.

The bookstore plays an important role in the final chapters of the novel. Possessing partial answers to the enigma of Kassoon and the Loop, to the impending invasion of the Iad Uroboros, to the secrets of Quiddity, the characters who have survived Jaffe's disastrous meddling with the Art try to restore their reality. The father of one of the League of Virgins joins the group and, after rescuing Jaffe, sets out to find out what he can about the only clue they have.

He heads for the nearest bookstore, the one "in the Mall." Initially, Hotchkiss finds the bookstore frustrating. Books, he believes, are "all lies" particularly the ones he finds in the Mormon Book Store: "volumes of stuff about revelation and God's work on earth"

(VII, 7, 627). Hotchkiss has come to this particular place, in all of Palomo Grove, to unravel a reference to Trinity; he ostensibly chose it because it was nearby, in the Mall. He checks the indices of books, locating a few references, then casting them aside when the comments on "Trinity" prove unenlightening (VII, 6, 627). Rather than the illumination he seeks, he finds only books on Motherhood: "pap and platitudes. There was nothing in the pages that made reference, even obliquely, to any Trinity. Only talk of motherhood as a divine calling, woman in partnership with God, bringing new life into the world, her greatest and most noble task." (VII, 6, 628).

When he opens a book called *Preparing for Armageddon,* he finally discovers what he wants. As Barker describes it, the book is a handbook for survival, geared to the Mormons' well-known belief in preparedness and reserving a year's supply of food and clothing. There is a twist, however. Among the natural disasters for which Mormons might justifiably be expected to prepare, Hotchkiss discovers that "the image that loomed largest amid this catalogue of final acts was the mushroom cloud"(VII, 7, 634); the caption to one photograph of a nuclear explosion notes that the first atomic bomb was detonated at "a location named Trinity" (VII, 7, 635).

One difficulty in Barker's presentation of this scene is that a book by that title exists. Philip Lawrence's *Preparing for Armageddon: A Critique of Western Strategy* was published in 1988 by Wheatsheaf Books in England and St. Martin's Press in the United States. One of the earliest reviews of the book appeared in *British Book News* (October 1987), suggesting that it was available in England in time for Barker to have seen it and possibly incorporate its title into *The Great and Secret Show*, published in 1989. In spite of its title, however, Lawrence's scholarly appraisal of nuclear weapons was not published by one of the parochial presses Barker emphasizes in his descriptions of the Mormon Book Store; nor would it be appropriate for a Mormon Book Store (several telephone calls found no LDS bookstores in Los Angeles, Thousand Oaks, and Simi Valley that stocked it).

When Hotchkiss discovers *Preparing for Armageddon,* the final bit of the puzzle Barker has constructed falls easily into place nonetheless. But the discovery is disconcertingly adventitious. Barker's characters scurry about to decipher the riddle hidden in the word "Trinity," specifying that they are looking for something other than the surface meaning of "Father, Son, and Holy Spirit." Hotchkiss races to the nearest bookstore...only to discover that it is stocked with religious books that should address the theological minutiae of countless historical and theological arguments on the nature of the Trinity. None of those arguments would have been of any help, of course, and his chances of accidentally discovering the true reference should have been quite small.

Instead, however, he thumbs through books published by one of the few major Christian denominations that does not accept the conventional "Trinity" (that is, "The union of three divine figures, the Father, the Son, and the Holy Ghost, in one Godhead") and whose works are frequently almost devoid of the word itself. Yet here he finds his answer…and, coincidentally, in a book unrelated to theology. While Mormons are well known for their Welfare Program, which includes the injunction to faithful members to store a year's supply of food, clothing, and other essentials, it is less accurately defined as an "apocalyptic" religion. In this context the title of the book Hotchkiss discovers, *Preparing for Armageddon*, is not recognizably Mormon at all. Mormons prepare for natural disasters, to be sure; perhaps some have in mind preparing for a nuclear exchange (if preparing for such a thing were possible)—one Mormon has even written a collection of short stories set in a post-holocaust Great Salt Lake Valley. But few LDS books purport to provide instructions for surviving "Armageddon"; few deal with nuclear war; and even fewer, if any, would assert that with the detonation of the first atomic bomb, "Mankind's last age began" (VII, 7, 634).

For Mormons, the "last age"—more accurately referred to as the "dispensation of the fullness of time" in Mormon literature—would have begun, not with the Atomic Bomb, but with Joseph Smith's vision. Barker's text, then, seems inaccurate in its representation of Mormon belief. Yet Hotchkiss finds a specific book, in this particular bookstore, at a moment of unendurable stress; and the book provides the key to the resolution of a very long novel:

> All he needed was that one word, *Trinity,* in some other context than Father, Son, and Holy Ghost. Here it was. The Three-in-One reduced to a single place—a single event, indeed. This was the Trinity that superseded all others. In the imagination of the twentieth century the mushroom cloud loomed larger than God. (VII, 7, 635)

This is at best a questionable generalization, considering the fact that Hotchkiss had to ransack entire shelves about God in order to find a single reference to the bomb.

There is nothing narratively unacceptable in Barker's resolution, however; Hotchkiss (and behind him, Barker) simply states his opinion as to the relative weight of God and atomics. The revelation that "Trinity" refers to the location of the first atomic bomb, coupled with already existing knowledge that Kissoon's loop holds time in stasis, leads inevitably to climax and *dénouement*. All of the pieces fit. The survivors meet at Trinity and foil (for the time being, at least) an invasion of Earth by the alien Iad Uroboros.

Ironically, however, Hotchkiss does not tell the others what he has discovered. Threatened by alien monsters, he runs for his life but hesitates just long enough to pick up the book he dropped moments earlier. With the word "Jesus" on his lips ("evoking the name of the Savior he'd long ago forsaken") and *Preparing for Armageddon* in his hand, he dies (VII, 7, 637). He is granted a fragmentary moment of hope when he hears the word "Kissoon"—repudiating his antagonism to all things religious, he disastrously misinterprets Kissoon's name as "kiss" and "soon." After consciously denying, if not denigrating and ridiculing, religious verities throughout the narrative, Barker suddenly grants a dying character the hope implicit in so many of the Mormon texts he gleefully cast aside: "Carolyn, waiting on the other side of death, lips ready to press to his cheek. It made his last moments bearable, after all the horrors" (VII, 7, 639).

Later, Grillo discovers the body and the book. At this point, Barker makes the text of *Preparing for Armageddon* explicitly LDS:

> It seemed to be a manual on how to survive the Apocalypse. These were words of wisdom from Mormon Brethren to members of the Church, telling them that all would be well; that they had God's living oracles, the First Presidency and the Council of the Twelve apostles to watch over them and advise them. All they needed to do was take of that advice, spiritual and practical and whatever the future brought could be survived. (642)

Again, the terminology is correct, but the content frustratingly skewed. While the presiding Councils of the church do urge members to prepare and to become self-sufficient, it is not in the overt context of surviving either Armageddon or a nuclear war. The passage seems to suggest that this highly conservative contemporary religion cannot match the unmaking that is in progress. Nothing the church teaches even approaches understanding the universe of *The Great and Secret Show*.

If Barker did in fact base this plot development on images gleaned from the real *Preparing for Armageddon,* the story veers even further from reality. According to C. P. Potholm's review, Lawrence's book

> focuses on the nuclear predicament and on the contribution the West has made to that predicament. He believes 'security' in the nuclear context is a myth and therefore is concerned about the future of humankind in the nuclear age. Lawrence also asserts that the risks of nuclear war far outweigh the advantages of mutual deterrence and lays major blame for the current nuclear situation with the US. Although his arguments are stimulating and challenging, the author does not wrestle sufficiently with the fact that whatever nuclear weapons have or have not done, the US and the Soviet Union have avoided war for almost 50 years. Lawrence is on firmest ground when he moved away from strategic doctrine and onto the moral plane. For him, the inherent immorality of nuclear strategy revolved around the assumption that the West would resort to mass murder (by nuclear attack) in response to Soviet mass murder (by nuclear attack). These considerations depend not on an analysis of whether nuclear weapons have kept the peace, but rather on whether the consideration of their use is ipso facto immoral.

Potholm's assessment seems accurate, given the images, attitudes, and information Barker needs to move his narrative in the appropriate direction, but it does not correspond to Mormon doctrine or the general tenor of Mormon publications dealing with either preparedness or the End of Things. In addition, Barker's book in some senses illustrates one of Lawrence's concerns:

> the issue of nuclear war is not one which individuals can readily confront as a possible reality. In this respect I have profound misgivings about some of the ways in which the issues are now being portrayed in film and on television. There is a danger, or so I believe, that the interest in nuclear war could take on the character of an entertainment. Thus the horror de-

picted becomes a fiction; it remains in the realm of the inconceivable" (14).

Barker does this to a degree. The 'reality' of nuclear weaponry, symbolized by the Trinity blast, is treated as peripheral to the 'super-reality' of alien invaders. The destruction caused by the Trinity bomb (and by extension all of its progeny) is treated as peripheral to, and in fact preferable to, the destruction humanity will face if the Iad break through.

Again, the key to the crisis is discovered accidentally. Grillo locates the book, flips through it, and serendipitously not only sees the photograph of the mushroom cloud but instantly understands its importance. But the scene is not yet over. As Grillo races back to Coney Eye, he considers the irony that the politicians who should be assembling weapons to destroy the invading Iad Uroboros were

> too pragmatic to think that their empire could be put in jeopardy by something that belonged on the other side of dreams? He couldn't blame them. He wouldn't have lent that notion a moment's credibility seventy-two hours ago. He'd have judged it a non-sense: like the talk of God's living oracles in the book on the seat beside him, an overheated fantasy. (VII, 7, 643)

The schizophrenic sense persists that Barker both wants the religious sub-text as part of his narrative, yet at the same time feels compelled to deny it.

Taking all of its elements into account, the episode seems unacceptable, at least to a reader familiar with Mormon history, doctrine, and publications. It is not only improbable, but it is disconcertingly inaccurate. Throughout the episode, Barker uses images, symbols, language of religion, but primarily to undercut it and to suggest its inability to explain the twentieth-century world. He asserts it, undercuts it, misrepresents it, and manipulates it, but ultimately offers nothing substantive to replace it.

Barker's vision of Cosm and Metacosm denies human conceptions of religion. It is a valid narrative and thematic approach, but in this instance, Barker sets up a straw-opponent, what becomes essentially a pseudo-religion designed and defined to meet his narrative requirements but which is spoken of as if it were a legitimate religious viewpoint. The effect is to subordinate religion to Barker's horrific vision; the text consciously places Jesus on a par with werewolves, comic book heroes, and stars of X-rated films (VI, 9, 489): "Presidents, messiahs, shamans, popes, saints and lunatics had attempted—over the passage of a millennium—to buy, murder, drug and flagellate themselves into Quiddity" (VII, 1, 527). More to the point, the desire for Quiddity impels humanity and "Made it create gods. Made it destroy gods" (527).

*The Great and Secret Show* ultimately fails to remain consistent to its own protocols. Barker forces his text to break with the external landscape in which he places his story, and intrudes the *names* of actual places, religions, and books into the text while inaccurately representing their *essence*. Because the book claims verisimilitude as a standard by virtue of its careful positioning in time and place, its failure to recreate those times and places accurately calls all in doubt. Reading it ceases to be an exercise in imagination and vision, and becomes instead a frustrating exercise in separating fictive truth from objective unrealities.

# WHO IS BILLY JONES?:

## SOME SUGGESTIONS
## TOWARD AN UNDERSTANDING

This is not a review.

This is not an objective, distanced, scholarly examination.

This is, quite blatantly, an enthusiastic appreciation of a book I enjoyed tremendously written by a young man whose work I have enjoyed for years…and who happens to be my son.

*Billy: Messenger of Powers* is a young-adult fantasy novel, the first in a multi-volume series, published through an inventive use of the internet. By accessing its site—http://www.whoisbillyjones.com/ —anyone interested may download an audio edition of the novel, read quite professionally by Andy Bowyer. The cost? Whatever the listener thinks is appropriate. The whole project is an intriguing innovation in online publishing that has thus far garnered over 100,000 hits internationally from Argentina, Australia, Belgium, Brazil, Canada, China, Denmark, Estonia, Finland, Germany, Hungary, India, Ireland, Israel, Italy, Japan, Malaysia, Mexico, Morocco, Netherlands, Norway, Pakistan, Poland, Portugal, Romania, Russia, Seychelles, South Africa, Spain, Sweden, Switzerland, Turkey, Ukraine, United Kingdom, and, of course, the United States.

But none of that really addresses the central question. It is window dressing, making the book extrinsically more interesting but failing to indicate the richness of the story itself.

As a young-adult novel, *Billy* provides its readers with an engaging hero—a high-school freshman who, like many of its readers, feels totally out of place. To make matters worse, he is small, all five-foot nothing of him, and subject to frequent forceful insertion into empty hall lockers. He feels helpless…until circumstances introduce him to unknown Powers and give him a thorough education in power, its rightful uses, and its abuses. What follows is a roller-coaster ride of events, characters, landscapes, situations, and emotions, resulting in a Billy who, although still physically small, has grown significantly in all the ways that are important.

It is a delightful novel, fast-moving, energetic, flavored by constant humor, both situational and linguistic. And well worth hearing.

But on other levels, it is even more provocative. For older listeners, it provides a treasure-trove of allusions, structural references, archetypal echoes, and imagistic resonances that create depth and an ever-shifting backdrop of cultural, religious, and social echoes.

At its most fundamental, *Billy* infuses an archaic trope with new vigor. The underlying structure of Billy's universe—or, more precisely, perhaps, *multiverse*—relies on the ancient classification of all matter as belonging to one or more basic elements: Earth, Air, Fire, Water. To the traditional four, the novel adds a fifth and sixth: Death and Life. Key characters represent Elements, at times even the *essence* of the Elements, exhibiting appropriate knowledge and powers. And, given the often contradictory characteristics of the Elements and the beings who personify them, *Billy*'s worlds stand on the perilous edge of war, exemplified by the unbridgeable gulf between Life and Death.

The novel expands upon this essentially Medieval/Renaissance world-view, including echoes of such crucial beliefs as the Music of the Spheres, an image for the fundamentally harmonic character of the universe when acting in concord to God's will; and the entire panoply of associations implied by humoral psychology, in which the overriding element in one's physical makeup parallels specific mental, emotional, and spiritual characteristics, including associations with colors, personalities, and age. Individual Powers dress, act, and think in accordance with their respective elements. Hence, one character is associated with Fire, wears red; is an active, vigorous young man; and is, appropriately, by profession a 'fireman.' The novel avoids making the identifications too blunt and obvious, but underlying each major character, one may see the Elements moving.

Upon this foundation *Billy* builds a second archetypal level, this one associated with the mythic history of King Arthur. Arthurian touches occur, apparently randomly, through most of the early part of the novel, but the final chapters reveal the close interweaving of myth with world-view, ultimately introducing—in much the same manner as Spenser's *Faerie Queene*—Arthur, not so much as acting character but as a promised presence in future books. Specific components of the mythos gradually reveal themselves as the novel progresses, until at its conclusion, they emerge directly to participate inexorably and seamlessly with the story. The novel handles the emergences adroitly, almost tantalizingly, until the Arthurian motifs crystallize sufficiently for younger listeners to become aware of them. The whole sub-structure is handled carefully and well, never overwhelming the surface story but supporting and enriching it.

In addition, *Billy: Messenger of Power* penetrates through the core of both the ancient Elements and the Arthurian mythos to an even more fundamental sequence of echoes. J. R. R. Tolkien once discussed Fantasy-as-genre as leading, in its highest moments, to a sense of *Eucatastrophe,* that is, a single moment of overwhelming joy that echoes throughout past, present, and future. For him, the best fantasy gives us a glimpse of the 'true' eucatastrophe, the Incarnation of Christ at the central point of human history. Whether overly Christian or not, specifically religious or not, high fantasy leaves readers in an emotional state that parallels that of the most intense religious experience.

*Billy* attempts—and to a large extent succeeds—in creating the sense that, underlying the surface story, with all of its archetypes and echoes, is a greater story, one dealing ultimately with redemption and regeneration. Scriptural allusions begin with the title itself, *Billy: Messenger of Power.* A *messenger* is "one who is sent out," an "apostle" in the earliest Greek and Latin senses of the word. There is a nicely comic sense in the juxtaposition of Billy's commonplace name with a word that mediates between him and "power." The allusions continue with references to a grand Council and an early battle that separated the Powers into forces of light—the Dawnwalkers—and forces of darkness—the Darksiders. The Dawnwalkers are committed to allowing humanity its freedom to act; the Darksiders to ruling and subjugating. There are Christic references throughout. There is an Anti-Christ, one who asserts himself as the true Messenger of the King. There is a revelation scene reminiscent of Christ's temptation on the pinnacles of the Temple or Moses' visions upon a high mountain. There is a sealed book, only one-third of which can be read. There is even a character swallowed by a whale *à la* Jonah.

Even given all of this, *Billy* carefully avoids being simply Arthur-warmed-over or Christic-imagery-sprinkled-about. It tells its own story, creates its own memorable characters, defines its own unique landscapes, and arrives at its own inevitable but satisfying conclusion. Yes, the villain gets away. Yes, there are clearly more books to follow, more weapons to discover. No, Arthur does not appear, but as in the early volumes of Susan Cooper's Arthurian sequence, the way has been opened. And no, Billy does not exactly get the girl in the end.

Taken as a whole and as the opening chapter in a much longer story, *Billy: Messenger of Power* does itself proud, especially for a first novel. It is readable, engaging, and rewarding.

And even if it was written by my son, I recommend it.

# AN ESSAY INTO LDS
# WRITERS AND THE FANTASTIC

## I. The Fantastic

Twenty-five years ago, I published a paper that explored some perspectives on the LDS church as expressed by science fiction, fantasy, and horror writers ("Refracted"). Over the intervening quarter of a century, I have explored works by that same community of writers, frequently explicitly but always implicitly from an LDS point of view. It seems time to complete the process with this essay and explore my perspectives on why LDS fantasists are drawn to these three genres. As with every essay in this collection, the conclusions reached are mine alone; I do not claim to speak either for all writers of SF/F/Horror or for the LDS Church. But as a member of both communities, as scholar/critic and poet/novelist, I would like to share some possibilities.

It has been frequently noted that there seems to be an unusually large number of LDS writers of the Fantastic—particularly of science fiction, but to varying degrees fantasy and horror as well—especially given the percentage of Mormons in the general population. To get even a minimal appreciation of the phenomenon, one need only consider the regional, nation-wide, and international successes of such writers as Orson Scott Card, Brandon Sanderson, Brandon Mull, Dave Farland (Dave Wolverton), James Dashner, Chris Heimerdinger, Tracy Hickman, Stephenie Meyer, M. Shayne Bell, Lee Allred, Scott Parkin, Glenn Anderson, and many others.

Curious as to how others might answer to the question "Why are LDS writers attracted to science fiction, fantasy, and horror?" I posted it online and invited responses. Most respondents were of a single mind, expressing their thoughts in different ways. One wrote regarding horror specifically:

> It's an outlet for the urges that all people have, but that we work so hard to ignore, overcome, or sub-

limate... If we write stories about really evil guys, we can express that bit of our humanity without endangering either ourselves or others, and we can also make the good win over evil every time...like we know it does.

Another concentrated on science fiction and fantasy:

For me, I think I would have gravitated to SF/F no matter my religion. Not horror, though. I don't do horror.

SF, at least Star Trek and many of the books from the 50's and 60's that influenced me, paint a hopeful, bright future that is better than what we have now, similar to the promises we are given in church. God is loving and just and we are here to be happy. Not many religions teach that doctrine. SF parallels many of the ideals embraced by LDS religion.

Current SF is too dark for my tastes. Nobody has morals, everyone dies pointlessly, evil is winning, etc.

I'm not as big into fantasy as I used to be, but it's a similar thing. Epic fantasy is about good vs. evil, right and wrong, and prophecy. Our church history is full of right and wrong, good vs. evil, and prophecy being fulfilled. Lots of parallels there. But fantasy has also gone too far down a dark path for me.

I guess what I'm saying is that I personally am attracted to the stories where good and evil are well defined, the future is a better place than the present, and the characters are driven by moral choices and when they choose poorly, they face serious consequences. It fits with my inner philosophies.

While I appreciated the responses and noted that they did indeed follow the lines I would have expected, I began to wonder how deeply one might explore the parallels between the Fantastic and LDS thinking before they began to break down. The more I thought, the more intriguing the possibilities became. The result is this essay.

My answer to the question stems from the nature of the LDS religion and teachings themselves. It has become almost a truism at the BYU Symposium on Fantasy and Science Fiction, that Mormonism itself is a science-fiction religion. This is not to say that it was conceived of and developed on science-fictional lines, such as was apparently the case with Golden Age SF author L. Ron Hubbard and his Church of Scientology (the name itself suggesting links with the 'science' element of science fiction). Rather, it is to suggest that in their overall outlines, many teachings of the LDS church find parallels or analogues in conventions and devices most often found in science fiction. While some of the more general characteristics— Heroes, Progress—may occur in the wider Christian community as well, others—especially beliefs in Other Worlds and Other Beings— seem more uniquely LDS.

Given these assertions, then, it may prove fruitful to explore—in general terms and, given the limits of time and space, briefly—a few of the more frequently recurring themes, motifs, and tropes associated with the Fantastic and their relationship to LDS theology and thought.

**HEROES**—We want a hero. The Fantastic gives us one. Whether it be a child preparing to combat insectoid alien invaders, or a badly injured man confronting a resurgent pagan goddess, or a young magician intent on defeating the greatest dark wizard ever—the Fantastic virtually insists upon a single hero (or occasionally a plucky group of survivors from some cataclysm or disaster), willing or unwilling, to battle insuperable odds and save a nation, a planet, or a galaxy. As a genre, the Fantastic is, like its predecessor classical Epic, structured around a belief that the actions of an individual can and must make a difference in the world. The conflict itself must be significant, beyond the fortunes of an individual; instead, it impinges upon the survival of an entire community. Occasionally, the hero may fail or even fall, but regardless, the struggle itself is worthwhile, uplifting, even redemptive.

The desire for a hero is not uniquely LDS, but our heritage *is* built around the concept of the individual serving, if not sacrificing, for the greater good of the community. We are raised on stories of Joseph Smith and other early leaders of the church, who faced ridicule, persecution, and ultimately death in the name of the restored Gospel. We value the memories of the men and boys who braved winter blizzards to rescue the stranded Martin and Willey handcart companies…and of the pioneers in those companies who gave up all to journey to Zion. We consider every missionary in the field a hero, struggling to save souls and build up the Kingdom of God on earth.

**OTHER WORLDS**—The Fantastic—particularly science fiction and fantasy—relies on the existence of other worlds, either literal, meta-phoric, or symbolic. Part of the apparatus of science fiction is the creation of landscapes that are themselves unknown, often unknow-able, into which is injected something or someone knowable and familiar whose story is meaningful to us as readers and whose ex-periences are intended to alter us in fundamental ways. These worlds may be planets millions of light years distant or millions of years in the linear future; they may resemble Earth closely enough for read-ers to identify with them and their inhabitants; or they may be so utterly different in makeup, in gravity, in overall environmental conditions as to force readers to make mental adjustments merely to read about them and vicariously experience them. They may be vir-tually congruent with Earth, separated from this world by the thin-nest of barriers, yet in essence unreachable to us except though the medium of scientific devices or magic. Regardless of how they ap-pear or where they are, these other worlds serve as proving grounds for values and virtues the writer wishes to explore further, in ways that would not be possible in stories set on our objectively known world.

Other worlds are essential to LDS thought, a belief in them re-quired by the scriptures we accept as God's word. The Book of Abraham tells us that there are worlds innumerable, some closer to the throne of God—a physical place in the Universe—than others. Joseph Smith, in a poetic version of one of his most stirring revela-tions, section 76 of the Doctrine and Covenants, reiterated this point:

> And I heard a great voice bearing record from Heav'n
> He's the Savior, and only Begotten of God—
> By him, of him, and through him, the worlds were all
>    made,
> Even all that career in the heavens so broad.
>
> Whose inhabitants, too, from the first to the last,
> Are saved by the very same Savior of ours;
> And are, of course, begotten God's daughters and
>    sons,
> By the very same truths and the very same powers.

One God, one Savior, a multiplicity of worlds. We know little of those worlds or their inhabitants; the particulars of who they are, what they look like, what language or languages they speak are ir-relevant to the fact that all of Creation is filled with worlds whose Creator is God and whose Redeemer is Christ—who, for reasons unknown to us, chose this world as the scene of His mortality.

THE JOURNEY/EXODUS—The existence of other worlds implies moving to or from them. George Slusser once defined the essential movement of science fiction as an Odyssean journey, or to say the same thing in terms borrowed from J. R. R. Tolkien, "there and back again." The journey may complete the circuit, as epitomized by Odysseus's travels from Ithaca to Troy and his long-delayed return. Or it may include only one leg of the journey, frequently an exodus outward toward a new world, a new home, as with Aeneas in Virgil's *Aeneid*. In non-LDS fantasists, the journey may find its end at the Dark Tower and the beginning of an infinite journey; or transport the reader from Transylvania to London and back again; or reach a final place to call home before doubling back on itself to encompass changes throughout the universe. In the context of LDS writers, it may entail children traveling to their grandparents' house...and from there further outward into the boundaries of a magical country, before they return. Or a remnant of colonists returning, after 30 million years, to the Earth that gave birth to their race.

The history of the LDS Church is itself a journey, beginning in Palmyra, New York and moving ever westward. The travelers settled in what appeared to be permanent homes, rearing structures and building temples, until forced by threats of genocide to journey again. First to the basin of the Great Salt Lake. Then to spread throughout the whole world. And finally to return to Salt Lake City, either physically or spiritually, as epitomized by the turning of the people, first to the Tabernacle, now to the Conference Center for the semi-annual conferences.

In a more fundamental sense, LDS theology is based on a journey. More specifically than most other denominations, LDS teachings identify a setting out from a particular place, an other world, if you will, with full knowledge that not all will safely return. The journey entails a life-long series of crucial events, each testing, altering, strengthening the individual. And finally the individual returns—back to our appointed places within the perfect place from which we all set out.

MIRACLES: SCIENCE AND MAGIC—The Fantastic thrives on that which cannot be explained except through science and technology or through the uncanny, the supernatural, or magic. In order to fit comfortably within the Fantastic, for example, a story must take as its premise "what if," and that "what if" in turn depends on a fundamental change in the way we perceive the world as operating. The change may be slight, almost superficial, a small extrapolation from that which we know in our everyday lives; or it may be world-altering in any of an almost infinite number of ways. Space flight to open new worlds, increased longevity through medicine; or, looking on the darker side, new diseases that destroy 99.4% of humanity, or developing nuclear weapons that eradicate almost all life or stimulate new, unexpected, potentially threatening forms of life—each can, in its own way trigger a science-fiction or horror story. With fantasy, the device may be even simpler—stipulating a world in which magic works, in which elves or fairies exist, in which ghosts and other revenants return to visit the living. In any event, the alterations seems, from our present perspective, essentially a miracle.

The LDS church accepts the reality of miracles. Much of its history incorporates literal miracles, from the seagulls that rescued the early pioneers from the devastation of crickets to the smaller, individual miracles that result daily from Priesthood blessings. It invites the miracles of medicine as they make our lives more bearable and our deaths more comfortable. It embraces what would have been to our forebears miracles of advanced technology in transportation and communications that allow present-day members worldwide to share directly in the teachings and testimonies of the General Authorities, creating a literal as well as a figurative community of the Saints. And we eagerly anticipate even greater advances that will further facilitate the spread of the Gospel.

THE OTHER/ALIENS (as either races or messengers)—Science fiction in particular focuses on the Other, the Alien, the non-human entity or entities who either come face to face with others like themselves or with representatives of the human race and, in doing so, transform humanity or are themselves transformed by humanity. Yet whatever their guise, the alien stands for, represents in the deepest senses of the word, the *human*. Aliens and their worlds become images of characteristics and traits that the writer wishes to examine, not in their otherness, but in human terms. We cannot perform social or scientific experiments on humans—our lifespan is too long to make such experiments feasible, even if they were morally justifiable. But we can create Others who are subjected to the conditions and demands we are interested in exploring, and through their imagined reactions assess the extent to which humanity meets or fails to meet expectations. The Other is at once interesting because it is different from us and because it *is* us, regardless of superficial variations of size, shape, or substance.

LDS theology takes seriously the concept of other races, other life forms, if you will, inhabiting the universes. Whether they are identical to humans or not, we assume a connection between ourselves and the peoples of innumerable other worlds. And in a deeper sense, we acknowledge the interactions between humans and aliens—angels and other divine messengers are like us and are not like us, yet they may visit us when necessary, and through their words and actions we are given standards of belief and behavior that we are to strive to reach. To equate heavenly messengers with science-fictional Others may sound strange. It seems more than odd, perhaps, to think of Moroni as an 'alien', for example; certainly he was not a "little green man" or a "bug-eyed monster" to be studied and understood. But just as certainly he was not merely human; in appearance and substance there were elemental differences between him and Joseph Smith. Even so, at core the similarities between the two far overshadowed the differences: both are spirit children of our Father in Heaven, both experienced the time of testing that is mortality; and both share the promises of eternity with God.

MONSTERS/DEMONS—The aliens/others we encounter through the Fantastic may be benign or malignant. They may have humanity's best interests at heart or they may wish our total destruction. When the latter is the case, we represent them as monstrous, either in scientific, fantastical, or horrific terms. The Fantastic lends itself as readily to darkness as to the light, and in some cases cannot exist without the representation of fear, terror, horror and evil. Some stories use the darkness to amplify the powers of light; others dwell on darkness to the exclusion of all else. In many cases, the monsters are of our own creation and directly reflect our unhealthy obsessions, vices, and desires; in others, they are external to humankind, appearing abruptly and with devastating consequences. In all instances, the monstrous, when truly identified as monstrous and evil, is to be combated at all costs.

Again, from its inception, the church has accepted not only the existence and interaction of God and angels with humanity, but of forces for darkness as well. Some are insubstantial. Joseph Smith recounts his own experience with darkness:

> After I had retired to the place where I had previously designed to go, having looked around me, and finding myself alone, I kneeled down and began to

offer up the desires of my heart to God. I had scarcely done so, when immediately I was *seized* upon by some power which entirely overcame me, and had such an astonishing influence over me as to bind my tongue so that I could not speak. Thick *darkness* gathered around me, and it seemed to me for a time as if I were doomed to sudden destruction.

But, exerting all my powers to *call* upon God to deliver me out of the power of this enemy which had seized upon me, and at the very moment when I was ready to sink into *despair* and abandon myself to destruction—not to an imaginary ruin, but to the power of some actual being from the unseen world, who had such marvelous power as I had never before felt in any being—just at this moment of great alarm, I saw a pillar of *light* exactly over my head, above the brightness of the *sun*, which descended gradually until it fell upon me.

The Doctrine and Covenants contains instructions on how to distinguish angels of light from devils in disguise (see Section 129). Records of the early church members refer to casting out of demons from those possessed, and literally and physically combating demons. This is not to say that the church is obsessed with the powers of darkness or sanctions liturgical exorcisms; nor that it recognizes the existence of werewolves, vampires, and other imagined creatures of the night; but rather that it believes firmly that where God is, Satan wishes to intrude and may try to do so.

FASTER-THAN-LIGHT—Space travel nearly requires faster-than-light travel, or at least something approximating it. Failing that, the science fiction story must take into account the decades, centuries, even millennia that would be required for a space ship to arrive at an extra-galactic destination. Such a journey may itself provide the basis for a provocative story combining elements of the SF journey, other worlds (the inner world of the starship itself), and possibly even aliens. The dream of opening the cosmos to human exploration/colonization, however, to a large extent depends on as-yet unknown technologies that would allow us to bridge the abyss of space.

Given the nature of the LDS conception of the universe, with Kolob, inhabited by God and angels, existing as a fixed point in space, the existence of faster-than-light travel becomes a given.

Heavenly beings sent as messengers to individuals on Earth must come from somewhere and do so instantaneously in order to deliver their messages and return to report. The currently known limitations of the physical, terrestrial body do not apply to celestial bodies, apparently including their ability to move at will through space as we understand it.

TIME TRAVEL—Need it be noted that time travel is a staple of science fiction, going at least as far back as Wells' Time Machine.

It would be less obviously a tenet of LDS teachings, perhaps, except for the belief that time itself is not necessarily linear—in fact, that it may be necessarily *non*-linear. Eternal entities are not subject to time as we understand it; the Book of Abraham facsimile 1 blends time and space in a curious way, equating one with the other, suggesting unique permutations of time and distance. And certainly Moses' vision upon the mountain and other scriptural accounts of revelation of distant times are at least partially explicable through the idea of time travel of some sort, allowing the prophets to see past, present, and future in essence simultaneously.

PROGRESS—The idea of progress as essential to human society and culture is primarily a modern one. For most of human history, the assumption has been that tomorrow will be the same as today. Little was expected in the way of social change or mobility; if a man was a farmer, his sons would expect to be—and be expected to be—farmers as well. If any social change was anticipated, it would probably have been retrograde. Yesterday was the Golden Age; tomorrow we will descend further into the Iron Age.

Within the past two centuries, however, that sense has completely inverted. Now the expectation is that tomorrow will be, must be different—and *vastly* different from today. We teach our children that the jobs for which they are preparing in college now do not yet exist. We are acclimated to such rapid-fire changes in technology, usually referred to as technological *advances*, that we take for granted marvels that would have astounded our parents or grandparents. We see—or have seen, until perhaps the most recent generations—the future as a consistent progression from where we are now to something unknown perhaps but greater, finer, more glorious.

To a large extent, science fiction requires progress. Space flight, planetary colonization, even the ubiquitous Galactic Empires depend for their existence upon a continued improvement in machinery, technology, and science. When the focus shifts to apocalyptic threats or realized horrors, the idea of progress is still implied; here is what we *could have been* but because of this mistake or that incursion of evil, that progress has been halted. Even in such stories, however, there is usually a concluding sense that in spite of the darkness and the horror, something good will emerge, frequently something demonstrably better that which existed before.

The sense of *progress* has been a touchstone of LDS thinking from the beginning. We use the term "Eternal progression" lightly, almost without thinking, usually never stopping to realize how radically different that view of human destiny is from nearly every preceding culture...and from most Christian denominations, for which Time and History do not progress infinitely but come to a definite End.

APOCALYPSE—In its literal sense, *apocalypse* means 'to uncover' or to 'dis-cover'. In its lexical senses, it broadens to encompass any widespread or global destruction, or simply a prophecy or revelation—a 'revealing'. Not all SF/F/H is apocalyptic, but there are sufficient examples to include it in a list of the most common characteristics. The sense of apocalypse may be based on a discovery or revelation that alters our perception of humanity (or of the Other). It may broaden to incorporate the destruction of planets or galaxies. It may detail the ending of a specific phase of human existence and the transformation of the race into something that is—to the reader—distinctly Other. It may in the most extreme examples, reach out to detail the end of the universe itself. In any of these cases, the apocalyptic gives the narrative a greater sense of tension, of suspense, and of significance for both the characters limned and the reader.

In the generalized Christian sense, *apocalypse* refers specifically to the Revelations of John, which are simultaneously prophetic and descriptive (symbolically or literally) of the End of Things. In the sense that Christianity itself is based on the belief in a cessation of this mortality, triggered by a cataclysmic battle between good and evil and followed by something else, substantially different from this life, all of its denominations are apocalyptic. As a literal belief, therefore, the apocalyptic intrinsically comprehends a deep, pervasive sense of oncoming darkness and potential horror, culminating in a *eucatastrophe*—a global and universal triumph of Good.

LDS beliefs support the sense of an ending. They are not obsessed by it; nor do the members calculate from biblical dates and perform complex numerology to determine the precise day of the Second Coming. We do, however, accept it as essential to our theology. But within the Plan of Salvation as presented by the church, there is a stronger sense of specificity than in many other Christian denominations. We adhere to the belief in a literal resurrection (itself a transformative event); a spirit prison, with both prisoners and ministers; a Second Coming that ushers in yet another transformation for humanity; a millennium; a final judgment; and an eternity in which to learn and progress. The LDS perspective on apocalypse includes pain and suffering, but it is also and more importantly a prelude to humanity as physically and spiritually more refined beings.

THE FUTURE—Paralleling the belief in Progress is the concept of the Future itself. Again, this seems to be a relatively recent phenomenon in human thinking. Many cultures and most Christian denominations see human life as coming to an abrupt end, climaxing in an Armageddon-style battle. Ancient cultures perceived the conflict as between cosmic forces, the gods and the giants in Norse culture, for example—the forces of order and stability combating the forces of darkness and disorder…and in the Norse mythologies at least, the giants win. *Beowulf* similarly ends with distinct foreshadowings of disaster; after the death of the great hero, the enemies will descend and destroy everything. Even within the Christian tradition, which sees an End of all things followed by a nebulous, ill-defined gathering of the righteous unto God, there is little sense of specifics about that future. On a secular level, after decades of developments that have suggested an inevitable future of greater leisure, wealth, and ease for humanity (or at least parts of it), recent movements in scientific and technological experimentation have resulted not only in miracles but also in an almost overwhelming sense of oncoming darkness. We have despoiled and polluted our planet until there is little hope for a bright future.

Science fiction can work against that. With the exception of alternate-earth stories about single changes in the past that have altered the course of human history, much science fiction looks to the future, whether it be positive or negative. To be sure dystopias occur, frequently due to human activities; but just as frequently, the core struggles in the stories result in the sense of renewed possibilities, if not for the entire race, then at least for a part of it willing to struggle against disaster.

LDS thinking is founded on a literal belief in a never-ending future, a concomitant to the belief that intelligences are co-eternal with God. What never began will never end but will continue as a distinct, individual being, as immortal as matter itself. What for other beliefs is the End of Times is for the LDS the Beginnings of a New Time, with specific promises and possibilities. Few if any SF stories, even the most optimistic, moves as far into the future as LDS theology, culminating, if you will, with the concept of humanity moving ever closer to Godhood.

INFINITY—There are no boundaries to space in science fiction. Stories have taken readers to the edges of the universe...and beyond into greater, unknown space. Multiverses with an infinite number of near Earths are common landscapes in both SF and fantasy. Change a single element of human past or present and a second version of that Earth splits off and continues on its own path through the future, until a single moment causes that world to split off as well. And on forever. Time and Space have no end in science fiction.

Or in LDS teachings. We are eternal; thus we belong to the infinite. We inhabit one of worlds innumerable; hence, if we taken the term literally, the space in which we dwell must continue infinitely.

HUMANITY AS CENTRAL—Within galaxies and universes unnumbered (even if we inhabit nothing more than an average planet orbiting an inconsequential sun in an arm of an inconsequential galaxy somewhere in the hinterlands of the universe), humans are central in the Fantastic. Humanity my be beneficent or malignant, arriving as savior or destroyers, but regardless of the positioning the narrative takes there is still the sense that humanity, more than any imagined alien races, holds a crux position. More crucially, perhaps, the Other in science fiction, fantasy, and horror *must* in some key ways resemble human nature, reflect human desires, live out human concerns. A truly alien Other would be ultimately unknowable to the readers—as was attempted in Stanley Weinbaum's "A Martian Odyssey." No matter the physical appearance or psychological makeup, the Other almost always reflects its readers...and its creator.

In LDS belief, humanity is in fact at the center of things. Not in the Renaissance view of humans as inhabiting the apex of a celestial hierarchy of Creation, placed only below the angels and God. Rather, humanity is the purpose behind the creation. This planet—and all planets—exists primarily to be homelands for immortal intelligences, once spirit children of God, now dressed in flesh and blood.

More fundamentally than these individual tenets, however, LDS teachings and philosophy are unusually and enormously liberating to a writer's imagination. Each person is seen as eternal; at the core rests an Intelligence that was neither created nor can be destroyed, but that has existed co-eternally with God Himself.

This belief diverges widely from the traditional view of human origins and destinies held by most Christian religions. For them, humanity is not in fact *eternal*; individuals come into being at a particular point in the gestation period—often held to be either the moment of conception or the moment of birth—when the spirit enters the body and both together become human. Before that, nothing.

This ties neatly with the conventional Christian view of time, that it had a specific beginning at the instant of Creation, whenever that is held to be, and that Time itself will have an end when all of humanity is judged, determined destined for Heaven or Hell, and the righteous are taken into the bosom of God. All things—with the single exception of God—have a distinct beginning and will, in some real sense, have a distinct ending. What happens after that point, when the righteous portions of the human race have been gathered into God, either literally, symbolically, mystically, or spiritually, is rarely explored. It is and will remain a mystery.

By its nature, this belief seems limiting, widening the already infinite-seeming gap between God and Humanity even further. God is different in essence, substance, and being from humanity, and nothing can be done to diminish that difference.

If, on the other hand, each individual shares infinity with God Himself, is in some way similar to if not identical with God—in essence, in potential—then the effects on the imagination would seem to be remarkable. Whatever an individual can imagine, whatever worlds, galaxies, universes, peopled with whatever alien races the Fantastic can suggest…God has in all probability already imagined them. Whether He has chosen to embody those imaginings with substance or actuality or not, to dress them for a space of time in pre-existent matter (itself as eternal as He) or not, an infinite God would already intellectually comprehend all things imaginable. Yet it is still within human nature—shared in specific particulars with God—to strive to envision those things.

The result, it would seem, would be a loosening of the imagination, a sense that anything conceived of is fair game for exploration…and the result would be an urge toward the Fantastic itself.

## II. The Peculiar Case of Horror

Throughout this essay the terms *science fiction*, *fantasy*, and *horror* have appeared as subsets of the Fantastic, often treated as through they were interchangeable. Without getting into the morass of definitions for each—attempts to do which are both innumerable and ultimately fruitless—suffice it to say, for the purposes of this essay, that essential differences occur among the three, along with substantial similarities.

What is equally important at this point, however, is that the differences are sufficient to suggest a parallel difference in the way horror is perceived and received by most of the LDS community.

In a recent exchange of emails on this subject, Stephen Carter of *Sunstone Magazine* commented:

> Horror, it seems to me, doesn't enjoy nearly the cachet SF/F does in Mormondom. It seems more a guilty pleasure than a public obsession. As a teen I often borrowed Stephen King books from my non-Mormon friend and hid them beneath my bed lest my devout mother find them. And there certainly isn't a horror writing conference at BYU.

Although there have been horror *panels* at the BYU symposium on science fiction and fantasy, Carter is correct in noting that horror as genre occupies a far smaller segment of the LDS writers' community, even among other aficionados of the Fantastic.

So…why horror?

In his 1981 study of horror fiction, *Danse Macabre,* Stephen King discusses three levels of horror:

> I recognize terror as the finest emotion and so I will try to terrorize the reader. But if I find that I cannot terrify, I will try to horrify, and if I find that I cannot horrify, I'll go for the gross-out. I'm not proud. (Ch. 2)

Revulsion—the Gross-out—is, as King suggests, relatively easy to accomplish: it requires sufficient blood and guts, with graphic descriptions, accompanied in many cases by graphic language. At this level the most vocal arguments against horror as genre take place. At the other extreme, true Terror, the moment that generates a frisson down the spine just before the monster is revealed, requires extraordinary facility with language, characterization, and setting to accomplish, and only a few masters—among them Poe and

Lovecraft, as well as King himself—create it consistently. When it occurs, and when Horror and Revulsion are used critically and carefully, such literature may demonstrate a number of useful traits.

At the thematic level perhaps, horror can be used metaphorically or symbolically. The literary monsters may stand for literal monsters that threaten everyday life. A vampire suddenly appearing in a small town and systematically preying on its inhabitations may easily transform into a condemnation of the contemporary sense of isolation that afflicts many if not most communities. People live separated lives; they do not notice the alterations in or absence of their neighbors until it is too late—the bonds of civility have already broken and the sense of community disappears.

The vampire may also be, and often is, sexualized until it exemplifies both the allure and the tragedy of uninhibited lust. By virtue of its existence—neither dead nor alive; its mode of feeding—penetration and bloodletting; and the inescapably body-oriented nature of its attacks—usually male upon female, the vampire can easily slip from a figure of horror into quasi-pornography, especially when the transmission of blood is described in loving, overly sensual detail.

The werewolf may represent the abrupt, inexplicable intrusion of death into a family or community. Unseen and unsuspected until it lashes out in rage and inflicts carnage on its victims, the werewolf parallels disease—cancer, for example—and its insidious rampage within a healthy body. It may stand for accident or fate; there is no cause, no rational or purpose behind its sudden eruption—it simply *is,* and by its presence disrupts order and security.

Most other literary monsters may serve parallel functions. Zombies epitomize the loss of agency and rationality; Amazons demonstrate the threat of sexual disparity; Creatures from Other Dimensions, including Lovecraft's Great Old Ones, embody the threat of the unknown, of the breakdown of reason and intellect into madness. Ghosts, Demons, the Haunted Place/Bad Place, and other denizens of darkness—each may in its turn speak volumes about the human condition.

On a more literal level, horror may work in a manner similar to classical tragedy. When written effectively, with an eye on creating terror rather than mere revulsion, horror may combine pity and fear to achieve a kind of Aristotelian *catharsis*—one focused on the purging of specific strong emotions, namely, fear itself. Horror allows the reader to confront an object or objects of pity, usually the victims, frequently innocent or inoffensive victims; and an object of terror, horror, or revulsion—the monster or monsters; and by juxta-position of the two legitimately *feel* fear in a safe, controlled environment. This fear may in fact be physically expressed, through a rise in heartbeat, increased rate of respiration, even a literal chill up the spine. In any case, the physical response allows the reader to *experience* and thereby *purge* the effects of fear without physical danger.

And finally, the reader of horror is more often than not exposed to the most literal sort of morality. Unlike in the experiential world, in the worlds of horror, evil, wrong, or even misguided actions have *immediate* consequences. Cause and effect are clearly linked. If a mad scientists creates a monster, eventually the monster will turn on its creator; at least as far back as Shelley's *Frankenstein*, this has been a *leitmotif* of horror fiction. The responsibility of creator to creature—and for the acts of the creature—in part defines the plot itself. If a teenage couple have illicit sex and thereby participate in an adult action without being prepared to accept the concomitant responsibilities, they die, frequently during the act itself. There is no reprieve, no opportunity for a second chance. Transgression leads to death.

It is possible for horror itself to be essentially immoral. Novels exist in which characters are introduced and almost immediately destroyed, merely for the sake of blood and gore. The monster itself becomes little more than a killing machine and the plot determined not by causal relationships among episodes but by the simple need for more blood. The horror of unrelieved revulsion, in other words, runs the risk of existing solely for the sake of that revulsion, with little thought of creating the more transcendent horror or terror. Such fiction verges on the immoral, if not the obscene, not through the representation of unacceptable language or events but because of its cavalier attitude toward characters and their lives.

On the whole, however, those writers most frequently cited as masters in the field—Poe, Lovecraft, King, Koontz, McCammon, and a handful of others—consistently provide tales that, however close they come to mere revulsion, ultimately lead the reader to a heightened sense of morality, of catharsis of fear, and of the relationship between story and life, between characters and the reader.

If horror provides at least these useful experiences, why not horror? Why does it not have the same cachet among the LDS audience as science fiction and fantasy?

In a recent afterword to his 1987 novel *Shadowfires,* Dean R.

Koontz considers the question of what constitutes horror and why it is so often shunned as a genre. One of his conclusions is that horror concentrates its images and effects on *death*—death as theme, as plot device, as indicator of character. And in large part, what he suggests holds true. The major "monsters" of horror fiction are, by and large, the Undead and the Walking Dead—ghosts, vampires, zombies, revenants of varying sorts, Lovecraftian Great Old Ones long since vanished from this plane and seeking to re-enter it. Even the werewolf is in some ways a figure intimately associated with death—although the lycanthrope is still alive, he is an outcast, an 'other' essentially dead to the larger community.

Death is the beginning and end of much horror. It triggers the appearance of the monster, either literally, as the monster is called from death; or figuratively, as its victims announce the presence of the monster. It is the punishment meted to the unwary, the unethical, the unrighteous. As noted above, teenagers who engage in sex before understanding the adult responsibilities implicit in the act are punished by death. Mad scientists—and often even inadvertent meddlers in the true order of the universe—suffer death at the hands—or claws, or teeth—of their creations. Even the innocent die, often in gruesome ways, in order to underscore the leveling power of horror…and of death. It is not accidental, of course, that so many horror novels sport black covers; the archetypical cover may be the first paperback edition of Stephen King's *'Salem's Lot,* almost pure glossy black, with no title, the embossed face of a girl…and a single crop of crimson blood. The essence of the novel was communicated forcefully and directly.

The overriding presence of death at least partially explains the lack of general enthusiasm for the genre in the LDS community. There are other elements that push LDS readers and writers away—among them the frequent exploitation of sex, the overt depictions of violence, the common use of harsh language—but the concern for death-as-theme overwhelms them. Even the most sexually restrained, the most vaguely violence-oriented, the most verbally unexceptional of horror tales (several of Lovecraft's more imagistic, atmospheric short stories come to mind) still remain largely outside the pale of LDS interest.

There is a good reason for this. Perhaps more than any other Christian denomination, the LDS Church minimizes the presence and effect of death. Unlike many church doctrines, LDS teachings see death, not as something to be feared but as a prerequisite step in an increasingly glorious sequence of progression and perfection. It is in fact an intermediate step in an eternal sequence, as necessary as birth itself. The Church does not glorify death by any means, nor does it ignore the grief and loss that accompanies death, but it does place the phenomenon in a context that ameliorates the consequences and effects of death.

On the most obvious level, itself symbolic of a crucial attitude, Latter-day Saints almost universally ignore the crucifix as an object of worship or of veneration, even as an object of frequent meditation. There are no crosses on LDS steeples, no representations of the crucifixion hanging in LDS chapels. Christmas pageants are common; Easter pageants occur far less commonly, and when they are presented, they often skip over the events on Calvary to concentrate on the Resurrection.

Similarly, LDS funerals tend to concentrate less on death and more on the overall plan of salvation. Few attendees wear black. Few openly and publicly mourn. Sadness there may be, and a sense of loss, but rarely outright, inexpressible grief. The general theme of LDS funerals seems to be "And should we die before our journey's through, Happy day! All is well!"

A religion that approaches death from this perspective might justifiably be wary of a literary genre devoted to death. It will be equally wary of open, often graphic depictions of the bringers of death, the various monsters and the human traits they represent. It will turn away from the darkness that such monsters both create and embrace, and instead far more willingly face the light.

# BIBLIOGRAPHY OF
# WORKS CITED AND CONSULTED

Aguirre, Manuel. *The Closed Space: Horror Literature and Western Symbolism.* Manchester: Manchester University Press, 1990.
Aldiss, Brian W. *An Age.* London: Sphere, 1969. Subsequently reprinted as *Cryptozoic.*
---. *Barefoot in the Head: A European Fantasia.* London: Faber, 1969.
---. *Report on Probability A.* London: Faber, 1968.
Anthony, Piers. *A Spell for Chameleon.* New York: Ballantine, 1977.
---. *Battle Circle.* 1975. New York: Avon, 1978.
---. *Castle Roogna.* New York: Ballantine, 1979.
---. *The Source of Magic.* New York: Ballantine, 1979.
---. *Split Infinity.* New York: Ballantine, 1980.
Atkinson, William C., trans. *The Lusiads.* by Luis Vaz de Camões. London: Penguin Books, 1952.
Baker, Howard. *Induction to Tragedy: A Study in a Development of Form in* Gorboduc, The Spanish Tragedy, *and* Titus Andronicus. 1939. New York: Russell and Russell, 1965.
Ballantine, Lee, ed. *Poly: New Speculative Writing.* Mountain View CA: Ocean View Press, 1989.
Barker, Clive. *The Great and Secret Show: The First Book of the Art.* New York: Harper & Row, 1989 [hardcover]. New York: Harper Collins, 1989 [paper]. In-text references are to Part, Chapter, and pagination from the paperback issue.
---. "A Telephone Interview with Clive Barker, Conducted 2/1/90," conducted by Tyson Blue. *Mystery Scene,* Vol. 29 (April 1991): 76-80.
Benson, Larry D., general editor. *The Riverside Chaucer.* 3 ed. Boston: Houghton Miflin Company, 1987.
Blessington, Francis C. *Paradise Lost and the Classical Epic.* Boston: Routledge & Kegan Paul, 1979.
*The Blood Review: The Journal of Horror Criticism* Vol. 1, no. 1 (October 1989).
Boston, Bruce. *All the Clocks are Melting.* Berkley CA: Velocities Chapbook Series, 1984.
---. *The Bruce Boston Omnibus.* Mountain View CA: Ocean View, 1987.
---. "Evolution of the Death Murals." *Isaac Asimov's Science Fiction Magazine* (September 1985).

---. "The Hunter: 20,000 A.D." *Amazing* (November 1982).

Bratman, David. Internet memo. 15 June 1995.

Brooke, C. F. Tucker. *The Life of Marlowe, and The Tragedy of Dido, Queen of Carthage*. 1930. New York: Gordian, 1966.

Burleson. Donald M. *H. P. Lovecraft: A Critical Study*. Westport CT: Greenwood Press. 1983.

Camões. Luis de. *Os Lus'adas.* 1572. English translation by Richard Fanshawe, 1655. See also: William C. Atkinson.

Candelaria, Frederick H. and William C. Strange, ed. *Perspectives on Epic*. Boston: Allyn and Bacon, 1965.

Card, Orson Scott. "America." *Isaac Asimov's Science Fiction Magazine* (January 1987): 22-53.

---. *The Call of Earth: Homecoming Volume 2*. New York: TOR, 1993.

---. *Capitol: The Worthing Chronicle*. New York: Baronet/Ace, 1979.

---. *Earthborn: Homecoming Volume 5*. New York: TOR, 1995.

---. "Ender's Game." *Analog* (August 1977): 100-134.

---. *Ender's Game*. New York: TOR, 1985.

---. *Ender in Exile*. New York: TOR, 2008.

---. *EarthFall. Homecoming Volume 4*. New York: TOR, 1995.

---. "Fantasy and the Believing Reader." *Science Fiction Review* (August 1982): 45-50.

---. "The Finer Points of Characterization, Part I: Just How Important Are These People?" *Writer's Digest* (October 1986), 26-28; "Part II: Creating Characters that Readers Care About" (November 1986). 37-38. "Part III: Making Your Characters Believable" (December 1986). 32-36.

---. *First Meetings: In Ender's Universe*. New York: TOR, 2003.

---. *The Folk of the Fringe*. West Bloomfield MI: Phantasia Press, 1989; New York: TOR Books, August 1990. All citations to the text are from the TOR edition.

---. "The Fringe." *The Magazine of Fantasy and Science Fiction* (October, 1985): 140-160.

---. "Hart's Hope" *Chrysalis 8*. Ed. Roy Torgeson. New York: Zebra, 1980: 75-201.

---. *Hart's Hope*. New York: Berkley, 1983.

---. "Hatrack River." *Isaac Asimov's Science Fiction Magazine* (August 1986): 54-80.

---. *Hot Sleep: The Worthing Chronicle*. New York: Ace/Baronet, 1979.

---. "Kingsmeat." *Analog Yearbook*. Ed. Ben Bova. New York: Baronet, 1978; New York: Ace, 1978. 191-201.

---. Letter. February 20, 1985.

---. "Lost Boys." *Fantasy and Science Fiction* (October 1989): 73-91.

---. *Lost Boys*. New York: HarperCollins, 1992.

---. *The Memory of Earth: Homecoming Volume I*. New York: TOR, 1992.

---. "On Sycamore Hill: A Personal View." *Science Fiction Review* (May 1985): 6-11.

---. *A Planet Called Treason.* New York: St. Martin's Press, 1979.

---. *Prentice Alvin: Tales of Alvin Maker, Book 3.* New York: TOR, 1989.

---. "Question and Answer" session. "XVth Annual Brigham Young University Symposium on the Influence of Science Fiction and Fantasy." Provo UT. March 27, 1997.

---. *Red Prophet: Tales of Alvin Maker, Book 2.* New York: TOR, 1988.

---. *Saints.* New York: TOR, 1988. See also *A Woman of Destiny.*

---. "Salvage." *Isaac Asimov's Science Fiction Magazine,* February 1986): 56-75.

---. *Seventh Son: Tales of Alvin Maker, Book 1.* New York: TOR, 1987.

---. "SF and Religion." *Dialogue* (Summer 1985): 11-13.

---. *The Ships of Earth: Homecoming Volume 3.* New York: TOR, 1994.

---. *Songmaster.* New York: Dial, 1980.

---. *Speaker for the Dead.* New York: Tor. 1986.

---. *A Woman of Destiny.* New York: Berkeley, 1984. See also *Saints.*

---. *The Worthing Chronicle.* New York: Ace, 1983.

---. *Unaccompanied Sonata and Other Stories.* New York: Dial, 1981.

---. *Wyrms.* New York: Arbor House. 1987.

---. *Xenocide .* New York: TOR, 1991.

Carpenter, Humphrey. *The Inklings: C. S. Lewis, J.R.R. Tolkien, Charles Williams, and Their Friends.* Boston: Houghton Mifflin, 1979.

Cawley, A. C., ed. *The Wakefield Pageants in the Towneley Cycle.* Old and Middle English Texts. 1958. Manchester: University of Manchester Press, 1963.

Chambers, E.K. *English Literature at the Close of the Middle Ages.* Oxford: Clarendon Press, 1945.

Chambers, E.K. *The Mediaeval Stage.* 2 vol. 1903. Oxford: Oxford University Press, 1967.

Christensen, Dan. "Stephen King: Living in 'Constant Deadly Terror.'" *Bloody Best of Fangoria* (1982): 30-33.

Christopher, Joe R. *C. S. Lewis.* Boston: Twayne, 1987.

Chute, Marchette. *Ben Jonson of Westminster.* New York: E.P. Dutton, 1953.

Clute, John. "C. S. Lewis." *Science Fiction Writers.* Ed. E. F. Bleiler. New York: Scribner's, 1982. 243-248.

Cohen, Hennig. "Herman Melville." Online at: http://people. brandeis.edu/~teuber/melvillebio.html. Rpt. from: *Dictionary of Literary Biography, Volume 3: Antebellum Writers in New York and the South.* Edited by Joel Myerson. pp. 221–45. Gale Research, 1979.

Collings, Michael R. "'Argument Not Less but More Heroic': Epic, Order, and Postholocaust Society in Piers Anthony's *Battle Circle.*" In *Phoenix from the Ashes: The Literature of the Remade World.* Ed. Carl B. Yoke. New York: Greenwood, 1987.

---. "Black Dandelions." *Dark Transformations: Deadly Visions of Change.* Mercer Island WA: Starmont House, 1990; Rockville MD: Borgo/Wildside Press, 2008.

---. "The Blood Burns. *San Fernando Poetry* Journal Vol. 4, no 1 (1982): 25. Rpt. in *Naked to the Sun: Dark Visions of Apocalypse.* Mercer Island WA: Starmont House, 1985; Rockville MD: Borgo/Wildside, 2007, p. 28.

---. *Dark Transformations: Deadly Visions of Change.* Mercer Island WA: Starmont House, 1990; Rockville MD: Borgo/Wildside, 2007

---. "The Epic of Dune: Epic Traditions in Modern Science Fiction." *Aspects of Fantasy.* Ed. William Coyle. Westport CT: Greenwood Press, 1986, 131-140.

---. *Fields of Starflowers, and Other Poems: Science Fiction, Fantasy, and Horror.* Thousand Oaks CA, 1988.

---. "The Gift of Christmastide." *All Calm, All Bright: Christmas Offerings.* Malibu CA: Zarahemla Motets/White Crow Press, 1995; Rockville DM: Borgo/Wildside Press, 2007, pp. 91-101.

---. *"Imago Christi:* Christ Figures in the Fiction of Orson Scott Card." *The Leading Edge* 14: 15-24.

---. *In the Image of God: Theme, Characterization, and Landscape in the Fiction of Orson Scott Card.* Westport CT: Greenwood, 1990.

---. *Naked to the Sun: Dark Visions of Apocalypse.* Mercer Island WA: Starmont, 1985; Rockville MD: Borgo/Wildside, 2007

---. "Refracted Visions and Future Worlds: Mormonism and Science Fiction." *Dialogue* (August 1984): 107-116.

---. "Science and Scientism in C. S. Lewis's *That Hideous Strength.*" *Hard Science Fiction.* Ed. George Slusser and Eric Rabkin. Carbondale IL: Southern Illinois University Press, 1985, 131-140.

---. *"The Stand:* Science Fiction into Fantasy," in *Discovering Stephen King.* Ed. Darrell Schweitzer. Mercer Island WA: Starmont House, 1985. 83-90.

---. "Vampire," in *The Blood Review: The Journal of Horror Criticism* Vol. 1, no. 1 (October 1989): 15-B.

---. "Words and Worlds: The Creation of a Fantasy Universe in Zelazny, Lee, and Anthony," in *The Scope of the Fantastic—Theory, Technique, Major Authors: Selected Papers from the First International Conference on the Fantastic in the Arts,* ed. by Robert A. Collins and Howard Pearce. Westport CT: Greenwood Press, 1985, 173-182.

Crews, Frederick. *The Random House Handbook,* 2ed. New York: Random House, 1977.

Crist, Judith. "This Week's Movies." *TV Guide* (April 30-May 6, 1983): A5-A6.

Davenport, W. A. *Fifteenth-Century English Drama: The Early Moral Plays and their Literary Relations.* Totowa NJ: Rowman and Littlefield, 1982.

Davidson, Clifford. "Introduction." *The Saint Play in Medieval Europe.* Ed. Clifford Davidson. Kalamazoo MI: Medieval Institute Publications, Western Michigan University, 1986, 1-10.

De Camp, L. Sprague, and Thomas D. Clareson. "The Scientist," in *Sci-*

ence Fiction: Contemporary Mythology, ed. Patricia Warrin, and others. New York: Harper and Row, 1978.

Delaney, Samuel R. Dahlgren. New York: Bantam,. 1980.

Delany, Samuel R. "Some Reflections on SF Criticism," Science-Fiction Studies, 25, 8, 3 (November 1981), 233-239.

Demaray, John G. Milton's Theatrical Epic: The Invention and Design of Paradise Lost. Cambridge MA: Harvard University Press, 1980.

Donaldson, Ian. The Oxford Authors: Ben Jonson. New York: Oxford University Press, 1985.

Donaldson, Stephen. Lord Foul's Bane. Garden City, New York: Doubleday, 1977 [Book Club edition].

---. The Illearth War. New York: Holt, Rinehart and Winston, 1977.

---. The Power That Preserves. New York: Holt, Rinehart and Winston, 1977 [Book Club edition].

Dozois, Gardner, ed. The Year's Best Science Fiction. New York: Bluejay, 1986.

Easton, Tom. "The Reference Library." Analog (December 1979): 168.

Engh, M.J. "Science Fiction Poetry: A Rejoinder." Star*Line. Rpt. from The New York Review of Science Fiction. 1988.

Fielding, Henry. The History of the Adventures of Joseph Andrews, and of his Friend Mr Abraham Adams. 1742. Ebook available through Project Gutenberg at: http://www.gutenberg.org/etext/ 9611 (Volume I) and http://www.gutenberg.org/etext/9609 (Volume II)

Frazier, Robert, ed. Burning With a Vision. Philadelphia PA: Owlswick Press, 1984.

---. Co-Orbital Moons: Poems of Science and Science Fiction. Mountain View CA: The Mountain View Press, 1987.

---. Perception Barriers. Berkley CA: Berkley Poets Workshop & Press, 1987.

Fredericks, Casey. "Revivals of Ancient Mythologies in Current Science Fiction and Fantasy," in Many Futures, Many Worlds. Ed. Thomas Clareson. Kent OH: Kent State University Press, 1977, 50-65.

Frye, Northrop. Anatomy of Criticism. 1957. New York: Atheneum, 1967.

Frye, Roland Mushat. Milton's Imagery and the Visual Arts: Iconographic Tradition in the Epic Poems. Princeton NJ: Princeton University Press, 1978.,

Gardner, John. On Moral Fiction. New York: Basic Books, 1978.

Glover, Donald. C. S. Lewis: The Art of Enchantment. Athens OH: Ohio University Press, 1981.

Green, Scott E. Contemporary Science Fiction, Fantasy, and Horror Poetry: A Resource Guide and Biographical Directory. Westport CT: Greenwood Press, November 1989.

Griffin, Brian, and David Wingate. Apertures: A Study of the Writings of Brian W. Aldiss. Westport CT: Greenwood, 1984.

Gummere, Frances. Beowulf. 1910. Online at: http://www.fordham.edu/halsall/basis/beowulf.html

Gunn, James. *The Road to Science Fiction: From Gilgamesh to Wells.* New York: New American Library, 1977.

Guthke, Karl S. *The Last Frontier: Imagining Other Worlds from the Copernican Revolution to Modern Science Fiction.* 1983. Translated by Helen Atkins. Ithaca NY: Cornell University Press, 1990.

Hainsworth, J. B. *The Idea of Epic.* Berkeley: University of California Press, 1991.

Halliday, F. E. *Shakespeare and His Critics.* 1949, 1950, 1958. New York: Schocken, 1965.

Hannay, Margaret. *C. S. Lewis.* New York: Ungar, 1981.

Harrison, G. B., ed. *Shakespeare: The Complete Works.* New York: Harcourt, 1980.

Heinlein, Robert. "Science Fiction: Its Nature, Faults, and Virtues," in *Turning Points: Essays on the Art of Science Fiction.* Ed. Damon Knight. New York: Harper & Row, 1977, 3-28.

Heldreth, Lillian Marks. "Alternative History Series." *SFRA Newsletter,* 184 (January/February, 1991): 50-52.

Hillegas, Mark. "*Out of the Silent Planet* as Cosmic Voyage," in *Shadows of Imagination: The Fantasies of C. S. Lewis, J. R. R. Tolkien, and Charles Williams.* Revised edition. Ed. Mark Hillegas. 1969. Carbondale IL: Southern Illinois University Press, 1979, 41-58.

Hogan, Patrick G., Jr. "The Philosophical Limitations of Science Fiction," in *Many Futures, Many Worlds.* Ed. Thomas B. Clareson. Kent OH: Kent State University Press, 1977. 260-277.

Hooper, Walter. "Preface," in *The Dark Tower and Other Stories by C. S. Lewis.* New York: Harcourt Brace Jovanovich, 1977, 7-14.

Howard, Thomas. *The Achievement of C. S. Lewis.* Wheaton IL: Shaw, 1980.

Hume, Kathryn. *Fantasy and Mimesis: Responses to Reality in Western Literature.* New York: Methuen, 1984.

Irwin, W. R. *The Game of the Impossible: A Rhetoric of Fantasy.* Urbana IL: University of Illinois Press, 1976.

Jackson, Rosemary. *Fantasy: The Literature of Subversion* New York: Methuen, 1981.

Jacobs, Karrie. "Waiting for the Millennium: Part II, The Interface Author." *Magazine: Metropolis Issue.* Netscape. July 1995

Joron, Andrew. *Force Fields.* Mercer Island WA: Starmont House, 1985.

---. "Poe + Isis: A Rejoinder to Engh." *Star*Line* Vol. 12, no. 3 (May/June 1989): 4-6. Rpt. from *Synergy 2.*

---. "Shipwrecked on Destiny Five." *Isaac Asimov's Science Fiction Magazine.* (May 1985).

---. "SF Poetry: A New Genre." *Star*Line.* Rpt. from *Portland Review* 1981.

Kates, Judith A. *Tasso and Milton: The Problem of Christian Epic.* Lewisburg: Bucknell University Press, 1983

Keeler, Greg. "*The Shining*: Ted Kramer Has a Nightmare." *Journal of Popular Film and Television* (Winter, 1981): 2-8.

Kenin, Millea, ed. *Aliens and Lovers*. Oakland CA: Unique Graphics, 1983.

Ketterer, David. *New Worlds for Old: The Apocalyptic Imagination, Science Fiction and American Literature*. Bloomington IN: Indiana University Press, 1974.

King, Stephen. "Books: The Sixties Zone." *Adelina* (June 1980): 12.

---. "Brooklyn August." *Io* 10 (1971): 147.

---. "The Dark Man." *Ubris* Spring 1969; *Moth* 1970: [n.p.]

---. *The Dark Tower: The Gunslinger*. West Kingston RI: Donald M. Grant, 1982. New York: Signet/New American Library, 1989.

---. *The Dark Tower I: The Gunslinger*. New York: Viking, 2003. New York: Signet, 2003.

---. *The Dark Tower VII: The Dark Tower*. New York: West Kingston RI: Donald M. Grant, 2004. New York: Simon and Schuster/Pocket, 2006.

---. *Desperation*. Hampton Falls NH: Donald M. Grant, August 1996. New York: Viking, September 1996.

---. "Donovan's Brain." *Moth* 1970: [n.p.]

---. "For Owen." *Skeleton Crew*. New York: Putnam, 1985. 359-360.

---. "Harrison State Park '68." *Ubris* Fall 1968: 25-26.

---. "Horrors!" *TV Guide* (October 30-November 5, 1982): 54-58.

---. "Night Surf." *Ubris* (Spring 1969): 6-10.

---. "On Being Nineteen (and a Few Other Things)." In *The Dark Tower I: The Gunslinger,* ix–xix. New York: Viking, 2003. New York: Signet, 2003.

---. "Paranoid: A Chant." *Skeleton Crew*. New York: Putnam, 1985: 241-244.

---. *The Regulators* (as Richard Bachman). New York: Dutton, 1996.

---. "Silence." *Moth* 1970: [n.p.].

---. *The Stand*. Garden City NY: Doubleday, 1978.

---. *The Stand: The Complete and Uncut Edition*. New York: Doubleday, May 1990.

---. *Stephen King's Danse Macabre*. New York: Everest House, 1981.

---. Untitled poem ["In the key-chords of dawn"]. *Onan* Jan. 1971: 69.

---. "Why We Crave Horror Movies." *Playboy* (January, 1981): 150-154, 237-246.

Lattimore, Richmond. *The Iliad of Homer*. Chicago IL: University of Chicago Press, 1951.

Lawrence, Philip K. *Preparing for Armageddon: A Critique of Western Strategy*. New York: St. Martin's Press, 1988. Sussex, England: Wheatsheaf Books, 1988.

Le Guin, Ursula K. *The Language of the Night: Essays on Fantasy and Science Fiction*. Ed. Susan Wood. 1979. New York: Berkley, 1982. See especially "Myth and Archetype in Science Fiction," 63-72.

Lee, Tanith. *Death's Master*. New York: DAW Books, 1979.

---. *Night's Master.* New York: DAW Books, 1978.

Leeming, David Adams. *Mythology: The Voyage of the Hero.* New York: Harper & Row. 1981.

---. *Flights: Readings in Magic, Mysticism, Fantasy, and Myth.* New York: Harcourt Brace Jovanovich, 1974.

Leggatt, Alexander. *English Drama: Shakespeare to the Restoration, 1590-1660.* London: Longmans, 1988.

Lewis, C. S. *The Lion, the Witch and the Wardrobe.* New York: Macmillan, 1950.

---. *The Magician's Nephew.* New York: Collier Books, 1970.

---. *Of Other Worlds: Essays and Stories.* Ed. by Walter Hooper. New York: Harcourt Brace Jovanovich, 1966.

---. *Out of the Silent Planet.* 1938. New York: Macmillan, 1965.

---. *Perelandra.* 1944. New York: Macmillan, 1968.

---. *The Screwtape Letters.* 1941. New York: Macmillan, 1956.

---. *The Silver Chair.* New York: Macmillan, 1953 [Book Club Edition].

---. *That Hideous Strength: A Modern Fairy-Tale for Grown-Ups.* 1946. New York: Macmillan, 1965.

---. *The Voyage of the "Dawn Treader."* New York: Macmillan, 1953 [Book Club Edition].

---. *Till We Have Faces: A Myth Retold.* 1956. Grand Rapids MI: Eerdmans, 1966.

Lovecraft, H. P. "The Outsider." *The Dunwich Horror and Others.* Selected by August Derleth. Ed. S. T. Joshi. Sauk City WI: Arkham House, 1963. 46-52.

---. "The Picture in the House." *The Best of H. P. Lovecraft: Bloodcurdling Tales of Horror and the Macabre.* Intro. Robert Bloch. 1963. New York: Ballantine, 1982. 30-36.

Lucie-Smith, Edward. *Holding Your Eight Hands.* Garden City NY: Doubleday & Co., 1969.

Macklin, Anthony F. "Understanding Kubrick: *The Shining.*" *Journal of Popular Film and Television* 9:2 (Summer, 1981): 93-95.

Macky, Peter. "Myth as the Way We Can Taste Reality: An Analysis of C. S. Lewis's Theory." *The Lamp-Post of the Southern California C. S. Lewis Society.* Vol. 6, no. 3 (July 1982): 1-7.

Manlove, Colin. *Christian Fantasy from 1200 to the Present.* Notre Dame IN: University of Notre Dame Press, 1992.

---. *Modern Fantasy: Five Studies.* Cambridge: Cambridge University Press, 1975.

Merritt Y. Hughes, ed. *John Milton: Complete Poems and Major Prose.* New York: Odyssey Press, 1957).

"Moby Dick: or, The Whale—Contemporary Criticism and Reviews." Online at: http://www.melville.org/hmmoby.htm#con temporary.

Murrin, Michael. *The Allegorical Epic: Essays in Its Rise and Decline.* Chicago, University of Chicago Press, 1980.

Nelson, Thomas Allen. *Kubrick: Inside a Film Artist's Maze*. Bloomington, IN: Indiana University Press, 1982

Nicolson, Marjorie Hope. "The Discovery of Space." In *Medieval and Renaissance Studies: Proceedings of the Southeastern Institute of Medieval and Renaissance Studies, Summer, 1965*. Edited by O.B. Hardison, Jr. Chapel Hill NC: University of North Carolina Press, 1966.

---. *Voyages to the Moon*. 1948. New York: Macmillan, 1962.

Palwick, Susan. "The Neighbor's Wife." *Isaac Asimov's Science Fiction Magazine* (May 1985).

Parrinder, Patrick. *Science Fiction: Its Criticism and Teaching*. New York: Methuen, 1980.

Perakos, Peter S. "Stephen King on *Carrie, The Shining*, Etc." *Cinefantastique* 1:8 (Winter, 1978): 12-15.

Poe, Edgar Allan. *The Complete Tales and Poems of Edgar Allan Poe*. Intro. Hervey Allen. New York: The Modern Library, 1938, 1965.

Potholm, C. P., II. Review of *Preparing for Armageddon: A Critique of Western Strategy*. *Choice* (November 1988): 567.

Quaglia, David. "*A Woman of Destiny.*" *West Coast Review of Books* (March-April, 1984): 42.

Rabkin, Eric S. *The Fantastic in Literature*. Princeton NJ: Princeton University Press, 1976.

Radford, Elaine. "Ender and Hitler: Sympathy for the Superman." *Fantasy Review* (June 1987): 11-12+.

Rees, Gareth. "Maps in a Mirror." Online. Netscape, July 1995.

---. "*The Worthing Saga* (Orson Scott Card)." Online. Netscape. 12 July 1995. Available: Gareth Rees@cl.cam.ac.uk.

Rose, Martial, ed. *The Wakefield Mystery Plays*. 1961. New York: Norton, 1969.

Rouse, A. L. *Christopher Marlowe: His Life and Work*. New York: Harper & Row, 1964.

Sage, Victor. *Horror Fiction in the Protestant Tradition*. New York: St. Martin's, 1988.

Sammons, Martha. *A Guide Through C. S. Lewis's Space Trilogy*. Westchester IL: Cornerstone Books, 1980.

*San Fernando Poetry Journal* Vol. 4, no. 1 (1982).

Scholes, Robert, and Eric S. Rabkin. *Science Fiction: History, Science, Vision*. New York : Oxford University Press, 1977.

Schow, David J. "Return of the Curse of the Son of Mr. King: Book Two." *Whispers* No. 17/18 (August, 1982): 49-56.

Shelley, Percy Bysshe. "A Defence of Poetry." Online at: Rpt. from *English Essays: Sidney to Macaulay*. The Harvard Classics. 1909–14.

Shirk, Dora M. "Interview with Orson Scott Card." *Westwind* [Norwestcon Alternacon Progress Report] (January 1987): 11-15.

"SK Criticized for References to Blacks." *Castle Rock* Vol. 4, No. 3 (March 1988).

Slusser, George Edgar. *The Space Odysseys of Arthur C. Clarke*. The Milford Series: Popular Writers of Today, Vol. 8. San Bernardino CA: Borgo Press, 1978.

Smith, Lucy Mack. *History of Joseph Smith.* 1901. Salt Lake City UT: Bookcraft, 1958.

Spinrad. Norman. "On Books: Science Fiction Versus Sci-Fi." *Isaac Asimov's Science Fiction Magazine* (December 1986): 178-191.

---. *Science Fiction in the Real World.* Carbondale and Edwardsville: Southern Illinois University Press, 1990.

Steadman, John M. *Epic and Tragic Structure in* Paradise Lost. Chicago IL: University of Chicago Press, 1976.

---. *Milton and the Paradoxes of Renaissance Heroism.* Baton Rouge LA: Louisiana State University Press, 1987.

---. *Milton and the Renaissance Hero.* Oxford at the Clarendon Press, 1967.

---. *Milton's Epic Characters: Image and Idol.* Chapel Hill NC: University of North Carolina Press, 1968.

Stevens, Martin. *Four Middle English Mystery Cycles: Textual, Contextual, and Critical Interpretations.* Princeton NJ: Princeton University Press, 1987.

Stone, Peter, and Sherman Edwards. *1776: A Musical Play.* New York: The Viking Press, 1970. Reprinted: 1982.

Straubhaar, Sandra Baliff. "Joseph Smith in an Alternate Universe." *Dialogue: A Journal of Mormon Thought* Vol. 21, no. 4 (Winter 1988): 171-172

Straubhaar, Sandy and Joe. "Science Fiction and Mormonism: A Three Way View." *Sunstone* (July-August 1981): 52-56.

Straubhaar, Sandy. "Science Fiction, Savage Mysogyny and the American Dream." *Dialogue: A Journal of Mormon Thought* Vol. 14, no 1 (Spring 1981): 115-116.

Surette, Leon. *The Birth of Modernism: Ezra Pound, T. S. Eliot, W. B. Yeats, and the Occult.* Montreal: McGill-Queen's University Press, 1993.

Suvin, Darko. *Positions and Presuppositions in Science Fiction.* Kent OH: Kent State University Press, 1988.

Tasso, Torquato. *Discourses on the Heroic Poem.* Translated with notes by Mariella Cavalchini and Irene Samuel. Oxford at the Clarendon Press, 1973.

Tem, Steve Rasnic. *The Umbral Anthology of Science Fiction Poetry.* Denver CO: Umbral Press, 1982.

Tillyard, E. M. W. *The English Epic and its Background.* 1954. New York: Oxford University Press/Galaxy Books, 1966.

Todorov, Tzvetan. *The Fantastic: A Structural Approach to a Literary Genre.* 1970. Trans. Richard Howard. Ithaca NY: Cornell University Press, 1975, 1980.

Tolkien, J. R. R. "On Fairy Stories." In "Tree and Leaf," *The Tolkien Reader.* New York: Ballantine Books, 1966. 3-84.

---. *The Silmarillion.* Ed. Christopher Tolkien. Boston: Houghton Miflin, 1977.

Trissino, Giovanni Giorgio. *L'Italia Liberata dai Goti.* 1547.

Turner, Frederick. *The New World: An Epic Poem.* Princeton NJ: Princeton University Press, 1985.

Twitchell, James B. *Dreadful Pleasures: An Anatomy of Modern Horror.* New York: Oxford University Press, 1985.

---. *The Living Dead: A Study of the Vampire in Romantic Literature.* Durham NC: Duke University Press, 1981

Walsh, Chad. "C. S. Lewis: Critic, Creator, and Cult Figure." *Seven* 2 (March 1981), 72-74.

---. "C. S. Lewis: The Man and the Mystery," in *Shadows of Imagination: The Fantasies of C. S. Lewis, J. R. R. Tolkien, and Charles Williams.* Ed. Mark Hillegas. Carbondale IL: Southern Illinois University Press, 1979. -

---. *The Literacy Legacy of C. S. Lewis.* New York; Harcourt, 1979.

---. *The Visionary Christian: 131 Readings from C. S. Lewis.* New York: Scribner, 1981.

Warrick, Patricia. *Science Fiction: Contemporary Mythology—The SFWA Anthology.* New York: Harper and Row, 1978.

Williams, Charles, and C. S. Lewis. *Taliessin Through Logres, The Region of the Summer Stars, and Arthurian Torso.* Grand Rapids MI: Eerdmans, 1974.

Wynne-Davis, Marion. "Titus Andronicus," in *Prentice Hall Guide to English Literature.* New York: Prentice Hall, 1990.

Young, Karl. *The Drama of the Medieval Church.* Oxford: Clarendon Press, 1933.

Zebrowski, George, ed. *Synergy.* San Diego CA: Harcourt Brace Jovanovich. Vol. One, 1987; Vol. Two, 1988.

Zelazny, Roger. *Nine Princes in Amber.* New York: Doubleday, 1970.

---. *The Courts of Chaos.* New York: Doubleday, 1978.

---. *The Guns of Avalon.* New York: Doubleday, 1972.

---. *The Hand of Oberon.* New York: Doubleday, 1976.

---. *The Sign of the Unicorn.* New York: Doubleday, 1975.

# INDEX

*1776* (play): 155
Achillean Hero: 233
*Adelina* (magazine): 137
Aguirre, Manuel: 48
Alcott, John: 124
Aldiss, Brian W.: 11, 14, 69, 99, 230
    *An Age* (U.S.: *Cryptozoic!*): 69
    *Barefoot in the Head*: 230
    Helliconia Trilogy: 99
    *Report on Probability A*: 230
Allegory: 57, 59, 82, 181, 194, 237
Allen, Blair H.: 40
Aliens, other peoples: 28, 51, 64-67, 88, 100, 101, 104, 170-171, 176, 193, 211, 234, 237, 243, 255, 265, 266, 268-269, 275
Allred, Lee: 263
Alternative earth: see, Worlds, other
*Amazing Stories*: 232
*Amityville Horror, The* (film): 126
*Analog Science Fiction and Fact* (magazine): 166, 176
Anderson, Glenn: 263
*Anthology of Speculative Poetry*: 232
Anthony, Piers: 10, 11, 14, 93-94, 156, 230, 232
    Battle Circle Trilogy: 156, 232
    *Split Infinity*: 93-94, 95, 97
    Xanth Trilogy: 93, 95, 97
*Antonio's Revenge*: 22-23
Apocalypse: 272-273
Archetype: 82, 183, 188-189, 192-194, 261
Aristotle: 179, 277
Arthur, Arthurian mythos: 37, 42-43, 260-262
*Asahi Shimbun* (newspaper): 129
Asimov, Isaac: 99, 108
    Foundation Trilogy: 99
Atkinson, William C.: 230-231
Bach, Johan Sebastian: 124
Bachman, Richard: see King, Stephen

Baker, Howard: 17
Ballentine, Lee: 33
  *Poly*: 33
Barker, Clive: 9, 244-258
  *Books of Blood, The*: 246
  *Cabal*: 246
  *Damnation Game, The*: 246
  *Great and Secret Show, The*: 244-258
Barlowe, Joel: 29
  *Columbiad*: 29
Bartok, Bela: 124
Beahm, George: 13, 105, 119
  *Demon-Driven: Stephen King and the Art of Writing*: 105
  *Phantasmagoria*: 119
  *Stephen King Story, The: A Literary Profile*: 13,
Beaumont, Francis: 20-21
Beethoven, Ludwig van: 124
Bell, M. Shayne: 263
*Beowulf*: 15-17, 18, 24, 29, 52, 162, 273
Bible: 29, 87, 88, 89, 103, 136, 151, 175-176, 197, 199, 216-217, 224, 261
Biggs, Margaret Key: 40
Bishop, Jim: 116
Bleiler, E.F.: 206
*Blood Review, The*: 42
*Bonanza* (television series): 150
Book of Abraham: 261, 266, 271
Book of Mormon: 36-37, 167, 172, 178, 183, 200, 212, 250-252, 261
Borgo Press: 108
Boston, Bruce: 33
Bowyer, Andy: 259
Bradbury, Ray: 106
Brigham Young Symposium on Science Fiction and Fantasy, "Life, the
  Universe, and Everything": 12, 25, 35, 47, 60, 145, 155, 165, 185, 195,
  228n, 235n, 244, 264-265, 276
Brontë, Charlotte: 149
  *Jane Eyre*: 149
Brontë, Emily: 53
  *Wuthering Heights*: 53
Browne, Sir Thomas: 152-153
Browning, Robert: 29
Burgess, Anthony: 123-124
Burleson, Donald M.: 188
*Burnt Offerings* (film): 126
Burton, Richard Francis: 230
Byron, George Gordon, Lord: 29
Byronic hero: 53

Perakos, Peter S.: 121
Philological Association of the Pacific Coast: 195
Phoenix: 63
Plagiarism: 212-213
Plan of Salvation (see also, Church of Jesus Christ of Latter-day Saints): 69, 177-178, 267, 273
*Playboy* (magazine):
Poe, Edgar Allan: 106, 119, 244-245, 277, 278
    "Fall of the House of Usher, The": 244
    "Masque of the Red Death": 245
    "Oval Portrait, The": 245
    "Pit and the Pendulum, The": 244-245
Pope, Alexander: 29
Pornography: 56
Potholm, C.P.:256-257
Parrinder, Patrick: 48
Pound, Ezra: 37n
Progress: 271-272
Prynne, William: 23
    *Histriomastix*: 23
Purcell, Henry: 124
Rabkin, Eric: 48, 49-50, 98, 100
Racism: 141-142
Radford, Elaine: 185-186, 187
Rees, Gareth: 210, 219, 224
Reginald, Robert: 108
Reiner, Rob: 130-131
Revenge tragedy: 19, 22-23
*Revenger's Tragedy, The*: 23
Rhysling Award (Science Fiction Poetry Association): 27, 32, 33, 60
Rimsky-Korsakov, Nikolai: 124
Romero, George: 237
Ross, Betsy: 199, 215
Rossini, Gioachino: 124
Rushdie, Salmon: 149
    *Satanic Verses*: 149
Sage, Victor: 48
Sai, Shuei: 129
Sammons, Martha: 81-82, 98, 102
*San Fernando Poetry Journal*: 40
Sanders, Ed: 112
Sanderson, Brandon: 263
Scale of Being: 89, 274
Schlobin, Roger: 108
Scholes, Robert: 48, 49-50, 98
Schow, David: 120, 124

Stewart, W. Gregory: 33
Stoker, Bram: 59, 117, 246
  *Dracula*: 52, 59, 246
Story: 31-32, 165-166, 180, 196, 207-209, 218, 220, 225-226
Straub, Peter: 9, 117, 119, 135, 143, 147
  *Black House* (with Stephen King): 135, 143, 147, 163
  *Talisman, The* (with Stephen King): 117, 135, 143, 147, 163
Straubhaar, Joe: 165-166
Straubhaar, Sandy: 165-166
Strauss, Johann: 123
Strauss, Richard: 123
*Sunstone* (magazine): 174, 232, 276
Sunstone Theological Symposium: 174
Supernatural: 45, 53, 57, 63, 163, 181, 226, 243, 267
Surette, Leon: 37n
Suvin, Darko: 228n
Sycamore Hill Writers' Workshop: 180, 220
Symonds, J. A.: 48
Szasz, Thomas: 112
Tem, Stephen Rasnic: 33, 61
  *Umbral Anthology, The*: 33, 61
Tennyson, Alfred, Lord: 20
Theological Science Fiction: 41, 62
Tillyard, E.M.W.: 229n
Time travel: 103, 271
Todorov, Tzvetan: 26-27, 44-45, 100
Tolkien, Christopher: 87n
Tolkien, J.R.R.: 10, 15, 87n, 91n, 99, 117, 162, 186, 206, 207, 209, 225-226, 261, 267
  *Ainulindalë*: 87n, 88n, 91n
  *Lord of the Rings, The*: 15, 99, 162, 208
  "Monster and the Critics, The": 162
  "On Fairy Stories": 225-226
  *Silmarillion, The*: 87n
Tragedy: 47
*Tribute* (film): 126
Trissino, G.G.: 229
  *L'Italia Liberata*: 229
Trumbo, Dalton: 123
Turner, Frederick: 228
  *New World, The*: 228
Twain, Mark: 22, 49
  "Man Who Corrupted Hadleyburg, The": 22
  *Mysterious Stranger, The*: 49
Twitchell, James B.: 48, 52, 53
*TV Guide*: 120

# ABOUT THE AUTHOR

**MICHAEL R. COLLINGS** is an Emeritus Professor of English at Pepperdine University and the author of over thirty volumes of poetry, novels, short fiction, bibliography, and studies of writers including Stephen King, Dean R. Koontz, Piers Anthony, Brian W. Aldiss, and Orson Scott Card. Many of his books have been published by the Borgo Press Imprint of Wildside Press, his most recent being *The Art and Craft of Poetry*, the science-fiction novel, *Singer of Lies,* and *The Nephiad: An Epic Poem in XII Books.* He lives and works in Idaho

9 781434 457929